TEN GREAT RELIGIONS.

PART II.

A COMPARISON OF ALL RELIGIONS.

BY

JAMES FREEMAN CLARKE.

He who only knows one religion can no more understand *that* religion than he who only knows one language can understand *that* language.

TYLOR. *Primitive Culture*, vol. i., p. 421.

BOSTON:
HOUGHTON, MIFFLIN AND COMPANY.
New York: 11 East Seventeenth Street.
The Riverside Press, Cambridge.
1883.

The Riverside Press, Cambridge:
Electrotyped and Printed by H. O. Houghton and Company.

To

J. PETER LESLEY AND SUSAN I. LESLEY,

IN MEMORY OF

MANY HOURS OF HAPPY INTERCOURSE,

This Book

IS AFFECTIONATELY DEDICATED.

PREFACE.

The first part of "Ten Great Religions" was published in 1871. The success it has met with is probably due to the fact that it contains in a compendium an account of the principal religions of the world, sufficiently full for the wants of those who are not special students of this subject. There exist many works on the separate religions, much more thorough, and which enter into a greater detail. But I suppose it would be difficult, even now, to find the chief facts in relation to all of them brought together elsewhere in a single volume.

The present work (based on twelve lectures given in the Lowell Institute in the winter of 1881–2) is on a different plan. Instead of describing and discussing each of the great faiths of mankind separately, it attempts to show what they all teach on the different points of human belief. We ask what each declares concerning

God, the Soul, the Future Life, Sin and Salvation, Human Duty, Prayer and Worship, Inspiration and Art. We consider what is the Idea of God in all religions, and ask how it began and in what way it was developed. In the same manner we seek to trace other phases of the religious life, from their simplest beginnings to their fullest outcome.

In pursuing this course of thought I have been often called upon to discuss the religions of the primitive or childlike races, a department of the subject not treated in the first volume. The importance and value of researches in this direction have of late years been more fully recognized than formerly. "The time has long since passed," says Brinton,[1] "at least among thinking men, when the religious legends of the lower races were looked upon as trivial fables, or as the inventions of the Father of Lies. They are neither the one nor the other. They express, in image and incident, the opinions of these races on the mightiest topics of human thought, on the origin and destiny of man, his motives for duty and his grounds for hope, and the source, history, and fate of external nature. Certainly the sincere expressions on this subject of even humble mem-

[1] *American Hero-Myths*, by David G. Brinton, 1882.

bers of the human race deserve our most respectful heed, and it may be that we shall discover in their crude or coarse narratives gleams of a mental light which their proud Aryan brethren have been long in coming to, or have not yet reached."

This class of primitive or childlike religions I have called Tribal, because they are usually developed by each tribe, and have not the characters of Ethnic or National religions, nor of Catholic or Universal religions. They show the first dawnings of the religious life with a singular uniformity, whether in the heart of Africa, among the islands of Polynesia, or within the Arctic Zone. The special race developments have not yet begun, and these primitive sentiments have not been differentiated under the formative influences of national life. As yet human nature is in its cradle, and the cry of the infant is the same all over the world. All this indicates that the law applies to religion which we find elsewhere, and that here too the progress of the race will be from monotony, through variety, to an ultimate harmony.

The present volume contains, as far as I know, the first attempt to trace these doctrines through all the principal religions of mankind. It is only an attempt, but it indicates at least, what I believe to be the best way of understanding the value of any belief, that of comparative theology. How much light has been thrown on human culture by the works of Tylor, Lubbock, Waitz, Brinton, Bastian, Lecky, and others who have adopted to a greater or less extent the methods of comparison!

I cannot expect that the views taken in this book in regard to different religions will be universally accepted. Most of the questions treated in it are still subjects for inquiry, and specialists differ among themselves on some of the most essential points. Was the system of Zoroaster fundamentally a monotheism? Haug says it was; Lenormant and others tell us, that though on his way to this conception, he did not reach it. Was Buddhism a reaction against Brahmanism, as most writers suppose? Or was it a development of Brahmanism, as Oldenberg and Kuenen tell us? Probably it was both. If it did not seek to abolish castes in India, it ignored them, and admitted men of all castes to its order. If it did not reject the Gods of the Hindu Pantheon, it passed them by. It developed an entirely new side of life. It taught humanity instead of piety; it ascribed salvation, not to sacrifices and sacraments, but to the sight of the truth. I therefore think I was right, when in the First Part of this work, I called Buddhism the Protestantism of the East.

In Chapter VI. I have suggested that there may be essential truth in the doctrine of Transmigration, once so generally believed. The modern doctrine of the evolution of bodily organisms is not complete, unless we unite with it the idea of a corresponding evolution of the spiritual monad, from which every organic form derives its unity. Evolution has a satisfactory meaning only when we admit that the soul is developed and educated by passing through many bodies, and not only accept the theory that our ancestors may have been apes or fishes, but the larger doctrine that we ourselves were probably once apes or fishes, and that we learned much in those conditions which is useful to us in our present forms.

I have added a list of some of the principal books on the subjects here treated, which have been published since the index of authors was prepared for the first part of this work.

This list begins with recent works on Buddhism. Then follow those on the Parsis and the Zend-Avesta; next a few titles on Brahmanism; then on the Religions of Assyria and Babylon. The list ends with titles of books lately issued on Primitive Religions, the Beliefs of China, the origin and growth of all Religions, and works bearing on the general subject.

In selecting the titles on Assyria I have had the assistance of Professor David G. Lyon of Harvard College; and in regard to Buddhism, I have been aided by Charles R. Lanman, Professor of Sanskrit in the same university. I have not attempted to make any exhaustive list of references, but merely to indicate for young students, not specialists, some of the more important sources of information.

Buddha, Sein Leben, Seine Lehre, Seine Gemeinde, von Dr. Hermann Oldenberg. Berlin, 1881.

Buddha, his Life, his Doctrine, his Order. (The same work translated by William Hoey), 1882.

Die Therapeutæ und ihre Stellung. By P. E. Lucius. Strasburg, 1880.

Lectures on the Origin and Growth of Religion, as illustrated by some points in the History of Indian Buddhism. By J. W. Rhys Davids. Being the Hibbert lectures, 1881.

The Buddhist Scriptures in Pâli. The Vinaya Pitakam. Edited by Dr. H. Oldenberg. Five vols.

The Angel-Messiah of Buddhists, Essenes and Christians. By Ernest de Bunsen. (London, 1880).

[This book is largely quoted by those who would derive the facts in the Gospels from the Buddhist legends. Its value in the eyes of a real scholar appears in the following extract from Kuenen's Hibbert Lectures: —

"The well-known volume on 'The Angel-Messiah, etc.,' no doubt teems with parallels of every description; but, alas! it is one unbroken commentary on Scaliger's thesis that errors in theology all arise from neglect of philology. A writer who can allow himself to bring the name Pharisee into connection with Persia, has once for all forfeited his right to a voice in the matter. The very title of the book should preserve us from any illusion as to its contents. The 'Angel-Messiah' of the Buddhists, who know nothing either of angels or of a Messiah!—and of the Essenes, of whose Messianic expectations we know absolutely nothing! By such comparisons we could prove anything."]

The Dîpavamsa. In the Pâli language. Edited with an English translation, by Dr. H. Oldenberg.

[This is the most ancient historical work of the Ceylonese. It gives an account of the conversion of Ceylon to Buddhism.]

The Miliñda Panha. Dialogues between King Milinda and the Buddhist Sage Nagasena. Pâli text edited by Trenckner of Copenhagen.

Das Evangelium von Jesu in seinen verhaltnissen zu Buddha-saga und Buddha-lehre, von Prof. Rudolf Seydel. Leipzig, 1882.

[Kuenen, (Hibbert Lectures, Note, page 334) says that Prof. Seydel divides the parallels between Buddhism and Christianity into three classes. The first class contains those which are purely accidental. The second class consists of those which show some dependence of one of the religions on the other. The third are of those which Prof. Seydel thinks show decidedly an influence of Buddhism on the origin of the Gospels. These last are five, and we can see by their weight, whether those of the second class are worth considering. The resemblances to which Seydel ascribes the highest degree of evidential value are —

1. The fast of Jesus before his temptation was borrowed, he believes, from a similar fast ascribed to Buddha. The oldest tradition (Oldenberg, page 114 Eng. ed.) is in the Mahâvagga, and says that Buddha fasted seven days, and then went to the fig tree. Later traditions make it twenty-eight days. Now as fasting was a religious act in all systems, there is no necessity of supposing one of them to have been borrowed from the other. And if the fast of Jesus is legendary, why not rather suppose it borrowed from the forty days' fast of Moses (Exodus xxxiv. 28) than the seven days' or twenty-eight days' fast of Buddha.

2. The next incident which Seydel thinks must have been borrowed from Buddhism is the question "Did this man sin or his parents, that he was born blind?" (John ix. 2) which Seydel thinks unmeaning, unless explained by the Buddhist doctrine of re-birth. On this Kuenen says that "nothing can be more obvious than to refer this to the Jewish-Alexandrian doctrine of preëxistence, which renders the Buddhist parallel quite superfluous."

3. The preëxistence ascribed both to Buddha and to Christ, though one of Seydel's five strongest points, he does not himself regard as conclusive.

4. The presentation in the temple (Luke ii. 22).

5. The sitting under a fig tree (John i. 46).

Of these last Kuenen says that "the difference seems to me quite to overbalance the resemblance. There is no parallel between the simple scene in the temple and the homage rendered to the Buddha-child." And in John i. it is not Christ but Nathaniel who sits under the fig tree, as the Buddha himself sat under the tree of knowledge. To sit under the shade of a tree is not such an extraordinary event as to make it necessary to believe it borrowed from one which happened in a far off land, five centuries before. Yet these five cases are the strongest that Prof. Seydel, after the most careful research, can find as proving that facts in the gospel were borrowed from Buddhism.]

Der Buddhismus und seine Geschichte in Indien. By Heinrich Kern. (Translated from the Dutch by H. Jacobi.) Leipzig, 1882.

Der Buddhismus in seinen Psychologie. Mit einer Karte des buddhistischen Weltsystems. By A. Bastian. 1882.

The Dhammapada. Being one of the Canonical Books of the Buddhists. Translated into English from Pâli. By F. Max Müller. 1881.

The Sutta-Nipâta. One of the Canonical Books of the Buddhists. Translated from the Pâli. By V. Fansböll. 1881.

[These two translations are contained in vol. x. of the series called "The Sacred Books of the East" — an admirable work, edited by Max Müller, and published at Oxford.

Of the Dhammapada Müller says, "I cannot see any reason why we should not treat the verses of the Dhammapada, if not as the utterances of Buddha, at least as what were believed by the members of the council under Asoka, 242 B. C., to have been the utterances of the founder of their religion."

Of the Sutta-Nipâta the translator says, "There can be no doubt that it contains some remnants of Primitive Buddhism. I consider the greater part of the Mahâgga, and nearly the whole of the Attha-Kavogga, as very old."]

Buddhist Suttas. Translated from Pâli by T. W. Rhys Davids, 1881. Vol. xi. of "Sacred Books of the East."

[This volume contains seven Suttas, which Mr. Rhys Davids considers to come to us from the third or fourth century before

Christ. They are quite interesting, and give a good idea of primitive Buddhism. Mr. Davids finds some points of resemblance between this literature and that of the New Testament; but agrees with Kuenen, in denying the latter to be in any way derived from the former.[1]]

A Catena of Buddhist Scriptures from the Chinese. By Samuel Beal. London, 1871.

The Romantic Legend of Buddha. By Samuel Beal. 1875.

[Mr. Beal has given us in these books much light on Buddhism in China—though a great deal more remains to be done. He informs us that the Buddhist Canon in Chinese consists of 1,440 distinct works, comprising 5,586 books. The monasteries in China contain a vast number of works which have never been collated by European scholars. As far back as the first century after the birth of Christ, while Christian missionaries were going West to convert Europe, Buddhist missionaries went East as far as China.]

The Wheel of the Law. Buddhism illustrated from Siamese Sources. By Henry Alabaster, 1871.

Buddhagosha's Parables. Translated from the Burmese, by Captain H. T. Rogers, 1870.

Buddhist Birth-Stories. Edited by Fausböll. Translated by Rhys Davids.

Buddha and Early Buddhism. By Arthur Lillie.

[An interesting book, by an independent thinker.]

Das Evangelium von Jesu in seinen Verhaltnissen zur Buddha sage und Buddha-lehre. By R. Seydel. Leipzig, 1882.

Lehre der Buddha. Senart.

Legend of the Burmese Buddha. (Life or Legend of Gaudama. By Bishop Bigandet. Rangoon, 1866.)

Lectures on the Science of Religion, with a paper on Buddhist

[1] See Appendix.

Nihilism and a translation of the Dhammapada. By Max Müller. New York, Scribner, 1872.

"The Parsis." (Article in the "Nineteenth Century," March, 1881.) "The Religion of Zoroaster." ("Nineteenth Century," January, 1881.) By Monier Williams.

Zoroaster und die Religion des Altiranischen Volkes. By Karl Geldner.

[Not yet published, but sure to be good.]

The Vendidad. Translated by James Darmesteter. (Sacred Books of the East, vol. iv.)

The Bundahis. Bahman Yast, and Shâyast la Shayast. Translated by E. W. West. (Sacred Books of the East, vol. v.)

The Supreme God in the Indo-European Mythology. By James Darmesteter. (Contemporary Review, October, 1879.)

Essays on the Sacred Language, Writings, and Religion of the Parsis, by Martin Haug. (English and Foreign Philosophical Library.) Houghton, Mifflin & Co., Boston.

Indian Wisdom. By Monier Williams. 1875.

Hinduism. By Monier Williams. 1877.

History of India from the Earliest Ages. By J. Talboys Wheeler.

Manual of Hindu Pantheism. (Jacob.)

Hinduism and its Relations to Christianity. By Rev. J. Robson.

Der Rig-Veda. By Adolf Kaegi. Leipzig, 1881.

["An admirable book," Professor Lanman.]

The Religions of India. By Auguste Barth. (Translated from the valuable "Encyclopedie des Sciences religieuses, Paris," by Wood, London, 1882.)

The Upanishads. Translated by Max Müller. (Sacred Books of the East, vol. i.)

The Sacred Laws of the Aryas. Translated by George Buhler. (Sacred Books of the East, vols. ii. and xiv.)

The Institutes of Vishnu. Translated by Prof. Julius Jolly. (Sacred Books of the East, vol. vii.)

The Bhagavadgita, etc. (Sacred Books of the East, vol. viii.)

A Manual of the Ancient History of the East. By F. Lenormant and E. Chevallier. London, 1879.

Histoire Comparée des anciennes Religions de l' Egypte et des Peuples Semitiqués. Par C. P. Tiele. Paris, 1882.

The Chaldæan Account of Genesis. By Geo. Smith. (New edition by A. H. Sayce, 1882.)

The Records of the Past. (Vols. 1, 3, 5, 7, 9, 11.)

[These contain numerous translations (one of which is given in the Appendix). Prof. Lyon, of Harvard University, informs me that though these contain mistakes, yet they have enough of accuracy to give a good general view of the literature.]

Babylonian Literature. By A. H. Sayce.

On the Religion of the Babylonians and Assyrians. By Sir H. C. Rawlinson, in George Rawlinson's "Herodotus," vol. i.

Die Keilinschriften und das Alte Testament. Von E. Schrader. Giessen, 1883.

Wo lag das Paradies? Von Friedrich Delitzsch. Leipzig, 1881.

Avesta, Livre sacre du Zoroasterisme traduit du Texte Zend, par C. D. Harlez. (Bibliothèque Orientale, vol. v.) Second edition. Paris, 1881.

Origin of Primitive Superstitions, etc., among the Aborigines of America. By Rushton M. Dorman. Philadelphia, 1881.

The Vicissitudes of Aryan Civilization in India. Kunte. Bombay, 1880.

The Origin and Development of Religious Belief. By T. Baring Gould. 1870.

[The merit of this work is that it is an honest attempt on the part of a High Churchman to see and accept all the facts of science and human experience, without flinching. Its defect appears to be that it does not succeed in reducing these facts to unity.]

Die Religion, ihr Wesen, und ihre Geschichte. By O. Pfleiderer. Leipzig, 1869.

The origin of Religion considered in the light of the Unity of Nature. By the Duke of Argyll. (Papers published in the Contemporary Review.)

Man's Origin and Destiny sketched from the platform of the Physical Sciences. By Prof. J. Peter Lesley. Second edition, enlarged. 1881.

[A work full of information and suggestion.]

Pre-historic Times and Origin of Civilization. By Sir John Lubbock.

Anti-theistic Theories. By Prof. Flint.

From Whence, What, Where? By James R. Nichols. 1882.

Finalité. Par Paul Janet. Paris.

Outlines of Primitive Belief among the Indo-European Races. By Charles Francis Keary, of the British Museum. 1882.

Hibbert Lectures, 1878. Lectures on the Origin and Growth of Religion, as illustrated by the Religions of India. By F. Max Müller.

Hibbert Lectures, 1879. Lectures on the Origin and Growth of Religion, as illustrated by the Religion of Ancient Egypt. By P. Le Page Renouf.

Hibbert Lectures, 1880. Influence of the Institutions, etc., of Rome on Christianity. By Ernest Renan.

Hibbert Lectures, 1881. Lectures on the Origin and Growth of Religion, as illustrated by Buddhism. By T. W. Rhys Davids.

Hibbert Lectures, 1882. Lectures on National Religions and Universal Religions. By A. Kuenen,

Brahmo Year-Book. Brief Records of Work and Life in the Theistic Churches in India. 1877, 1878, 1879, 1880.

Prolégomènes de l'Histoire des Religions. By A. Réville.

The Faiths of the World. St. Giles' Lectures, Edinburgh, 1882.

Primitive Culture. By Ed. B. Tylor. 2 vols. 1871.

Researches into the Early History of Mankind. By E. B. Tylor. 1870.

The Myths of the New World.

The Religious Sentiment.

The Maya Chronicles.

American Hero Myths.

The above four works are by Daniel G. Brinton, M. D., of Philadelphia.

The Shu-King, the Shi-King, the Hsiâo-King. By James Legge. (Sacred Books of the East, vol. iii.)

The Chinese Classics. The Analects, Great Learning and Doctrine of the Mean, by Confucius. By James Legge. Worcester and Chicago.

[See also a series of excellent Manuals by Legge, Rhys Davids, and other eminent scholars, in a series published by the Church of England Missionary Society, called "Non-Christian Religious Systems." This series includes Confucius, Hinduism, Islam, Buddhism, etc.; and does *not* include any narrow or prejudiced bias against these religions.

See, also, articles on Brahmanism, Buddhism, China, etc., in the ninth edition of the Encyclopædia Brittanica. Also, numerous articles of value in recent numbers of the Contemporary Review, Nineteenth Century, Fortnightly Review and other periodicals. Those on the Religious Prospects of Islam (by Rev. Malcom Malcoll, Prof. Monier Williams, etc.); on Ancient Egypt, by R. S. Pool (Contemporary Review, 1881); on the New Development of the Brahmo-Somaj (by Wm. Knighton, Contemporary Review, October, 1881, answered by Sophia D. Collet, Contemporary Review, November, 1881), The Babylonian Account of the Deluge (Nineteenth Century, February, 1882), may be quoted as examples of the ability and learning which go into these periodicals.]

Oriental Religions, and their Relation to Universal Religion. By Samuel Johnson. Boston: Houghton, Mifflin & Co.

[In three volumes, on India, China, and Persia; the last volume not yet published.]

Philosophical Library. Houghton, Mifflin & Co.

Vol. IX. Outlines of the History of Religion. By C. P. Tiele.

Vol. X. Religion in China. By Joseph Edkins.

Vol. XII. The Dhammapada. Translated from the Chinese by Samuel Beal.

Vol. XVI. Selections from the Koran. By E. W. Lane.

Vol. XVII. Chinese Buddhism. By Joseph Edkins.

Philosophy of Religion. By John Caird.

The Native Races of the Pacific States. By Hubert Howe Bancroft.

[An important work of great extent, and full of valuable information.]

In the Appendix to this volume will be found interesting extracts from some of the works above referred to.

CONTENTS.

CHAPTER I.

INTRODUCTION. — DESCRIPTION AND CLASSIFICATION.

CHAPTER II.

SPECIAL TYPES. — VARIATIONS.

CHAPTER III.

ORIGIN AND DEVELOPMENT OF ALL RELIGIONS.

CHAPTER IV.

THE IDEA OF GOD IN ALL RELIGIONS, ANIMISM, POLYTHEISM, PANTHEISM.

CHAPTER V.

IDEA OF GOD IN ALL RELIGIONS. — DITHEISM, TRITHEISM, AND MONOTHEISM.

CHAPTER VI.

THE SOUL AND ITS TRANSMIGRATIONS, IN ALL RELIGIONS.

CHAPTER VII.

THE ORIGIN OF THE WORLD, IN ALL RELIGIONS. EVOLUTION, EMANATION, AND CREATION.

CHAPTER VIII.

PRAYER AND WORSHIP IN ALL RELIGIONS.

CHAPTER IX.

INSPIRATION AND ART IN ALL RELIGIONS.

CHAPTER X.

ETHICS IN ALL RELIGIONS.

CHAPTER XI.

IDEA OF A FUTURE STATE IN ALL RELIGIONS.

CHAPTER XII.

THE FUTURE RELIGION OF MANKIND.

APPENDIX.

TEN GREAT RELIGIONS.

SECOND PART.

CHAPTER I.

INTRODUCTION. — DESCRIPTION AND CLASSIFICATION.

§ 1. Object of the present Volume. § 2. The Science of Religion. § 3. Religious Aspect of the World B. C. 1100. Egypt. India. Greece. Persia. Buddhism. § 4. Definition of Religion. § 5. Religion is Universal. Exceptional Cases examined by Mr. Tylor. § 6. Religious Statistics of the World. § 7. False Classifications of the Religions of the World. § 8. A better Method of Classification. Tribal, Ethnic, and Catholic. § 9. Ethnic Religions are confined to Special Races, are not founded by a Prophet, are Polytheisms, and do not lay Stress on Morality. Catholic Religions spread beyond the Boundaries of Race, are founded by a Single Prophet, are Monotheisms, and inculcate Morality.

§ 1. *Object of the present volume.*

THE first part of this work, published some years since, was chiefly analytical and descriptive. It endeavored to give a distinct account of the character and history of the Ten Great Religions of the World. The purpose of the present volume is to compare them with each other, in order to learn what each teaches concerning God, the Soul, the Origin of the World, Worship, Inspiration, Right and Wrong, and the Future Life. We shall consider this important, interesting, but complex and difficult subject — the Comparison of the Religions of Mankind — to see wherein they agree and wherein they differ; to learn, if we may, something of their origin, whether from earth or heaven; to see what measure of truth each may contain, and what is likely to be the future religious history of our race.

Everything becomes more intelligible when compared with something else of the same sort. It has been well said that "he who only understands one language does not understand *any* language." The same thing, to some extent, may be said about religion. We cannot look on any religion with indifference.

It is thought by many, I know, that science, in its immense activity, large sweep, and vast demands upon our intelligence, has permanently called away the attention of thinking men from the world within to the world without. But science in its deepest sense includes all knowledge; it cannot be confined to the study of the outward world. It takes for its domain the whole range of phenomenal existence, the entire circuit of human experience. It is compelled, by the necessity of its nature, to observe and analyze all phenomena, and endeavor to bring them under law. Positive knowledge includes the facts of the soul as well as those of sense, — and Auguste Comte, having begun by declaring that all questions of theology must be repudiated as insoluble, ended by constructing a private theology of his own.

For a time many scientific men may stand aloof from religion, but the same immortal nature is in them as in all other men. The same questions must arise in their souls as in others to whom knowledge has never unrolled her ample page, rich with the spoils of time. Blame no honest man for his doubts. Better than blind assent is conscientious denial; better than the passive acceptance of the most important truth is the loyalty to truth which refuses to speak until it can see. "There is more faith," says Tennyson, "in honest doubt than in half our creeds;" and Milton said long before that if a man believes only because his pastor or his church says so, though his belief be true, he himself is a heretic, so that the very truth he holds becomes a heresy. Still, the soul of man is not fed by doubt, but by belief; the intellect lives by faith, not by denial. Agnosticism may be an important medicine for a temporary condition, but knowledge is the food by which we grow.

§ 2. *The Science of Religion.*

Is there such a department of knowledge as "The Science of Religion," or such a method as "The Scientific Study of Religion"? If there is such a method, it must consist in the faithful study of the facts, and a careful generalization from those facts. It must be free from prejudice for or against any system. Instead of condemning a religion for its polytheism, its idolatry, or its superstitious practices, it must endeavor to find the source of those practices in human nature, or in the environment. Thus only can we reach what may deserve to be called a "Science of Religion."

Physical Science has been described as consisting of three steps: (1.) Observation of facts; (2.) Induction of laws from those facts; (3.) Verification of these laws by experiment. Observation of facts alone does not constitute science. Induction and observation without verification do not constitute science. If these three factors are applicable in religious investigation, then religion can become a science, but not otherwise.

The facts of consciousness constitute the basis of religious science. These *facts* are as real, and as constant as those which are perceived through the senses. Faith, Hope, and Love, are as real as form, sound, and color. The moral *laws* also, which may be deduced from such experience are real and permanent, and these laws can be verified in the daily course of human life. If this is so it will make the Science of Religion possible.

The Science of Religion is equally hostile to two opposite assumptions. One is the assumption that nothing is real and certain, but that which can be verified by sensible experience. Spiritual experiences are as much facts as those which are perceived by the senses. The other assumption is that of the Theologians, who attempt to build a science of religion on the authority of the Church or the Scripture. There may be, and no doubt is, a legitimate authority belonging to both; but this is not to be assumed, but to be demonstrated.

The whole realm of spiritual exercises; the sense of sin and pardon; prayer and its answer; the convictions, trusts, motive-powers, illuminations, inspirations of holy souls, may and ought to be carefully examined, analyzed, and verified. Then it will be seen what part are illusion, and what part reality. When this is accomplished, but not sooner, there will be a Science of Religion.

§ 3. *Religious Aspect of the World about 1100 B. C. Egypt, India, Greece, Persia, Buddhism.*

In order the better to see what the problem before us is, let us take a brief glance at the religious history of the race.

Let us suppose ourselves, about 1100 years before Christ, to be making a visit to Egypt. It is before the time of the Trojan war — of course, long before the time of Homer, to whom that war was a tradition. It was before the time when David founded the Hebrew monarchy. The largest part of Europe was sunk in barbarism. But the land of Egypt had been a highly civilized nation for several thousand years. Suppose ourselves to be ascending the Nile in one of the numerous vessels which then navigated it.

We find its banks crowded with villages; and vessels covering the water, propelled by sails and oars, and carrying corn or building-stone, from one part of the country to another. Splendid buildings, the walls covered with carved figures and hieroglyphic inscriptions, rise successively along its shores, one vast city after another coming in sight. Groups of pyramids appear, rising out of the plain like mountains, not, as now, ragged and torn, but covered with polished slabs of glittering marble, red granite, or yellow limestone. As we continue to ascend the yellow river, now at the height of its annual inundation, we at last reach Thebes, the capital of the Upper Empire. It stands on a circular plain ten miles across, surrounded by a belt of hills, a vast collection of temples, palaces, obelisks, and majestic tombs. Two colossal statues rise above the river shore, their feet covered with the water of the inundation. Karnak, on the eastern bank, is a city of temples. While we gaze at these marvellous buildings, we see processions of priests passing along the avenues. We ask the meaning of the ceremony, and are told that Egypt is the land of religion. Every day has its festival, every town its god and temple. Sacrifices, prayers, incense, processions, begin and close the year. The deities, we discover, are innumerable. Great triads of gods, superior to the rest, are worshipped under different names in the different provinces. Every year the Festivals of Osiris and Isis renew the mourning for the Divine Sufferer, and joy at his resurrection. The tombs are resplendent with mosaics and brilliantly colored paintings. The dead are more cared for than the living: their resting-places are carved out of solid rock and filled with rich furniture and ornaments. One supreme being, above all other deities, is worshipped as the maker and preserver of all things. The hymns and ritual of the dead, the belief in the transmigration of souls, in the day of judgment, in the trial of the soul before Osiris, make the future life almost as real as the present. But with these grand ideas, and their inspiring truths, are mingled strange notions, which cause the Egyptian worship to be looked upon with astonishment and contempt by other nations. In the holiest place in some temple, when the rich golden or purple hanging was withdrawn, you would find a cat, a crocodile, or a dog as the apparent object of worship. But before you indulged your scorn for their puerile adoration, you might listen to the solemn priest, who would say, "Do not think we *worship* these animals. Each of them is a symbol of a divine thought of the Creator. We reverence the Creator in his work. We dare not make a statue in the likeness of God; we take the creatures of his hand as signifying his character. It is to avoid idolatry, to avoid making anything in the image of God, that we place these creatures in the shrine."

Such was the religion of Egypt during thousands of years, running back into the darkness of prehistoric times. Let us now suppose ourselves transported across the continent of Asia and dropped into Northern India. Here, we meet with another race, speaking a different language, worshipping other gods. Here, descending from the great plateau of Asia, they have brought into the Punjaub their sacred hymns to Varuna, to Indra, to Agni; to the Sun, the Heavens, the Dawn; to Fire, Air, and all the elements. Here also has grown up a vast priesthood, temples, sacrifices, prayers. Here ascetics torture their bodies in hopes of getting an ecstatic glimpse of God. Here they retire into the desert, forget the world, immerse themselves in long contemplation, and commune with the Spirit of the Universe. Time disappears — Eternity is in their mind and heart. They are hoping to escape from themselves and to be absorbed in God. Such was, and such in its essence has continued to be, the faith of the Hindus to this hour.

Once more change the scene. It is 670 years later, 430 before Christ, and now we are in Greece, assisting at Athens at the Pan-Athenaic Festival. All Greece has come to worship the Virgin Goddess in this fair city of her choice.

The city of Athens, the eye of Greece, is in its glory. It is the age of Pericles. That age had made Athens the centre of the highest civilization of the world (B. C. 445–431). The three great tragic poets, Æschylus, Sophocles, and Euripides, are all Athenians, and their plays are performed every day before the people. The greatest of architects and sculptors, Phidias, has just completed the noble buildings and statues which crown the Acropolis. Socrates, thirty-eight years old, is teaching and conversing with all whom he meets in the streets of Athens. Anaxagoras, one of the philosophers who first taught in Greece the doctrine of one Supreme Being, of one passionless Divine mind who formed the world out of chaos, has just been accused of impiety for denying the gods of Olympus. On the hill of Areopagus, opposite the Acropolis, Pericles has recently, with consummate eloquence and pathos, defended Aspasia from the same charge.

And now we stand and view the procession as it passes: old men leading the way, carrying green branches of olives; then a band of soldiers with shields and spears; then strangers from other lands, each with a boat in his hand, to show that he came from far; next the women with pots of sacred water on their heads; then a choir of young men singing hymns; next to them, select virgins of noble families, carrying in baskets the sacred implements of sacrifice; then other girls bearing umbrellas. So the procession winds its way up to the Acropolis, the sacred hill, covered with temples, all bright in the sunshine, gleaming with polished marble, in fair proportion and matchless beauty. And now we stand before the Parthenon, with its unapproached majesty, its long colonnades, its pediment covered with noble statues of superhuman size, all enriched with vivid colors, giving it an air of festive gayety.

On our left, raised on a high base, is the grand Phidian statue of Pallas, seventy feet high, with long lance and lofty helmet, looking far away over the Ægean Sea. The procession moves up the steps, encircles the temple, walking around it behind the columns; then the virgins take the *peplos,* the dress they have woven for Pallas, and put it on the recumbent statue of the goddess, with its ivory limbs and golden robes, in the Erectheum.

The Egyptian worship was sombre and mysterious, making death and another world its central ideas. But how bright and joyous was that of the Greeks, bringing down their gods to enjoy with them the happy festivals which rounded their cheerful year!

Again the scene changes. We now go back to the East and come to Persia, where we find still another form of religion.

The great monarchy of Persia, founded by Cyrus 100 years before, is now at this period, 430 years before Christ, already tending toward its decline. A hundred years later, it is to fall before the triumphant march of Alexander and his Macedonians. But now it still retains the ancient faith of Zoroaster, though modified by the developments of a thousand years. Herodotus describes it as it existed at the period of which we speak. In his insatiate desire for knowledge, he had gathered up all that he could learn of Persia, and says: "It is not customary for the Persians to have idols, temples, or altars. They offer sacrifices on the summits of mountains, not erecting altars or kindling fires, but they carry the animal to a pure spot, and there the sacrificer prays for the prosperity of the empire, the king, and all others." "The Persians believe fire to be a god."

Herodotus we find to be correct. Here are no temples, no altars, no idol worship of any kind. The Supreme Being is worshipped by one symbol, fire, which is pure and purifies all things. The prayers are for purity, the libation the juice of a plant. Ormazd has created everything good, and all his creatures are pure. Listen to the priest chanting the litany thus: "I invoke and celebrate Ahura Mazda, brilliant, greatest, best. All-perfect, all-powerful, all-wise, all-beautiful, only source of knowledge and happiness; he has created us, he has formed us, he sustains us." "He belongs to those who think good; to those who think evil he does not belong. He belongs to those who speak good; to those who speak evil he does not belong. He belongs to those who do good; to those who do evil he does not belong." This is the religion of the great race who founded the Persian Empire.

To these worshippers life did not seem to be a gay festival, as to the Greeks, nor a single step on the long pathway of the soul's transmigration, as to the Egyptians; but a field of battle between mighty powers of good and evil, where Ormazd and Ahriman meet in daily conflict, and where the servant of God is to maintain a perpetual battle against the powers of darkness, by cherishing good thoughts, good words, and good actions.

After other centuries have passed, if we come again into Asia, we find a new religion which, born in India and afterward expelled from thence, has converted by its zealous missionaries nearly the whole of the East. Buddhism is a religion which has been said to believe neither in God, nor the soul, nor in a future life. We shall examine these charges hereafter. But now go into the heart of Tartary and you will find thousands of monks living peacefully among the fierce tribes of the desert, kind, self-denying, engaged in daily worship and prayer. Their monasteries extend through Burmah, Thibet, China, and Japan. They teach their simple faith to millions of human beings, seeking to escape from the evils of time into the perfect rest of an eternal world.

Come down still later, to the sixth century after Christ. We are now in Arabia. It is mostly peopled by wandering tribes, divided from each other, roaming among the deserts of the vast peninsula, in search of pasture for their flocks. So they had roamed for a thousand years, hardly known to the civilized world, exercising no influence upon it. So they might have roamed for a thousand years longer. But a man appears among them with a fixed idea, a religious conviction, faith in one Supreme Being, one great master, and with an abhorrence for all inferior worship. His belief, after years of toil, he succeeds in spreading. He unites these children of the desert into mighty armies. They pour out like a flood, and sweep across Africa to the Atlantic, sweep over Syria and Persia into India, and at last as far as China. It seems to the world that its day of doom has come. But, after this outbreak of conquest, follows an outbreak of invention, thought, study. Great scholars arise among them, wonderful artists, who carve stone till it looks like lace. Scientific inventions follow in all directions. Europe goes to school to Asia, it reads Aristotle in Arabic, it learns astronomy, chemistry, and medicine at Cordova. The whole of this mighty flame which lit up the world during many centuries was kindled in the thought of one man, who really believed in God with all his soul. Such is the power of religious ideas.

Thus everywhere on the surface of the earth, from the earliest times, we find religions; each great nation and race, Egypt, India, Persia, Greece, Arabia, having its own special faith. Where did they come from? What is their value? Wherein do they differ? Wherein do they agree? Such are some of the questions we shall try to answer in this work.

Besides the religions I have specified there are of course many others, such as that of China, Judaism, the Scandinavian belief and worship, the state religion of ancient Rome, the strange forms and faith of the Assyrians, Babylonians, Phœnicians, Carthaginians, the religion of the Druids, and those found on the continent of America when it was discovered, the worship of the Mexican and Peruvian Empires. Lower down are the more primitive forms of religion, the tribal worship of ghosts, evil spirits, genii. Thus we see the whole world from the earliest times engaged in the worship of Unseen Powers.

How shall we bring this chaos into order? How extricate some system out of this confusion? Our first attempt must be to classify these varieties under some more general form. Then we can compare them together to find wherein they agree, and wherein they differ, and learn what there is of truth or error in each.

§ 4. *Definition of Religion.*

But first let us look for some simple, yet comprehensive definition of religion. Passing by others, I will for the present take this: "Religion is the worship and service by man of Invisible Powers, believed to be like himself, yet above himself." This definition includes what is called "Animism," or the worship of departed human souls, and also at the other extreme many forms of Pantheism. Spiritual Pantheism personifies the All of Things, making the universe full of feeling, consciousness, vitality, and purpose. Spinoza, the arch-Pantheist, declares that we must "love God as our supreme good," that "we love God and are blessed." Shelley, another Pantheist, has a hymn to "The Spirit of Intellectual Beauty," which he addresses as a being who can hear and answer; "an awful loveliness, which can give more than words express."

He says: "Let thy power supply calm to the life of one who worships thee." Even Fetichism is included in our definition, for the savage believes that the rude stone or block which he looks on with superstitious reverence, has an unseen spirit acting through it. It is the spirit which is feared or propitiated, and not the block. So we say that "Religion is the tendency in man to worship and serve invisible beings, like himself, but above himself." This supposes and includes the belief that there is a communication between the worshipper and the being worshipped, by which good or evil may come; that these beings can hear prayer and receive service, and in turn can send down help or hindrance, as they are pleased or displeased with their worshipper. Dr. Hedge says that "Fetichism is not materialism; but it is one of the first proofs of a spirit in man akin to the divine, that he can thus invest inferior and even inanimate creatures with the attributes of Deity." And through all the long ascent of thought from these humble idolaters to the worshipper of Him who is "above all, through all, and in all," "in whom we live, and move, and have our being," there is this one element in common, the faith in unseen powers above us, but not far from us, with whom we can speak, who can hear and answer prayer. No matter how much these thousand religions of the world may differ, they agree in this testimony;

that man has a natural inborn faith in supernatural powers with whom he can commune, to whom he is related, and that this life and this earth are not enough to satisfy his soul.

§ 5. *Religion is Universal. Exceptional Cases examined.*

Religion is so universal a phenomenon, that it may safely be said to belong to human nature. Though there may be tribes so debased as to manifest little or no religious tendency, we still call man a religious being. It would not affect our argument if such entire absence of the supernatural faculty should be verified in certain instances of depressed organizations.[1] As a matter of fact, however, no such instance has been found, certainly not verified. Mr. Tylor, in his work on "Primitive Culture," asks whether there have been any

[1] See, among other works, *Das Religionswesen der rohesten Naturvölker, von Gustave Roskoff. Leipzig: Brockhaus*, 1880.

In this work we find that Waitz considers the lowest races to be the Australians, Bushmen, Hottentots, and the inhabitants of Terra del Fuego. Peschel (*Völkerkunde*) regards some of the Indians of Brazil (Botucuden) as the lowest. Darwin, Fitzroy, and Wallis say that the people of Terra del Fuego are below all others. Burchell is of opinion that the Bushmen, D'Urville that the Tasmanian and Australian, Dampier and Forster that the people of Mallicollo, Owen that the people of the Andaman Islands (in the Bay of Bengal) are at the bottom. Lubbock gives this place to the Lapps. Others give it to the "Digger Indians." For authorities and references see also *Pfleiderer's Religions Philosophie*, Waitz *Anthropologie*, Sir John Lubbock's *Prehistoric Times*, Quatrefages' *Human Race*, Livingstone's *Journeys in South Africa.*

tribes of men so low in culture as to have no religious conceptions whatever? He replies by saying that no evidence has been brought forward of the existence of such tribes. He adds that the very writers who assert the non-existence of religious ideas among certain savages not unfrequently *give evidence themselves to the contrary.*[1] He quotes Dr.

[1] For Bushmen, see Burchell and Campbell (*Second Journey in Africa*). Livingstone is satisfied that the Bushmen worship a male and female deity. Arbousset says (Arbousset et Danmas, *Voyage d'Exploration*, etc.) that they believe in an invisible man in heaven, to whom they pray before going to war. As to the Hottentots, Sir J. Lubbock quotes Le Veillant, who says, "they have nothing which approaches the idea of an avenging or rewarding deity." But Waitz declares that Nott and Gliddon's comparison of the Bushmen to the Ourang outang is a "shameless exaggeration, made in the interest of slavery." Waitz thinks it is unjust to say they have no idea of religion; they worship the moon with dances and songs, etc. Kolb (*Journey to Cape of Good Hope*, 1719) declares they have religious ideas, believe in a divine creator and ruler, and call him "the great Captain." The moon is their visible God, but their invisible God they name "Jouma Tik-quoa," or "God of Gods."

As to the people of Terra del Fuego, Darwin (*Descent of Man*) says they have no religion. But he describes their blowing into the air to keep away evil spirits. Phillips, a missionary, complained of the heat of the sun, and a native exclaimed: "Do not say that; he will hide himself, and it will be cold."

As to the inhabitants of the Andaman Islands (see *Uncivilized Races*) they also are said to have no trace of religion. But Quatrefages informs us that the authors who assert this on the strength of Mowatt's testimony (*The Andaman Islanders*), overlook the evidence of Michael Symes and Day. The first reports what was told him by Captain Hockoe. Day tells us what he himself saw. Both state that the Mincopies worship the sun and moon, and the genii of the woods, waters, and hills as agents of those higher powers; that they believe

Lang as declaring that the aborigines of Australia have no idea of a divinity, no object of worship, no idol, "in short, that they have nothing whatever of the character of religion or religious observance to distinguish them from the beasts that perish." This statement of Dr. Lang has often been quoted as of high authority and as proof that men may exist with no trace of religion. But Dr. Lang himself states that these very tribes attribute smallpox to the influence of an evil spirit; that they propitiate him by an offering of honey, and sometimes by human sacrifices. Another traveller among these same savages, Mr. Ridley, says that he everywhere found among them definite tradi-

in an evil spirit who sends the storms; and that they believe in a future life.

The Tasmanians are denied, by Nidon and Dove (Lubbock), to have any religion. But Tylor quotes opposite opinions. Bonwick, *Daily Life of the Tasmanians,* describes various religious ceremonies, and says they believe in the ghosts of the departed. The Esquimaux and Greenlanders are classed by Sir J. Lubbock as people with no religion. But it is certain that they believe iu a great number of spirits. One is called an Innua, or possessor of the air, who also commands the people through sorcerers, as to what they must not do. There are also "Spirits of the Sea," "Spirits of the Fire," "Spirits of the Mountains," "War-spirits," and a mighty "Wind-spirit."

The religion of the Lapps is described by Klemm (*History of Culture*). They have Gods of the Sky, of the Thunder, and other elementary deities. They also worship the sun, and water.

The North American Indians are said, by Sir John Lubbock, to "have no religion, nor any idea of God." This is fully contradicted by many writers, and the opinion is now known to be without foundation. See, for example, the careful investigations of Brinton and Bancroft,

tions concerning supernatural beings, of whom one is the creator of all things and another the source of evil. Mr. Moffat, while declaring that the tribes of South Africa have no conception of a future life, himself gives the name used by them for the ghost or shade of the departed. In regard to South America, another writer, Felix de Arana, declares that the native tribes have no religious notion of any kind, and then presently states that the Payaguas bury arms and clothing with their dead to be used by them in another life, and that the Guavas believe in a being who rewards good and punishes evil. Evidently when these writers assert that such tribes have no religion, they mean they have no highly developed and organized religion, no systematic theology. They call them irreligious, just as the early Christians were called atheists by the Romans, because they had no public religion like that of Greece or Rome, no temples, altars, or sacrifices. We are too apt to say that a man has no religion who has a religion different from ourselves, that a man has no Christ who believes in another form of Christianity than ours, and that a man is without God who worships the Deity by other forms than our own. Socrates was called an atheist because his conception of the Deity was higher than that of his contemporaries. Spinoza was called an atheist because he believed there was nothing except God in the universe of being.

A similar narrowness of judgment is shown by those who assert that certain savage nations are wholly destitute of religion.

After examining these statements, Mr. Tylor concludes thus: "So far as I can judge from the immense mass of accessible evidence, we have to admit that the belief in spiritual beings appears among all low races with whom we have attained to thoroughly intimate acquaintance."

§ 6. *Religious Statistics of the World.*

Look at the map of the world. The population of our earth is supposed to amount to about 1,392,000,000. Of these about 100,000,000 are what are called Pagan or Heathen, by which is meant the lowest order of religious belief. Next to these is the chief surviving Polytheistic Religion, that of the Brahmans, numbering about 175,000,000. Then comes the religion of Buddha, which, with the system of Confucius, embraces some 420,000,000. The Mohammedans number 201,000,000, and the Christians, including Roman Catholic, Greek Church, Protestant, and smaller bodies, amount to about 388,000,000, — in all 1,284,000,000. The whole of Eastern Asia is occupied by the Buddhists, India by the Brahmins, large parts of Africa, Australia, and the South Sea Islands by the Pagan tribes, parts of Europe, Asia, and Africa by the Mohammedans, the largest part of Europe and America by Christians. The two monotheistic religions — Christianity and Islam — are believed by nearly half of the populations of the earth.

It may be said, however, that man outgrows all supernatural religion as he becomes more fully unfolded intellectually; that then, science, art, literature, humanity, take the place of God as the object of devotion and service. To see if there is any pronounced tendency in this direction, let us take the instance of the United States, — a country in which intellectual development has been carried further among the masses than anywhere else, unless we except parts of Germany. In 1850 there were in the United States 38,000 church buildings; in 1860 there were 54,000; in 1870 there were 63,000 (and 72,000 active organizations). In 1850 the buildings would accommodate 14,000,000 of persons; in 1860, 19,000,000; in 1870, 21,000,000. The value of church property in the United States in 1850 was $87,000,000; in 1860 it was $171,000,000; and in 1870 it was $354,000,000. The property had more than doubled in ten years, and these years included the whole Civil War. This would not be so remarkable in those States where there is a religious establishment, and where churches are built and supported by taxation. But in the United States church accommodations were provided by the free act of the people themselves for more than half the population, which was then less than 39,000,000, including the young and old, the sick, and those kept from church by all other causes. For this 39,000,000, 21,000,000 of church sittings were provided, and this in the land where 70 per cent. of the youth go to school, and in which over 1500 millions of copies of newspapers are published annually. Thus far the progress of education has not hindered the progress of religion. If anything can show that man in the highest state of culture yet attained continues to be a religious being, as he was in the lowest — these statistics will go far in that direction. Thus a survey of the history of the world brings us to the same conclusion with that of the Apostle, that God "has made of one blood all nations of men to dwell on all the face of the earth, having determined their appointed times and the bounds of their habitation, that they should seek the Lord, if haply they might feel after him and find him."

§ 7. *False Classifications.*

Paul here intimates that the Creator has not only implanted in man the tendency to feel after God, but also the capacity of finding him. It would much diminish our confidence in this statement if we were compelled to believe that the vast majority of the race had utterly failed of finding their Maker. Such, however, until recently, with few exceptions, has been the teaching of Christian theology. Christianity, we were told, is the only true religion; all others are wholly false, as bad as atheism or worse. Mohammedanism is a soul-destroying imposture; Buddhism is a denial of God and immortality; the idolatries of the poor heathen are the worship of devils; the heathen are not feeling their way upward to God, but downward to eternal ruin.

Of course, when we had thus divided the faiths of mankind by making one true and all the rest false, these false religions were deemed hardly worth studying, and were deprived of interest. Who cares much for the difference between one kind of falsehood and another? Nor can we say that man has a religious nature, if the vast majority of human beings have never found God. We could hardly assert that sight was a natural human function, if the greatest number of men were born blind. How much more large, generous, and just, how much more full of inspiration is the faith of Paul, that God has made *all men* to feel after him and find him, and that he has never left himself without a witness anywhere in the world?

The old classifications of the religions of the world were such as these:

True and False Religions.

Natural and Supernatural.
Paganism and Revealed Religion.
Spiritual Religion and Superstitions.

But such is not a scientific method; for, instead of beginning with the facts, it sets out from a theory. It judges every question beforehand. It also destroys our interest in the study, if we assume that the peculiarities of the great majority of the religions of the world are errors and falsehoods, having no special meaning or significance. But if we believe with Paul, that all the races of men are seeking after God, the case is different. Then the whole of the religions of mankind become at once full of interest to us; they all contain some elements of divine faith. At all events, in the study before us, we have only one interest, that is, to find what they really are, and to compare them together to discover their relations. Within a few years the opportunity for such study has vastly increased. Great progress has been made in the knowledge of the oldest religions. The writings on the Assyrian and Egyptian monuments have been deciphered, translated, and published. Many of the sacred books of the Brahmins, Buddhists, Chinese, and ancient Persians have become accessible by the labors of European scholars.

In beginning this study it is desirable, after defining religion, to find the true way of classifying the religions. This will be our first step out of confusion, comparing them in order to distribute them into classes. The old classification, as we have seen, was to divide them into true and false, — Judaism and Christianity being true, and all the rest false. But this classification assumes at the beginning the very fact which should appear, if at all, as the result of an inquiry. We wish now to find out what there is true, and what false in each. This classification, therefore, will not suffice. The same thing may be said of the division into natural and supernatural religion, — rational and inspired, and the like. All these assume at the beginning what ought to come out at the end, if it comes out at all.

§ 8. *A better Classification. Tribal, Ethnic, and Catholic.*

The only true method of classification is to base it on observed facts. If we look at the facts we shall immediately see that the less highly organized religions, which show an undeveloped ritual, priesthood, and creed, without sacred books, with no religious architecture or music, and which exercise little influence on the worshipers, belong to the undeveloped races, — those whom we usually call *savages*. I do not like the word savage, for it carries with it a touch of contempt and the absence of sympathy. Let us call them *childlike* or *primitive races*. They have not yet attained to national existence; they exist in tribes. The first class of religions, then, will be *Primitive Religions* or *Tribal Religions.*

Next we shall discover that many of the great religions of the world are confined to nations, each religion belonging to *one* nation, and never going beyond its limits. Thus, the religion of Egypt for many thousand years was confined to Egypt alone; the Assyrian religion to Assyria; that of Greece to the Hellenic race; that of Rome to the Roman people; that of Confucius to China; that of Brahmanism to India; that of the Eddas to the Scandinavian or Teutonic races. They never went beyond their boundaries, nor wished to go beyond them. You never hear of missionaries from Egypt trying to make converts in Europe to Osiris or Isis. Egyptian temples were to be found in Rome in later times, but they were for the use of the Egyptians living there. Indeed, it was a maxim in antiquity that each man *ought* to worship according to the religion of his nation, for religion was a *cult,* not a belief.

Therefore the second division in our classification will comprise the Religions of Races or Nations. I say races *or* nations, to meet the fact that sometimes two or three nations of the same race would hold the same religion, as, for example, the Lacedemonians and Athenians, both belonging to the same Hellenic race, and both adopting one Pan-Hellenic religion. We will call our second class *Ethnic Religions*, from the Greek word *ethnos*, which means nation, and also race.

But now we find another order of religions which manifest a tendency to overpass the boundaries of race, and to make converts outside. These are religions which have a belief, and in which worship follows faith. Such was the Jewish religion, which had confidence that the world must at last worship Jehovah, and that all the Gentiles would come to believe in him. Hence it was a missionary religion, compassing sea and land to make proselytes. Such also, as we know, is Christianity, which believes in converting the world to Christ. Such also is the religion of Mohammed, which, beginning as an Arab religion, has converted the Turks, the Persians, the Egyptians, Hindus, and many other races. Such, too, is the religion of Buddha, which sent out missionaries very early, and converted the people of Nepaul, Ceylon, Persia, Thibet, China, Japan, and other countries. There is reason to believe that the system of Zoroaster was also a missionary religion, and part of the strength of Cyrus consisted in the zeal of the conquering race to spread its religion among other nations.

These missionary religions, then, we will call *catholic*, that is, having a tendency to universality. Of the ten principal religions of the world, five are ethnic and five catholic. The religions of

Egypt, Greece, Hindostan, Rome, and Scandinavia are ethnic; those of Moses, Buddha, Zoroaster, Mohammed, and Jesus are catholic.

§ 9. *Other distinctions between Ethnic and Catholic Religions.*

We observe at once that another distinction appears, — the ethnic religions all grew up without any prophet as their founder; the catholic were each founded by a prophet. The first class were evolved out of the national life; the second class were taught by an inspired soul. This distinction also is worth noticing, for it can hardly be accidental.

Comparing again the ethnic and catholic religions, we notice yet another striking distinction between them. The religions founded by Moses, Buddha, Zoroaster, Mohammed, and Christ all teach with more or less distinctness the *unity* of God, recognizing one supreme power as the object of worship. On the other hand, the ethnic or evolved religions, as those of India, Egypt, Greece, Rome, and Germany, were *polytheisms,* with very little tendency toward unity. That the three religions of the great Semitic family, namely, those of Judaism, Christianity, and Mohammedanism, teach the unity of God there can be no doubt. But this is also true in a less degree of the doctrines of Buddha and Zoroaster.

Another distinction between ethnic and catholic religions is the greater morality and humanity in the latter. In ethnic religions there is very little connection between the service of God and that of man. Religion, in them, is divorced from morality. But in the catholic religions the opposite tendency is very apparent, though in different degrees, some of them showing much more of it than others.

Thus in the mythology of Greece, as found in its poets, there is no evidence that the gods required or expected righteousness and mercy from their votaries. Not possessing these qualities themselves, they could hardly demand them of others. Capricious, willful, jealous, envious, revengeful, licentious, as they are represented to be by the poets, having their favorites in whom they take an interest, but indifferent to the general welfare of mankind; interfering only occasionally in human affairs, usually from some personal motive, there is little moral influence to be derived from their worship.

The religion of Rome was essentially a state religion, concerning itself very slightly with the virtues of private life. That of Scandinavia made salvation to depend on courage: the brave soldier would go to Valhalla, and the rest of the world to Nifelheim, or the under world. Of the essentially moral defects of Brahmanism, and the exceptional moral merits in this regard of the religion of ancient Egypt, we will speak hereafter. It is certain, however, that religion and morality are much more closely united in the prophetic or catholic religions than in the ethnic. Moses and the Prophets, Mohammed, Buddha, Zoroaster, Confucius, all inculcate a serious personal law of goodness. This connection reaches its full harmony in Christ's placing together in one formula the duty of love to God and love to man, making these two forms of the same essential love.

All of these systems have their roots, however, in humanity and its needs; all have contributed to the education of man, and all, as we may hope, are finally to be reconciled and harmonized in that ultimate synthesis of faith, the universal religion. It will be one object of this work to endeavor to see how this universal religion shall arrive; whether by a further evolution of existing religions till they meet on a common plane, or by the substitution of some new faith wholly different from them all.

I shall accomplish what I wish to do in this book if I can bring myself and my readers into fuller sympathy with all forms of human nature and all shades of human belief. Without losing sight of the difference between Truth and Error, we may sympathize with all our fellow-men who are feeling after God. We shall have the spirit described by the poet when he speaks of the man: —

> "Slave to no sect, who takes no private road,
> But looks through Nature up to Nature's God;
> Pursues that chain which links the immense design,
> Joins Heaven and Earth, joins Mortal and Divine.
> Sees that no being any bliss can know
> But touches some above, and some below;
> And knows where Faith, Law, Morals, all began,
> All end, in love to God and love to man.
> For him alone, Hope leads from goal to goal,
> And opens still, and opens on the soul.
> Grasps the whole world of Reason, Life, and Sense
> In one close system of Benevolence.
> Wide and more wide, the o'erflowing of the mind
> Takes every creature in, of every kind.
> Earth smiles around, with boundless bounty blest,
> And heaven beholds its image in his breast."

CHAPTER II.

SPECIAL TYPES. — LAW OF DEVELOPMENT.

§ 1. Every Religion has its own Special Type. Two false Theories. § 2. Race and Nationality. § 3. Increased knowledge of Ethnic Religions during the last Century. § 4. Unity and Persistence of Type in Each Religion. § 5. The Typical ideas of Brahmanism, Buddhism, the Zend-Avesta, and the Religion of Egypt. § 6. Corruptions and Degradations of each Religion foreign to its original Type. § 7. Affirmations true; Negations false. § 8. Simplistic Systems are Short-Lived. Coördinated antagonisms necessary for continued Development.

§ 1. *Each Religion has its own Special Type. Two false Theories.*

THE subject of this chapter will be the special character, or type of each religion; that which distinguishes it from every other, and enables it to do a special work, different from every other; that which constitutes its power and its weakness, makes it acceptable to some and distasteful to others, develops a polar force which attracts or repels; its one special note which allots it a place in the great harmony of the coming universal religion of mankind.

I wish to show that each religion has this type of its own, to which it adheres as long as it lives and acts effectually, and also how we determine what this type is.

Each religion has a type of its own, to which it adheres during its whole growth and development.

Two views are opposed to this: (1.) The old Christian theological division, which put in one category all gentile or ethnic religions, calling them pagan, heathen, idolatries, superstitions. Because of this view no attempt was made to discover the character of each, as they were accounted equally false and worthy only of contempt. They were regarded, not as natural growths of the religious nature, but as monstrous deformities, proceeding from sin, and containing only error. (2.) In the reaction from this extreme some minds have gone to the opposite extreme. The reaction from the view which made all systems of faith outside of Christendom equally false, has produced the doctrine that they are all equally true. Similarities and resemblances have been found, and diversities ignored. The ethnic scriptures have been searched for parallels; these have been put side by side, and the conclusion has been easily drawn that all these faiths are essentially one, — possibly some a little better than others, — but all teaching the same essential truths concerning God and nature, man and morality, sin and pardon, immortality and retribution.

A scientific study of the faiths of the world will show both these two theories to be false. It will show that the same law applies to religions which is found to prevail in the other departments of nature; that the law of development is from the homogeneous to the heterogeneous; from chaos to cosmos; from monotony to variety; and that the great order and harmony of the universe results always from the concord of these varieties in mutual adaptation and coöperation. It would be a very poor concert in which there were fifty instruments all striking the same note and playing the same part. The harmony of the universe, like that of a chorus or a symphony, consists in the consenting varieties which accord in one divine union of agreeing though different parts.

That this is so can be only proved by extensive study, by collecting and comparing facts, and making the induction when all these facts have been ascertained.

The law of man's progress, in all the departments of human activity, has been from monotony to diversity, and by combined diversities to final coöperation and union. (1.) Monotony; (2.) Diversity; (3.) Harmony,—these are the three steps of human progress, in the development of races, nations, industries, literature, science, art, mental and moral character.

§ 2. *Race and Nationality.*

Some philosophical historians, like Buckle, have ignored wholly the fact and influence of race, and attributed all the varieties of mankind to the influence of climate, soil, and external conditions. Others, like Knox, have said that "race is everything." The two views must be combined. The power of climatic conditions is no doubt great; but many facts show that it never succeeds in breaking down the original type of a human family. The Jews, Arabs, Teutons, Kelts, Negroes, Mongols, preserve the same characters for thousands of years, under wholly different external circumstances. This shows that there was an unexplained divergent tendency implanted in man, which caused manhood to branch into races just as the tree branches into limbs, and then subdivides again into other smaller limbs. History shows us the original Aryan race in Central Asia, differentiating itself, according to this law, into seven great branches, which have continued to this day, viz.: the Hindu, Persian, Latin, Greek, Keltic, Teutonic, and Slavonic varieties. Another, the Turanian, has divided itself into the Mongols, Tartars, Turks, Magyars. Another, the Semitic, has branched into the Assyrian, Babylonian, Phœnician, Jewish, Carthaginian, and Arab tribes. All this has been proved by linguistic affinities.

But the law of differentiation does not exhaust itself in the lower ethnological divisions. It works on into the production of nationalities. The growth of national character is something which belongs even to modern history. We may be said to have seen this differentiation going on under our own eyes. We can observe in modern history the development of such distinct human types as the Italian, Spaniard, Frenchman, Englishman. A mixture of races, under new conditions, results in a new, distinct style of character — different from either — as when oxygen and hydrogen unite and produce water. The Englishman and Frenchman have characters of their own, and by some process of assimilation each citizen takes on more or less of his persistent national type. Here, in America, we see an American type gradually taking form, which, a hundred years hence, will have become another distinct and self-maintaining national type of character.

And so, too, within any race or nation, every new access of inward life shows itself in a new opening out of divergent forms of mental activity. So it was in Greece, when the wonderful Hellenic life-impulse suddenly developed such original forms of art and literature. Greek architecture, with its different orders, arrived. Greek statuary came, and rose to a sudden perfection. Plato and Aristotle developed systems of philosophy which have persistently dominated human belief to this hour. Homer invented the Epic. Herodotus and Thucydides discovered History; Pindar the Ode; Æschylus and Sophocles, the Tragedy; Aristophanes, the Comedy; Demosthenes and others, Oratory. What a branching out of the mind was here, and how these forms of literature, having been once developed, have persisted to this hour!

The same may be said of human arts and occupations. In this direction we call it "the division of labor." But it is the same law at work here. All the trades and professions of civilized society are differentiations of the homogeneous life of the savage, who does a little of everything, into the classified life of society, where each man works in his own branch of industry and so coöperates with the rest toward the harmony of the whole. Look at a great city, and see the whole combination which has grown up, not by any will of man, but by the working of a steadfast social law, which brings together just so many mechanics, so many tradesmen, so many professional men, so many bankers, engineers, writers; and so builds up a system of harmonious united coöperation.

I have gone over this rather detailed description of the unfolding of human life from monotony to diversity, and from diversity to harmony, to show that there is nothing to surprise us if we find that religion also pursues the same course, and that each one develops a style of its own.

But every religion has its accretions of incongruous material, its temporary relapses and revivals, its corruptions and reformations; and we must therefore inquire how we are to find that one special quality which belongs to it through all these changes. How shall we know what is a genuine development of the religion, and what is an addition from some outside influence?

§ 3. *Increased knowledge of Ethnic Religions.*

Fifty years ago, it would have been almost impossible to compare the religions of the world so as to detect their difference and resemblance. At that time little interest had been taken in this study. And yet it would seem evident, that Christianity which proposes to preach the Gospel to every creature, ought to be interested in knowing the beliefs and habits of the nations which it attempts to convert. In fact the growing interest of human beings in each other, is one of the most striking marks of modern civilization. The immense impulse given to the progress of our race in modern times by the invention of printing, the discovery of America, the Renaissance, and the Reformation itself, came from a growing interest of man in man. Printing was invented because writers wished to be read by larger multitudes; they no longer said with Horace: "I hate the profane vulgar, and beg them not to read my poems." America was discovered, because of the dim desire in the human soul to know all that belonged to the globe. The old world was large enough for the ancients; the greater heart of mankind in the fifteenth century sent explorers round the Cape of Good Hope, and across the stormy Atlantic to seek new lands and new men. The Renaissance meant the intense desire which pervaded Europe to know what men thought, said, wrote in the old world. Every one studied Greek that he might read Homer, Plato, Sophocles, Demosthenes. The Reformation was a revelation of the worth of every man as man, in the sight of God. It taught that every soul could go directly to God, without priest, ritual, or altar standing between. The discoveries and inventions of our time have not only brought men nearer to each other, but have themselves been indications of the desire of men to be brought nearer to each other. The steamship, railway, telegraph, testify that man every day becomes more interesting to man. On every such invention might be written the words, "Sacred to man."

Not the least among these discoveries have been those made in the direction of human language. The linguistic discoveries of the last century have added a new world to the domain of knowledge.

The whole world of Sanskrit literature was a sealed book to Western scholars, till the time of

Sir William Jones.[1] He was a good lawyer and writer on law. He published a work on "The Law of Bailments," which alone, according to Judge Story, "would have given him a name unrivaled in the common law for accuracy, learning, and power of analysis." When appointed a judge in Bengal, in 1783, he plunged with ardor into Sanskrit studies, and revealed to mankind the magnificent literature of ancient India. Since his time a succession of European scholars have followed in this path, till now, by their translations and commentaries, we can know as much of Brahmanism as of the Religion of the Jews.

As Sir William Jones led the way in the study of Sanskrit, Anquetil du Perron in like manner opened to Europe the ancient religion of Zoroaster.[2] The Zend-Avesta, which he was the first to translate into any European language, has since been studied by a multitude of scholars, like Spiegel, Haug, and others; and we are now able to understand the character and type of this system, which, through the great Persian Empire, exercised so great an influence in human history.

In the same way the languages which contain the Sacred Books of Buddhism have become known

[1] See, for the account of Sir William Jones and his work, *Ten Great Religions*; Part I., page 78.

[2] See for an account of Anquetil du Perron, *Ten Great Religions*, Part I., page 178.

to Europe, and this system also, in its origin and development can now be understood. And out of all these linguistic studies has arisen the modern science of comparative philology, which has thrown so much light on the relationship of races and nations. We now know more about the source of the Greek and Latin languages than the Greeks and Romans themselves knew. The same roots and grammatic constructions being in the Sanskrit, ancient Persian, Greek, Latin, Keltic, Teutonic, and Slavic languages, show that these seven are all branches of one original tongue; that this ancient tongue, which long ago perished, was spoken by a people inhabiting the high plateau of Central Asia; that this primitive race (who have left no other monument of their existence but these languages derived from that mother speech) were a pastoral people, but not nomadic; that they had houses, oxen, horses, sheep, goats, hogs, and domestic fowls; that they possessed the plow, the corn-mill and various tools, the decimal numeration, doors, windows, and fire-places in their homes, and that their year was of three hundred and sixty-five days.

How do we know all this, and much more than this, concerning this ancient Aryan race? They have left no record of their existence, except the unwritten airy sounds, the fugitive and winged words, which afterwards were found hidden in later languages, like fossils in some old strata of antediluvian rock. We know it by the modern science of comparative philology. That shows us certain things which have the same or similar names in the seven derived types of language. Thus, when we learn that house is in Sanskrit dama, in Zend demana, in Greek domos, in Latin domus, in Irish dahm, in Slavonic domu, from which root also comes our English word domestic, we may be pretty sure that the primitive Aryans lived in houses, and called them by a root-word from which all these have been derived. When we learn that boat was in Sanskrit nau, in Zend nawah, in Greek naus, in Latin navis, in old Irish nai, in old German nawa, we learn that they knew something of what we call in English *nau*tical matters, or *nav*igation.

In the same way we have learned about their emigrations, — that the two oldest branches of the Aryans left the high plateaus, east of the Caspian Sea, and descended from Aryana; the Hindus into the valleys of the Indus; the old Persians into Northern Persia; that the Latins preceded the Greeks, both passing south of the Caspian and Black Seas, and poured along the northern shores of the Mediterranean; that another flood of emigration went north of the Caspian, and entered Europe through Russia; that the Keltic races led the way, followed by the Teutonic and Scandinavian tribes, and finally by the Slavic people. All this, of which the ancients knew nothing, has been made known to us, during the last half century, by European scholars. If you had asked an ancient Greek the derivation of the Greek word thugateer, daughter, he could not have told you. But we could tell *him,* for we find in the Sanskrit its congener, thuckteer, which means both daughter and milkmaid, — showing that among that people it was the custom of the daughters of the house to milk the cows.

All this and much more has come from the studies in which Sir William Jones led the way.

§ 4. *Unity and Persistence of Type in each great Religion.*

We have spoken of the type of each great religion. Is there any rule by which to ascertain that type? In every faith there is something transient, and something permanent; something essential, and much that is accidental. But, in order to compare two or more systems of religion, it is necessary to be able to distinguish that which is essential in it from that which is non-essential. Thus idolatry has prevailed, both in Brahmanism, Judaism, and Christianity; but it would be unfair to contend that in either instance these were the natural and legitimate outcome of the faith. No support for idol-worship can be found in the sacred books of either sect; neither in the Old or New Testament, nor in the Vedas. It is an extraneous accretion, not a natural outgrowth. On the other hand, there may be a logical development of what, in the origin of the faith, was only a germ. Thus Christianity is essentially a missionary religion, though the Church at Jerusalem was at first reluctant even to receive the Gentiles into their body. It seems to have had little sympathy with Paul's efforts. And yet it is on record that the founder of the religion, on many occasions, expressed his interest in the outside world, and directed his disciples to go and preach the Gospel to every creature. The same spirit appeared in the successful attempts to convert the German tribes; and in the more distant missionary efforts undertaken, both by the Roman Catholic and Protestant branches of the church, which are kept up to the present day. The rule, therefore, which may be laid down for determining the typical character of each religion can be thus stated: "Whatever marks are found in the system at its origin, and which continue with it through all its changes, may be regarded as belonging to its idea, and as a part of its essence."[1]

Thus considered, it will be found that each of the great faiths which we are considering has its

[1] This corresponds to the famous definition of Catholic Unity by Vincentius Lirinensis: *Quod ubique, quod semper, quod ab omnibus.*

one essential and central idea, to which everything else is subordinate. All that persists in the religion is in harmony with this idea, and seems to grow naturally from it.

In the First Part of this work, I have placed opposite to the title-page a diagram intended to indicate in a general way the special type of each of the "Ten Great Religions." Eight are arranged around a circle, showing how they fill up the rounded circumference of religious tendency. They stand opposed and related thus: —

Brahmanism.	*Egypt.*
Spirit.	Body.
Substance.	Form.
Unity.	Variety.
Zoroaster.	*Islam.*
Freedom.	Fate.
Right and Wrong.	Divine Will.
Struggle.	Submission.
Scandinavia.	*Greece.*
Nature as Force.	Man.
Independence.	Beauty.
Battle.	Development.
Buddhism.	*Confucius.*
The Individual.	Society.
Nature as Law.	The Past.
Progress.	Conservatism.

This, however, is a suggestion, which is liable to

be altered and corrected on further study. Thus, it might be more accurate to consider the Teutonic faith as opposed to Buddhism, and the activity of the Greek mind to the quiet of China. These last might then stand thus: —

Scandinavia.	*Buddhism.*
Nature as Force.	Nature as Law.
Individualism.	Association.
Struggle.	Repose.

Greece.	*China.*
Development from within.	Discipline from without.
Progress.	Conservatism.
Beauty.	Order.

These differences originate in race, and are as permanent as race. There is no more persistent factor in human affairs than that of race. Nationalities grow and decay, but the social tendencies remain. After the Roman empire had fallen, the race tendency to strenuous organization reappeared in the Roman Catholic Church. It was Roman imperialism revived, with the Pope for an emperor. The vast Keltic emigration from Asia, which had swept over all of Europe before the arrival of the Teutonic tribes, had impressed their qualities on all the nations derived from them. One of these qualities was readiness to submit to a chief, a tendency which resulted in Cæsarism and the Papacy, and is seen at this time in loyalty to leaders in politics and religion. Wherever the Keltic blood is found to-day, these traits manifest themselves. On the other hand, the Teutonic race, in all its ramifications, tended to independent thought and action, to individual rights and personal freedom. Hence Protestantism originated with the German races, and holds its own now only among those nations who are descended from that stock. The strength of Protestantism is in Germany, Holland, Norway, Sweden, Denmark, England, and the United States. In these nations the German blood predominates. The strength of the Roman Catholic Church is in these other nations who are most permeated by the Keltic blood: France, Ireland, the Latin states, and their descendants in South America. Ancient Greece had a much smaller tincture of this blood than Italy, and thus it offered a constant resistance to Roman imperialism; and the Greek Church of modern times, next to Protestantism, is the chief antagonist to the Roman Papacy.

How races originate no one is able to say, nor is it important to decide. This differentiation of mankind into tribes may have come from some law of variation originally implanted by the side of the law of heredity. All the members of the great Aryan stock, Hindus, Persians, Greeks, Romans, Kelts, Germans, and Slavs, have some common marks in which they agree. All the Semitic varieties are united by similar common resemblances. This appears in their social customs, their personal qualities, and their religions. Among the Semitic nations God is seen as a personal unity of will. Among the Aryans he appears as unity in variety. Among the Turanians, the unity is lost in the variety. The Turanians (Mongols, Tartars, etc.) have therefore never succeeded in founding any great religion, for they have borrowed Buddhism from the Hindu-Aryans. Pure polytheism cannot hold together; it is naturally disintegrated into a multitude of separate modes of worship, in which each God is independent of every other. The polytheism of Egypt was rooted in a mysterious unity behind the variety. The polytheism of Greece had a supreme council of deities on Olympus, among whom Zeus was the omnipotent chief. The tendency of Aryan piety was away from polytheism toward pantheism; that of the Turanian belief was in the opposite direction, from polytheism toward atheism. The first of these tendencies is seen among the Hindus and Greeks; the last in the systems of Confucius and Buddha. Judaism and Mohammedanism regard the Deity as the one alone, the Supreme Will, above nature as its maker and ruler. Christianity was able to become a universal religion by effecting a harmony between Aryan and Semitic thought, in its doctrine of the Trinity. The meaning of the Trinity is unity in variety, the unity of spirit in the variety of nature; God, not only above all, but also through all, and in us all. The Father was regarded as the creative power above nature, the Son as the divine intelligence within nature, and the Spirit as the life in the soul of man. The practical object of this doctrine was to make possible a union of Semitic and Aryan thought. As a formulated doctrine it is now outworn, and its need is gone. But at the time when it came, it no doubt met a want, and did an important work. By modifying the strict unity of Judaism, it satisfied the needs of Aryan thought. But if we apply to this doctrine our rule, as stated above, we shall see that it is no essential part of Christianity, since it was not found in the system in its origin in the teachings of Jesus and his Apostles, and has never been universally accepted by the church.

Four great religions, which a century ago were virtually unknown to Western scholars, have in our time been fully revealed. The work of Sir William Jones, of Anquetil du Perron, of Champollion, and of Burnouf, has been continued by a host of scholars. We now are prepared to examine and understand the religions of India, of Persia, the Buddhism of the East, and the teachings so long hidden in the hieroglyphics of Egypt.

But unless we can obtain some clue to the germinal and radical idea of each system, our minds will be dissipated in a vast multitude of details. Somehow we must find our way to the centre, and seen from that point all will become clear and harmonious.

§ 5. *The Typical ideas of Brahmanism, Buddhism, the Zend-Avesta, and the Religion of Egypt.*

(*a.*) *The Essential Idea in Brahmanism.* It seems impossible to doubt that the most fundamental conviction in Brahmanism is the reality of spirit, and that spirit is the only reality. All existence is phenomenal, and is rooted in spirit, which is essence. Spirit is substance; it is one; it is the Para-Brahm: above all things, through all things, the reality in all things.

In the "Ten Great Religions," Part I., pages 116–123, I have quoted from the ancient Hindu philosophy passages which support this view. Innumerable others might be found to the same effect. The Vedanta philosophy makes the Deity say, "I am the great Brahma, eternal, pure, free, one, constant, happy, existing without end. He who ceases to contemplate other things, retires into solitude, annihilates his own life; he understands that spirit is the one and the eternal. The wise man annihilates all the things of sense, and to him they do not exist." "The world," says Sankara, "is Not-Being. It is appearance without reality, a delusive show." The Vedanta says: "From the highest state of Brahma to the lowest condition of a straw, all is illusion." The soul is a part of God himself.

Such was ancient Brahmanism; it was faith in pure spirit. Its worship was contemplation and adoration. The idolatry and polytheism which came afterward make no essential part of it, though they came by a natural reaction from an extreme spiritualism.

It was the worship of spirit, spirit as seen in all nature. Its hymns and prayers, its epics, its philosophy, were all intensely spiritual. The joy of a Hindoo in the beginning was worship; and his joy to-day is worship. The tendency of the system has always been towards pantheism, making God the only reality, and absorption in him the highest good. Hence it has run largely into abstract thought and contemplation. It produced the first anchorites, who wished to shuffle off the flesh by the most extreme mortification of the body.

The same tendency to spiritual worship exists unchanged in the Hindu mind to-day. That curious phenomenon, the Brahmo sect, is a testimony to the permanence of this type. This body originated with Ram-Mohun-Roy, a very noble Hindu reformer. His object was to persuade his countrymen to forsake idolatry and become monotheists, and he appealed to their ancient scriptures to prove that their uncorrupted religion was a pure monotheism.

An offshoot of this system is that of which Chunder Sen is the head. His doctrine is that all the great religions of the world are one. He speaks with profound respect of Jesus Christ, as the chief teacher of the human race, above all other prophets. I quote a passage from a recent discourse of Chunder Sen: —

"Remember your creed, one God, one Scripture, and one family of prophets. Love the one true God, and worship him every day. By daily worship make your lives holy. Attain communion with the saints of heaven inwardly in your minds. Eat their flesh and drink their blood, and turn your bodies into vessels of holiness. In your lives show the reconciliation of perfect wisdom, perfect asceticism, perfect love, perfect devotion, perfect conscience, perfect joy, and perfect holiness. Be not satisfied with the fraction of any one virtue. Do not covet the prosperity and pleasure of this world. Preserve your lives with the food that comes from mendicancy. Be happy in others' happiness, and sorry in others' sorrow. Regard all mankind as one family. Hate not, nor regard as aliens, men of other castes and other religions. Be ascetics, but live in the world in the midst of other men, and let them live in you. And let both them and yourselves live conjointly in God. There is salvation in unity, and peace in unity. Go in all directions, east and west, north and south, and preach the New Dispensation. Let no regard for men cause you to mix with the dispensation what does not belong to it. If any men meet you as enemies, let the peace of your prayers descend on their heads. Be poor and patient in spirit. Conquer contention with peace. Let peace and purity flow into the place where you go."

The following "Garland of a Hundred Names" is a list of titles of the Almighty adopted by the New Dispensation as suitable to their theistic worship, the titles of the Creator as taught by eclecticism: —

God, Lord, Holy, Great, Father, First Cause, Supreme Spirit, Almighty, All-Merciful, Saviour, Friend of the Poor, Moral Governor, Deliverer of the fallen, Absolute Substance, Primary Force, Life of life, Bodiless, Formless, Divinity, Adorable, Ancient, Giver of success, Dispenser, Triumphant, Heavenly King, Master, Eternal, Infinite, Self-caused, Self-existent, Resplendent, Excellent, Omnipotent, Omnipresent, Omniscient, Ocean of Love, Fountain of Joy, Captain of the vessel of life, Destroyer of danger, Extinguisher of sorrow, Lord of hosts, Abode of Beauty, Charmer of the soul, Awful, Conqueror of Death, Providence, Teacher, Creator, Preserver, Immaculate, One, All-witness, Smiling Mother, Light of Truth, Sea of Nectar, Necklace of the devotee, Crown of the martyr, Glory of the saint, All-Seeing, Beautiful Eye, Defender of the weak, Blissful, Self-manifest, Consoler of the distressed, Healer of the soul diseased, Everlasting, Chastiser of the wicked, Perfect, Inexorable Judge, Light of the eye, Supreme Intelligence, Guide, Priceless treasure, Heaven of peace, Without a second, Enchanter of the world, Queen of the Universe, True, Gratifier of pure desires, Household Deity, Bread of life, Endless Space, Supporter of the ascetic, Infinite Love, Water of the thirsty heart, Sovereign of all nations, Joy of the worshipper, Sender of prophets, Eternal scripture, Harmony, Inspirer, Matchless, Ever-living, Immanent, Invisible, Unfathomable, Comforter, Architect, Sun of Righteousness, I am.

In our time, when so much of Western Philosophy has committed itself to a sensationalism which makes the very idea of the Infinite and Eternal world an impossibility, it is a refreshment to find this majestic Indian literature, beginning a thousand years before our era, raising its solemn and venerable voice in testimony that eternity is the great reality, and that the human soul is made to believe in the living God. This faith is not anything artificial, but a native instinct. The great Hindu race stands in the world to testify, through thousands of years, that man belongs not only to time and sense, but to that also which transcends all the things which are seen and temporal. This is the place of India and of the great Brahmanic beliefs in the history of religion.

(*b.*) *The Essential Idea in the Worship of Egypt.* The ancient Egyptians covered the walls of their temples and tombs with pictures and carved inscriptions. They also wrote down the details of their lives on innumerable rolls made of papyrus. They carved on the marble casings of the pyramids, on the walls of public buildings, on the obelisks and columns, the deeds of their kings, the writings of their poets, and their Sacred Hymns; every spot of wall was covered with this indelible writing. The Hindus, living for eternity, cared little for the events of time, and had no historical records. The Egyptians, with an exactly opposite tendency of thought, seemed to consider every earthly event as providential and therefore sacred. So they recorded everything. But their writing was unintelligible to all but themselves. Neither the Greeks nor Romans, while masters of Egypt, were able to read this writing. It appeared to them an unattainable secret, a hopeless mystery. And so it continued till the younger Champollion, born in 1790, made the greatest discovery of modern times in the domain of history, by deciphering and translating the Egyptian hieroglyphics. Numerous scholars have followed in the path opened by him; and now the hieroglyphics of ancient Egypt may be translated with as much certainty as the writings of the classic authors.

The religion of India saw God pervading all

nature, but especially to be found dwelling in the soul of man. Union with him was union with Infinite Spirit, — the substance of the Universe, the only reality. Time and the things of earth are of no account, — only Eternity is true.

But the Egyptian religion looked for God in the opposite direction; in time and space; in bodily organization; in the wonder and mystery of all forms of life; in the instincts of animals. Animal-worship merely meant the sight of God's thoughts as embodied in each creature. Embalming was preserving the body to receive the soul once more after its long transmigration; at least, such is the opinion of some competent judges. No nation ever laid such stress on the hereafter as the Egyptians. Their whole religion seemed to revolve in a circle around the life to come.

This life to come was a continuation of bodily existence, an extension of time and space relations into another world. It involved a long series of transmigrations into various animal forms; a long struggle with a succession of demoniac enemies; a kind of Pilgrim's Progress toward a final Paradise.

Every organized existence was to the ancient Egyptian a manifestation of the Divine Idea. If India saw God wholly above Nature, as an absolutely Supernatural Being, — Egypt beheld him immersed in Nature, — a perpetual Creator, pouring life and beauty into all visible things. And the mission of Egypt in religious history was to develop this idea of the one Divine Life in all natural existence.

No doubt the conception of one Supreme Spiritual Being, above time and space, made a part of this system. But it was the esoteric element, the hidden mystery, the secret belonging to the inner circle of adepts. From the popular worship it was reserved by the priests, as something too abstract for the sensuous temperament of the people. In this race the African element predominated so largely that their religion tended constantly to embody itself in outward facts and forms; in temples, processions, pictures, and the worship of Gods with human qualities.

(c.) *The Essential Idea in the Worship of Zoroaster.* The radical thought with the great prophet of Persia is that of the eternal distinction between right and wrong,[1] and the duty of contending for the right against wrong. The Gods and good men are on one side in this great battle of time, the demons and bad men on the other. The soldier of Ormazd contends against Ahriman by good thoughts, good words, and good actions.

This is the warlike element which reappears from time to time in all religions. According to this view religion is not rest, but battle. But it is

[1] See *Ten Great Religions*, Part I., pp. 132, 133.

a battle with invisible foes, fought with no earthly weapons, but with the free power of a righteous soul.

(*d.*) *The Essential Idea of Buddhism.* The system of which Sakya-Muni was the founder, is at present a vast mass of metaphysics, ritual, and outward forms. But its central idea is very simple. It is as moral in its way as that of Zoroaster. But it is not a moral struggle for right against wrong, in the hope of a triumph of good. It is simple obedience to natural law. It is first discovering and then submitting to the laws of the universe. In this system the nature of things is the supreme power, and this nature of things is on the side of goodness. Every good act is rewarded, every bad one punished, with inevitable certainty. Every time one does right he goes up, whenever he does wrong he goes down.

To sum up briefly these types, we may say: —

1. Brahmanism is faith in spirit, as the only substance, — a substance which gives unity to all phenomena.

2. The faith of ancient Egypt was at the opposite pole of thought. It saw the divine in variety, not unity; in body, not spirit; in form, not substance.

3. The Scandinavian religion saw the divine in nature, appearing as force, making life a battle and placing morality in self-reliance.

4. The antagonist system to this was that of Greece, which saw the divine manifested, not in nature, but in man, having its essence in the beautiful and its morality in natural human development.

5. The system of Zoroaster was the worship of free will in the creator and the created, and its morality consisted in the free struggle of right with wrong, inspired by the hope of an ultimate triumph of good over evil.

6. I find the opposite pole to this system in that of Mohammed. Islam means the worship of one God as supreme will, whose law is fate, and whose service is submission.

7. Buddhism is the deification of the human soul, saved by the knowledge of the laws of nature. Buddhism makes morality consist in progress, by obedience to natural law as revealed by Buddha.

8. The religion of Confucius is reverence for the past, and his morality is conformity to the highest proprieties and conventions, as established by superior persons.

9. The essence of Judaism is the worship of one Supreme Spiritual Being, the Maker and Lord of all things. Its morality is obedience to his law, which consists in loving and serving God and man.

§ 6. *Corruptions and Degradations of each Religion, foreign to its original type.*

When we succeed in grasping and holding the radical motive of each system of belief, we are able to see that much historically connected with it is an adventitious accretion. Such phenomena are either not to be found in the religion in its origin; or else have not continued to belong to it during its subsequent development. No doubt there is a reason why they came. They are not to be considered as accidental. Nevertheless they do not belong to the type, but are corruptions or unessential additions to it.

Thus I do not consider as essential to Brahmanism the caste system, idolatry, the Indian Triad, the incarnations of Vishnu or its developed polytheism. None of these appear in the Vedas. The powers of Nature are there worshipped, but as manifestations of something deeper, namely, the spirit which pervades all Nature. These may be shown to be the logical growths out of an extreme and one-sided spiritualism, but do not belong to its essential character.

In fact, we may say, generally, that the corruptions and degradations of each religion are not the natural outcome of its type, but of the one-sided and exclusive development of that type. Monasticism belongs to the type neither of Buddhism nor Christianity, but consists in making the saving of the individual the end of all being. So the caste system and hierarchal authority in Brahmanism, in the religion of Egypt and in mediæval Christianity belong not necessarily to either system; but they are the logical result of making the worship of God the main duty of man; that is, of the assumption that man was made for religion, and not religion for man. For as soon as we yield to this assumption, the all-important question becomes this: "What is the right service of God?" And this throws all the power into the hands of the priesthood, whose business it is to see that worship is ritualistically correct.

§ 7. *Affirmations True; Negations False.*

Of all the systems of belief which have had a widespread hold on mankind, this may be posited: that they are commonly true in what they affirm; false in what they deny. The error in every theory is usually found in its denials, that is, in its limitations. What it sees, is substantial and real; what it does not see is a mark only of its own limited vision. The ground of this principle is that what we affirm is usually the result of our knowledge; while what we deny merely indicates our ignorance.

The best illustration of this principle of the essential truth of the affirmative side of any system of thought, and that errors are usually in denials, may be found in the ideas of the religions which we are examining.

Brahmanism, as we have seen, is faith in spirit as the only substance, which gives unity to all things.

In asserting this, it bears witness to a great and eternal truth. The substantial reality of spirit, as below all things, — substance in all forms, unity in all variety, — this is the great reality which it was the mission of the Hindoo mind to discover and declare, and which it knows and declares to-day with as strong a conviction as at first. Through all its sacred and profane literature, — in the Vedas and the Upanishads, the Baghavat-geeta and Sakoontala, the great epics and the great philosophies, — there runs forever this stream of faith in the absolute and supreme reality of spirit.

But when Brahmanism left this safe ground of assertion and affirmation, and went on to deny the reality of time and space, soul and body, nature and human personality — calling all these Maya or illusion — it committed its fatal error, from which many evil consequences have proceeded. In the interest of piety, it lost the basis of morality; in its aspiration toward the unseen and eternal it weakened the springs of human energy, and prepared the way for that effeminacy of temperament which has now, during many hundreds of years, made this great race the slaves first of native tyrants, and afterward of Mohammedan or European rulers.

Buddhism was a reaction from this one-sided Hindu spiritualism. It came to assert the reality of the human soul,[1] and of the external universe. These two assertions, or affirmations, are its great merit. Like Brahmanism it is true in what it sees; false in what it omits to see. It is right in asserting nature, wrong in omitting spirit; right in affirming time, wrong in denying eternity; right in positing the finite form, wrong in neglecting the infinite essence; wise in its sight of creation, foolish in its ignorance of a Creator; and as Brahmanism generated an imperfect civilization by its ultra-spiritualism, so Buddhism generates an imperfect civilization by its ultra-naturalism. Both of them are arrested civilizations, lacking the principle of continued progress.

§ 8. *Simplistic systems are short-lived in their vital energy. Antagonisms necessary for a long-continued development.*

A single, one-sided view of life soon exhausts its power of developing character. Antagonisms of thought are necessary to progress; and the most wonderful developments of national power and in-

[1] The current opinion, that Buddhism denies the reality of the soul, will be considered hereafter.

tellect are brief and evanescent if not sustained by this continued antagonism of opposing but not contradictory ideas.

This, for example, appears again in two other forms of rapid national development, both wonderfully exuberant for a time, though springing from very opposite religious ideas, I mean those of Greece and of Islam. I have already spoken of the rapid rise and sudden decline of the Hellenic genius. During about two hundred years this splendid fire flamed up, and then faded away. So it was with the equally wonderful, though not so original, blossoming-out of Arab art, science, and literature. The passage of two or three centuries saw the beginning and the end of this strange phenomenon.

The idea in the Greek religion, which was one source of Greek development, was the sight of something divine in human nature. The Greek gods were men, human beings, divine men and women, living only a little way off, on the summit of Olympus, occupied with human loves and hatreds, feastings and jests, wars, contrivances, deceptions. They were in no sense supernatural, hardly alarming. They interfered but seldom in human affairs, and if one of them became angry with a mortal, some other god was sure to step in and befriend him. Each one represented some human quality carried to its perfection: human wisdom, courage, beauty, skill, adroitness, genius, geniality; these found their apotheosis in Pallas-Athene, in Ares, Aphrodite, Hephaistos, Dionusos, Phœbus-Apollo.

In this anthropomorphism there is something true. There *is* a divine element in human nature; there is something godlike in man. Besides the instincts which he shares with the animals, that which is essentially human is something which makes him akin to Deity. Man is the son of God, and amid all his sin, folly, ignorance, and weakness, the sparks of the divine fire are never wholly quenched. He is capable of aspiration, generosity, courage to defy death in a good cause, capable of devoting himself to truth, and to the worship of the infinite beauty. This fact of the divine element in humanity, the Greeks saw; and this was the chief source of that wonderful development of human faculties which came between the time of the battle of Marathon, B. C. 490, and the reign of Philip of Macedon, B. C. 360, or in about one hundred and thirty years.

This sight of the capacities of human nature was the great inspiration of Grecian development, which was made possible by the liberty belonging to Greek institutions, and the favorable position of the race as to climate and geographical conditions. But why, then, was the period of development so brief, and so soon arrested? Climate and geography have remained the same till to-day; the race remains the same. What has become of the Greek genius?

> "Eternal summer gilds them yet;
> But all, except their sun, is set!"

The cause of the rapid decline of Greek civilization is to be found in the perpetual internecine struggles and wars of the Hellenic tribes. Outward force failed to destroy them while they were united — want of union was their ruin. Freedom without union was their danger. The human polytheism of Greece secured their freedom, but left them without union. The Pan-Hellenic festivals were not enough. They needed to be bound together as the Jews and Mohammedans and Christians have been bound together by the worship of one supreme God. They had in their faith the forces of humanity and freedom; they needed those of unity and order, — some common law, some binding morality. This is my explanation of the rapid fall of Greek civilization.

It may be said that Islam, which possessed this unity, had an equally brief career of progress. That is true. The religion of Mohammed is the exact opposite to that of Greece. If the Greek faith was inspired by humanity, variety, and freedom, that of Islam taught unity, submission, and the absolute sovereignty of one God. Every Mohammedan was the servant of the one true God, and his mission was to convert the world to Allah, and to his prophet. This great hope inspired and united the tribes of Arabia, and is the only explanation we have of that prodigious development of art, science, literature, which followed the conquests of the Saracens. These Arab races had been sleeping in their deserts for a thousand years, a nullity in the affairs of the human race. A religious idea awakened them, and vitalized them into amazing activity. They ran their strange career for a couple of centuries, and then faded again into apathy.

We perceive that Islam, like the Greek religion, like those of India and Persia and Rome, like Buddhism and the system of Confucius, has seen one side of truth, — but failed to see the opposite. Islam saw God, but not man; saw the claims of deity, not the rights of humanity; saw authority, failed to see freedom, — therefore hardened into despotism, stiffened into formalism, and sank into death.

The chief superiority of Christianity to other religions, as I shall hope hereafter to show, is not that it taught what had never been known before; not that it contains only truth, while all the rest contain only error; but that it is all-sided, all-embracing, hospitable to all truth. It is not exclusive but inclusive. Each of the other great religions give us one side of truth. Christianity, by a deeper inspiration, allies itself with all truth.

But we shall be in the fullest sympathy with the spirit of Jesus, if in these studies of other religions we look for truth rather than error, for good rather than evil. We shall not be able to understand them, so long as they seem to us only the work of priestcraft; only an outbreak of superstition; only the exhibition of human weakness and error. The larger view is the truer view. Each represents the aspirations of the soul toward God; each comes from the highest, not the lowest part of man's nature; each contains some essential truth; and each has conferred on the world some lasting blessings. They have all been, and all are, indispensable to the development of mankind. They make a part of the education of the world. We need them all; God needed them all; they have been His property since the world began. Every earnest seeker, every sincere thought, is a blessing to the world. The moral of our study is that of Mr. Emerson's beautiful poem, "Each and All": —

> "All are needed by each one,
> Nothing is fair or good alone."

CHAPTER III.

ORIGIN AND DEVELOPMENT OF ALL RELIGIONS.

§ 1. Two ways in which religions begin: suddenly, under the influence of a Prophet; or gradually, out of a national tendency. § 2. Religions derived from previous religions, by imitation or reaction. Influence of the Greek upon the Roman Theology; of the doctrines of Egypt on the teaching of Moses; of Buddhism on Christianity; of Judaism and Christianity on Mohammedanism. § 3. Origin of all religions. Three answers. Transformed sensations cannot give to us the Idea of the Infinite. § 4. Belief in disembodied spirits the first form in which the religious nature manifests itself. § 5. The world of Dreams, and its influence. § 6. Why do Primitive Races fear Ghosts? § 7. Demoniacal Possession and Exorcism. § 8. In all childlike races religion is the same. Animism the first step in religion. § 9. The next step upward gives Polytheism. The Vedic Hymns. The Character of Polytheism. § 10. Arrested and progressive Development. The point of religious development reached by Zoroaster. § 11. When Polytheism degenerates, it becomes Idolatry. The relapse of Brahmanism. That of Egypt. How Religions Decay. § 12. The Mexican Religion at the Time of the Conquest was the degenerate form of an anterior Monotheism. Its mixture of pure moral teaching and terrible superstitions.

§ 1. *The two ways in which Religions begin.*

THE origin of religion is a question which has been much discussed of late. Three courses of the Hibbert Lectures in England have taken this for their subject. The first was by Max Müller, the second by Renouf, the third by Rhys Davids, all eminent Oriental scholars. The last work of Herbert Spencer examines the same subject.

This question, however, is really two questions. One asks wherein is the root and source of RELIGION; the other inquires how each special religion began; in what movement it had its origin.

Looking for a moment at the second of these topics, we find that *Religions* begin very differently. Some are slowly unfolded by a gradual process out of the life of a nation or race. This is the fact with what we have called Ethnic religions, as those of Egypt, India, Greece, Rome, Scandinavia. So far as we can see, these all gradually took form, in accordance with the character of the nation or race.

But the other class, which we have called Catholic religions, come more abruptly; not so much by development as by a kind of crisis. These all proceed from the personal influence of some inspired soul. They are prophetic religions. Thus arose, not slowly, but in a few years, the systems of faith and worship taught by Zoroaster, Buddha, Moses, Christ, Mohammed. The beginnings of religions, therefore, greatly differ, according as they grow out of a national tendency, or are taught by some inspired prophet.

§ 2. *How religions are derived from previous religions?*

Another question in regard to the beginnings of specific religions is this: Are they ever derived from each other? Does one ever originate in another? It is certain that one national form of belief or worship may be greatly indebted to another. Thus the religion of Rome was largely borrowed from that of Greece. Creuzer affirms as a prominent fact that there was a concourse of Oriental, Pelasgic, Samothracian, and Hellenic elements in the religion of Rome. The Romans were, no doubt, an imitative people, with very little originality. They borrowed and begged their stories about the gods, from Greece or elsewhere. Jupiter was a transformed Zeus, Apollo was Phœbus under another name, Venus was Aphrodite, Mercury was Hermes, and so on. But, as Hegel long ago remarked, these resemblances are superficial; the two religions were radically different. The Roman gods were prosaic persons, with little character of their own; in fact, servants of the state and performing various useful offices. There was a Jupiter Pistor, presiding over bakers. There was a goddess of ovens; another, Juno Moneta, who took care of the Roman coin. There was a goddess who presided over *doing nothing*, Tranquillitas Vacuna. So that, after all, the Roman religion and worship had each a character of its own, wholly different from that of Greece.

It is sometimes asserted that Moses borrowed his monotheism and the Jewish ritual from Egypt, because he was learned in all the wisdom of the Egyptians.

The sacred books of Egypt taught the unity and spirituality of God, the immortality of the soul, and a future judgment, besides a morality of justice and mercy. The Jewish priesthood was in some respects like that of Egypt, and the two rituals had some analogy with each other. But here again the resemblances are on the surface, the differences are radical. The doctrine of the divine unity was a secret doctrine in Egypt, but it was made by Moses the public faith of the nation. The polytheistic idolatry, which constituted the public worship of the Egyptians, Moses made a crime. And the doctrine of a future life, which played so large a part in Egyptian faith, is nowhere distinctly taught in the Books of Moses. The striking fact in regard to the two religions is not that they resemble each other, but that they differ so essentially.

The resemblances between Buddhism and mediæval Christianity are so great that it seems at first as if one must have copied from the other. We find, in both, monks living in monasteries, mendicant orders taking the three vows of poverty, chastity, and obedience, telling their beads on a rosary, going about begging, with bare feet, shaven crowns, and a rope round the body. We find in Buddhism and mediæval Christianity, bells, images, and holy water, a service in a dead language, choirs, priests, processions and incense, abbots, monks and nuns, the worship of saints and angels, confession, fasts and purgatory, reverence for a divine mother and child, relic-worship, pilgrimages to the shrines of saints, and even a pope in each, with his triple tiara. And yet history shows us that neither could have borrowed from the other, that there was no contact or intercourse between the two systems, but each developed these remarkable coincidences of ritual independently of the other, out of common human needs and human tendencies. This proves how unwise it is to infer from similarity of form in any two systems that one was derived from the other.

Islam, perhaps, more than any other faith, derived its essential doctrines from preceding religions. Nearly every dogma in the Koran is taken from Judaism or Christianity. And yet Mohammedanism came, not as a continuation of these, but as a reaction against them. It was a revolt against the narrowness of Judaism and the laxity of the Christianity of that region. Especially, it was a declaration of the unity of God against the saint-worship of the East in those days.

In fact, a new religion is much more likely to come by a reaction against an old one than an imitation of it. Christianity was a reaction against the dead formalism of Judaism. Islam was a reaction against the dead formalism of Eastern Christianity. Protestantism was an anti-sacerdotal and anti-ritual reaction against the formalism of mediæval Christianity. And so, Buddhism was a reaction against the sacerdotalism and ritualism of Brahmanism. It rejected the whole system of caste and salvation by a priesthood. It taught, as Luther taught, salvation by faith. It made all men equal before God, as Protestantism made them equal. Its ritual came later, after its early energy of faith had begun to decay. For as spiritual life goes out, forms come in. When the ship of faith can no longer pursue its voyage over the storm-tossed sea of life, it comes to anchor in the quiet harbor of ritualistic worship.

Special religions, therefore, begin either as growths out of a national life and national character, by the original influence of some great prophetic soul, or by a reaction against something one-sided and extreme in an existing faith.

§ 3. *Origin of all religion.*

But when we come to the origin of all religion, and ask whence religion itself arose, there are three answers: an original Supernatural Revelation; a Natural Revelation by religious ideas planted in human nature; or the transformation of the experience of the senses into something higher by a process of evolution. Of the first we shall not speak, but briefly consider the two others.

The philosophical theory that there is nothing in the human consciousness beside transformed sensations, is obliged to deny to man a religious nature. It has even led a certain school of thought to deny that we possess ideas which certainly appear to be not only universal but necessary — such as Cause, Substance, the Soul, the Infinite. Nothing which cannot be derived from sensation is allowed to exist as knowledge. There are two things which all mankind think that they know, namely, their own existence, and the existence of an outward world. But since these are not derived from sensation, it has been thought necessary to deny their existence. We certainly do not and cannot know the reality of an outside world by sensation alone; all that sensation reveals is its phenomena: form, color, resistance, and so forth. Therefore John Stuart Mill, faithful to his sensationalistic philosophy, has defined our knowledge of the outside world to be merely "a permanent possibility of sensation," giving us not even sensation, but only "a possibility of sensation" in place of a real universe. Herbert Spencer denies that we have, or can have, in our mind, any conception of the Infinite, or of Creation, or of a First Cause. These three are all, he says, *un-*

thinkable. I do not stop to answer his argument, which has been sufficiently refuted by Mr. Martineau and others. I merely call attention to his philosophical position, to show how absolutely necessary it was that he should trace the origin of religions to some outward perception, coming through the senses. He therefore derives them from dreams. A savage dreams, he says, and his dream seems real. He gets the notion of another world, and of his own possible existence therein, and of his existence apart from his body. Hence the belief in ghosts, ancestral spirits, ancestral worship and the like.

The truth in this view I shall attempt presently to show. Meantime I merely remark that we certainly have in our minds *now* the conception of a Supreme Power, of an Infinite Creator, a First Cause, a just, holy, benevolent being — all-wise, all-good, all-powerful. These ideas are not derived from sensation; then they must have come some other way. The brook does not rise higher than its fountain. No sensation of hardness, color, smell, taste, form, can by any transformation become thought, will, memory, love. Something must be added to it not there before. There is no objection to the theory which assumes that everything in nature and the soul was evolved from a nebula, provided we grant either that everything evolved was first involved, or else that everything not there has been added since. Assuming that undeveloped man has in his soul the germs of a religious nature, just as he has the germs of a rational, moral, and social nature, let us inquire next how they are unfolded, in what way they first manifest themselves, and through what processes they pass to their highest manifestations.

§ 4. *Belief in disembodied Spirits the lowest form in which Religion manifests itself.*

Those who have searched most deeply into the nature of tribes in the lowest state of development can generally trace a belief in one Supreme God. But this monotheism is latent, not active. The active prominent form of religion among such savages is dread of ghosts, and fear of malignant powers. The idea of a ghost comes to them from the instinctive consciousness that the soul within them is independent of the bodily life, and will survive it. Ghosts are supposed to be souls without bodies — beings who can see without eyes, hear without ears, strike without a hand — who can think, feel, love, hate, remember, be angry. In short, they are men *minus* the body, and *plus* the power of suddenly appearing and disappearing, going and coming with rapidity through far distances. This belief is universal among the lower races. How did it come? The so-called modern Spiritualists will say, "From the fact that there *are ghosts*, and that they have been seen by these people." But putting aside this explanation as thus far unverified, how could this universal belief arise? The explanation is easy enough if we believe that man is conscious of an immaterial and immortal soul, which is his real self, his ego. That this ego is not body is proved to him because he knows it, not through his bodily sense, but by his consciousness; because this ego, or soul, thinks, feels, loves, hates, remembers and foresees, hopes and fears; that this ego thus exercises certain powers which are separated by an impassable gulf from physical sensations. Though wholly unacquainted with the simplest philosophic or metaphysical definitions, every man is quite sure that his soul and its phenomena cannot be described in terms of matter; that a thought cannot be said to be white or black, hard or soft; that pain cannot be weighed in scales, nor pleasure measured by a foot-rule; that you cannot say of hope, memory, or love that they are squares or triangles, fragrant or odorless; that you cannot attribute the taste of sweet or sour to the imagination. These distinctions may be hidden from the wise and prudent, but are certainly known to babes.

Knowing thus the essential character of soul and its distinction from body, the primitive or childlike man assumes that death, which dissolves the body, does not destroy the soul. His soul continues to exist as a disembodied spirit. Until he obtains some theory of a distant Heaven, or underground Hades, or Tartarus, he very naturally supposes that the disembodied spirits remain near by. They are believed to appear by night, because in the dim shadows of darkness many objects may assume the aspect of a human form. They disappear at day, because in the daylight no such error is possible.

§ 5. *The world of Dreams and its influence.*

Thus primitive religion begins with a belief that we are surrounded by an unseen world of spirits like ourselves. Then the wonderful phenomena of dreams suggests another step of belief. Dreaming is so common that we do not often consider what a very strange fact it is in our life. We spend nearly a third of our life in a world of imagination, not reality. We walk in an imaginary world, see and converse with imaginary beings, encounter and escape imaginary dangers. We awake convulsed with terror, glad with mysterious joy, troubled by forebodings. If we did not forget the largest part of this experience, we should probably find that our sleeping life is much more rich in excitement, adventure, and suggestion than our waking hours. To the child-man, to whom the outward order of the visible universe is so imperfectly known, the realm of dreams seems probably more real than it does to us. Dreamland is a vast domain, close by, which he enters every night with his soul, leaving his body behind. When he leaves his body *wholly* behind at death, he naturally believes that his soul enters some such world as that of dreams. Hence, in addition to his belief in spirits, comes a conception of a spirit-land. As *he* enters the dreamland every night, and comes from it to *his* earth-world every morning, he can see no reason why the spirits should not sometimes leave their dream-home and enter his waking-world.

§ 6. *Why should primitive races be afraid of disembodied spirits.*

But why should primitive man be afraid of ghosts? Why should supernatural beings be conceived as more often malignant than beneficent. For the same reason that he distrusts strangers. Most primitive peoples imagine the strangers who first come to their shores to be enemies, bent on rapine and devastation. Their unhappy experience has taught them that most strangers are their enemies. The condition of chronic want in which these people so often live — exposed to hunger, cold, poverty — leads them to invade each other's territory for plunder. But there is another and perhaps more potent reason for their fear of spirits. A universal intuition of the reason gives to all men, as soon as the intelligence awakens, some conception of cause and effect, — in other words, assures them that nothing can take place without a cause. Now all causes are divided into physical and spiritual — those which act through the great machine of nature, and those which originate in will, whether human or superhuman. The progress of knowledge tends to relegate more and more of the causes working around us, to the realm of nature. When an epidemic breaks out, we do not ascribe it to a malignant spirit, but to imperfect drainage or bad air. When a tornado sweeps away a town in Iowa or Kansas, we do not say that a demon of the air has done it, but explain it by some meteorological antecedents. The great fires which desolated Michigan are not ascribed to the anger of Agni, but to the long previous drought. But to the mind of the uncivilized man, unstored with these explanations, which are our commonplaces of knowledge, every unusual, sudden, unexplained disaster is supposed to be the immediate work of an evil spirit. As a man, he must believe that every event has its cause; as an uneducated man, he is unacquainted with physical causes, and so assumes spiritual causes for any uncommon event. Common events do not disturb him. When he throws a stone into the air and it falls again, he neither thinks of this as the work of a spirit, nor as the result of gravitation; but he simply says, "It falls because it is heavy." The causes for common events in the outward world he finds in the nature of things. But strange, unexpected events he ascribes to the spirit-world; and, as these are mostly disasters and misfortunes, he believes in malignant spirits more than in good ones. The supernatural, invisible beings around him are like the men around him, capricious, irritable, violent. These characteristics he finds even in men of his own tribe, but every time he meets a stranger he is apt to encounter an enemy. The supernatural world is full of such strangers, hence he fears more than he hopes from their interference in his affairs. But how can he ward off these dangers? Who can tell what can placate the hostile invisibles? Some of his tribe think they know what ought to be done, hence sorcery and sorcerers. Among the childlike races these are universal. It is exactly the same motive which leads so many among ourselves to take quack medicine and call in quack doctors. An ignorant man, in his distress, will believe any one who declares with great confidence that he can certainly help him. That is all that the child-man does. He believes in his sorcerer or medicine-man.

§ 7. *Demoniacal possession and exorcism.*

The same belief in evil spirits and their power we find in the time of Christ among the Jews, with whom some forms of disease, as epilepsy and insanity, were supposed to be the work of demons. And no wonder, for such diseases seem to show a kind of possession. A change of mental and moral character is a well-known symptom in cerebral disease. The generous man becomes avaricious, the peaceable man quarrelsome, the cheerful man gloomy, a sweet temper grows morose and suspicious; hence the notion of demoniacal possession. In malarial disease, a man may be helpless from fever every third day, and apparently well during the two intervening days. Does not this diabolical periodicity naturally suggest that an evil spirit comes and goes on these occasions? The man, among the undeveloped races, who knows how to drive away such demons, is the sorcerer. Hence the universal practice of sorcery among the child-like races.

Belief in demoniacal possession and sorcery has continued until a recent period, even in the Christian Church. The sorcerer in Christendom received another name, and was called an exorcist. The change of name certainly marked a development of the idea into a higher form. The sorcerer among ethnic races uses magical processes, and not only casts out evil spirits, but invokes them in order to injure an enemy, or to destroy the life of his foe. The Jews, who were the principal exorcists in ancient times, professed to cast out demons partly by adjuration and partly by the use of a certain root called Baaras.[1] After Christianity prevailed, the Christian exorcists were considered the most powerful. By the name of Jesus, and the sign of the cross, they thought they could cast out the demons who had resisted the enchantments of the Pagan exorcists. All the early Christian fathers believed in this power. Tertullian, in the midst of a fierce Pagan persecution, makes a deliberate offer to test the whole question between the two religions by the ability of the Christians to cast out any demon who may have taken possession of a sufferer. He declares "If we Christians cannot make the demons confess aloud their diabolical character, we will consent to be put to death on the spot." Abuses of this custom caused a council in the fourth century to limit the exercise of exorcism to an order in the church called exorcists, who were regularly ordained. Every heathen, at his conversion, was supposed to be possessed by an evil spirit, which must be cast out before he could be baptized. The exorcist breathed on him, made the sign of the cross on his forehead and breast, and said: "Exi, immunde spiritus, et da locum spiritui Sancto Paraclito." "Go out, evil spirit, and make room for the Holy Spirit, the Comforter." In the Roman Catholic Church exorcism is still practiced, not only on

[1] Josephus, *Antiquities*, viii. 2. § 5.

enurgumens (or possessed persons), but the oil and water are exorcised before being blessed, in the baptism of infants. The exorcist is the third of the minor orders in the Roman Catholic Church. Exorcism in the Christian Church was, however, never used, as in ethnic religions, to torture and kill one's enemies; it was not connected with mysterious magical operations, and it has now nearly passed out of Christianity, lingering in the Catholic Church rather as a tradition than as a living belief.

§ 8. *Religion not differentiated in childlike races. It is Animism.*

We see that in all childlike races religion is the same. It is not as yet differentiated. Though these races are widely separated, and have never come in contact with each other, nor with educated man, they hold a uniform faith. This universal religion which embraces the tribes of Australia, the Hottentot and Bushman of South Africa, the islanders of the Pacific Ocean, the tribes of North America and South America, and the Esquimaux of Greenland, is Animism. All these races believe in a soul, which exists after the body dies, and in a world of spirits, from which departed souls may return to earth; in beneficent or malignant influences from the supernatural world, in conjurors and sorcerers, and the power of magic.

Apart from all theory about the origin of religion, this we see, as a matter of observation, to be the beginning of religion. The first supernatural notion of the undeveloped man is of the continuance into a supernatural world of that mysterious entity which we call soul. It is a very natural inference that not only the souls of ancestors are in that world, but that other kindred and more powerful spirits are there too. Hence the universal primal belief in superhuman and supernatural powers, who interfere for good and evil, occasionally or constantly, in human affairs.

This primitive belief evidently comes from within, not from without. All undeveloped races believe in ghosts; but whether ghosts are ever actually seen or not continues very doubtful. The belief, therefore, which is so universal and so strong, does not arise from any outward facts known to be certain and universal. It is developed from within, from the supernatural element in man, the power of soul, which, even in the lowest state, is *above* nature, — the power of thought, contrivance, energetic will, persistent desire, which can bend and alter outward things to serve its purpose.

§ 9. *Polytheism is the next step upward from Animism.*

The next stage in the historic development of religion takes us out of Animism into Polytheism.

Two changes now appear: first, that whereas Animism comes chiefly from the consciousness of the powers of the soul within us, polytheism is mainly derived from the observation of nature about us. The root of faith remains the same, a belief in other personalities like ourselves. But the character of these personalities is a conception taken from the phenomena of the outward universe. Some things man can do, other things are evidently above his power; these last must be the work of higher beings. The primitive man sees that he depends on powers higher than anything in himself. He cannot make the sun rise or set, summer come or go, fruits ripen, rain fall, yet without these events he cannot live. There is a higher power which causes the sun to shine, the God of light. There is another power which collects the clouds and sends the rain, the God of wind and storm. Hence comes nature-worship, as the second stage of religious development, but differing among different races, according to the type of the race, and the geographical position. The Vedic hymns adore one spiritual power, which dwells in the sun, the air, or the fire, and in other elements of nature. The number of these deities is differently given in different hymns. One ancient commentator makes them three deities. Many texts declare that there are thirty-three; others assert that there are three hundred, or three thousand. Sometimes these gods are said to be the children of heaven and earth (Dyaus and Prithivi), "whose marriage," says Albert Reville, "forms the foundation of a hundred mythologies." So Homer, Æschylus, Sophocles, and Euripides call earth the "Universal Mother." So too, as Tacitus tells us, the ancient Germans called the earth "Mother."

The Vedic hymns are addressed in turn to "Varuna," the all-surrounding sky; to "Indra," god of storms; "Agni," god of fire; "Surya," the sun; "Ushas," the dawn; "Yama," god of death; to time and night, and to other beings representing physical power and change. God, as manifested first in one then in another natural phenomenon, was the central idea of this polytheism. The gods were personified, but were not persons; behind them all was the universal spirit, and, therefore, each was alternately worshipped as the supreme, omnipotent God.

If the Vedic polytheism represents God *in* nature, worshipping the manifestation, the ancient Egyptian polytheism represents God *behind* nature, and the Greek polytheism gives us God wholly detached from nature and developed into human beings, with human passions, experiences, and enjoyments. The Greek gods are men, full of human life; the Vedic gods are the powers of nature; the gods of Egypt are abstract symbols.

But through all the polytheisms of the earth there runs this one conviction, that the whole outward universe is filled with spiritual powers. Behind all matter is spirit; above all that we see, is the unseen; the phenomena which pass before our eyes in nature do not come from any iron fate or any blind chance, but from intelligence, purpose, a will that chooses, a heart that desires, a mind that creates. In all polytheisms there is unity and variety; in some of them the unity is more pronounced, in others the variety.

§ 10. *Arrested and progressive development. Point reached by Zoroaster. The Duad.*

Animism thus develops itself naturally into polytheism. But at this point, in some religions, the development is arrested; in others the movement goes forward. The Vedic religion passed on into Brahmanism, which was the worship of a Triad — Brahma, the Creator; Siva, the Destroyer; and Vishnu, the Restorer — in which the circle of change was completed. Some of the Vedic prophets and sages were occupied with the problem of creation. Out of this came in one part of India the worship of Brahma. On another class of minds the destructive force of nature laid a stronger hold. Where the first saw life, growth, adaptation, development, the second class of thinkers saw decay, war, death, destruction. The worship of Siva originated in the latter view. As Brahma represented all the creative powers of nature, so Siva represented all the destructive forces of nature. Then came the Vishnu worship as another step. Admitting that there is creation and destruction in nature, it is evident that there are also forces which restore and renew, and maintain the harmony of the world. The antagonistic forces of nature are brought again into peace, and, after all struggle, a great unity and harmony remain supreme. This is represented by the Triad worship as we find it in the Hindu religion.

The ancient Persian race, in the religion of Zoroaster, did not for a long time reach this conception of a supreme existing harmony, but saw in nature only perpetual war.

Zoroaster, a highly moral person, saw evil as a hateful power, very present and real, and to be fought with forever. To him good and evil represented everything in nature. A fearful elemental and spiritual war is forever going on around us, and we are to be soldiers of the good. We have to fight on the side of Ormazd, King of Light, against Ahriman, Prince of Darkness. In the present age there will be no end to this terrific war, in which all the powers of the universe are engaged, on one side or the other. But in the last days, after this age has come to an end, good will triumph and all evil disappear, transformed into purity, truth, and love. The religion of Zoroaster, then, may be considered as the primitive religion which had passed up through a Polytheism like that of the Vedic system into a dualism, where it was long arrested, chiefly by the vast influence of this great prophet.

§ 11. *Degenerate polytheism becomes idolatry. How Religions decay.*

While the development of the Persian religion was long arrested in the Duad, and that of India for a time in the Triad, other Polytheisms degenerated into idolatry. Idol-worship is polytheism pushed to its extreme limits. In this degenerate system, which has so widely prevailed, the unity in nature-worship has been wholly overcome by the variety. The divine powers have been detached from the All of Things, and become independent local deities, each worshipped in his own home and at his own altar. Such were Baal and Ashtaroth in Syria, Juggernauth and Rudra in India, Osiris and Typhon in Egypt, Artemis at Ephesus, Aphrodite at Cyprus and Corinth. In this form of worship, passions, instead of being restrained, are deified. Each man worships the God after his own heart, and so justifies his own limitations. He makes his gods not merely like himself, but like his lower self, his one-sided self.

Social religions, like social institutions, are subject to dilapidation and relapses. Many religions stand before us in history as majestic ruins. When you penetrate the thick jungles of Yucatan, and come on the ruins of Palenque, you find vast structures, covered with carved ornaments and mysterious symbols, indications of a lost race, a forgotten creed, and a long-buried civilization. So it is with many religions, as they emerge into the light of present knowledge from the profound night of an unknown past. Instead of being arrested at an upward stage of development they have all the mark of being the decayed remains of purer and nobler religion. In the case of Hinduism, we have the whole story of this rise and progress, followed by a decline and fall. We see it commence in a pure nature-religion, which is a thinly-veiled Monotheism. We see it developed into a vast system of philosophies, ethics, literature, art. Meantime a priesthood has grown up and acquired supreme control. Under its influence a complicated theology is developed and a ritual formed. As the first stage appears in the Vedic hymns, the second is seen in the laws of Manu, the three great systems of philosophy, the poems of Kalidas, and the two epics. Then followed the third period of gradual dilapidation, when worship became idolatry. Theology degenerated into the myths of the Puranas, and the pure morality of earlier times disappeared in ceremonial sacrifices offered to a Pantheon of cruel or voluptuous deities. In this case we see the process of dilapidation and decay which has been going on for thousands of years. The decay has been going on, but dissolution has not come. Life still remains in this religion, and the possibility of revival. The heart of India is still full of reverence for the unknown God, who is behind its idolatries; it is still held by its ancient Vedas, as by an anchor, to a better faith. It is, therefore, a dilapidated and relapsed, but not a dead religion.

A worse fate befell the religion of Egypt. Highest in the earliest period, it gradually degenerated to the hour when it finally disappeared and passed away forever. It began in a pure monotheism, as is positively affirmed by Herodotus, and confirmed by De Rougé and Renouf. It declared that God is the only One, whose life is Truth, that He has made all things, and that He alone has not been made. "More than five thousand years ago, in the valley of the Nile, the Hymn began to the Unity of God, and the immortality of the soul, and we find in the last ages Egypt arrived at the most unbridled polytheism."[1] "The sublimer parts of the Egyptian religion are demonstrably ancient," and "its last stage was by far the grossest and most corrupt." The oldest inscriptions emphasize justice, mercy, love of right, hate of wrong, kind-

[1] P. Le Page Renouf, *Hibbert Lectures*, 1879, p. 91.

ness to the poor, reverence for parents, But in the later periods these high moral ideas disappeared from the monuments. Epicurean notions come in. The Litanies of *Ra* on the royal tombs of the XIXth dynasty are already pantheistic,[1] and the editor of these litanies, M. Naville, remarks that the pantheism which had taken possession of Egyptian thought had abolished the ideas of right and wrong which appear earlier, and notably in the Book of the Dead. The reverence for animals, which was at first symbolism, became pure idolatry. Even the grand faith in immortality is lost in an Epicurean denial of a hereafter. A dead wife addresses her husband thus from the sepulchre: "O my brother! my spouse, cease not to eat and drink, to enjoy thy life, follow thy desires, and let not care enter thy heart, as long as thou livest on the earth. For this is the land of darkness and abode of sorrow. No one awakes any more to see his brethren, nor knows father nor mother. I long for water. I long for air."

Both in the religion of India and in that of Egypt, this process of degeneracy may probably be traced to the influence of a priesthood which had become the ruling power in the state. An established priesthood is apt to lay more and more stress on ceremony and ritual, on the letter that kills rather than on the spirit which gives life. A like tendency in Judaism put a stop to its natural

[1] Renouf, p. 234.

development, and made the reform necessary which took place in Christianity. The same hardening of the life of Christianity into an extreme magnificence of worship, under a caste of priests, compelled the Reformation of Luther. Such a revival may still come in India. There the reformer may appeal to the records of the primitive religion in the Vedas, as Luther appealed to those in the New Testament.

§ 12. *The Mexican Religion the degenerate form of a higher faith.*

Having seen the course taken by these two great nature religions, — that of Egypt and India, where we have been able to pursue historically their decline from a primitive form of Monotheism to a corrupt Polytheism, — we can imagine what the course has been in other systems of whose historic development we are ignorant.

Take, for example, the Mexican religion as it was found at the time of the Spanish conquest. This Aztec system bears all the marks, not of one evolved from a lower condition of development, but of one lapsed from a higher. As described by Prescott, it had an elaborate ritual, a powerful priesthood, magnificent places of worship, and a developed theology. "The priests," says Prescott, "had digested as thorough and burdensome a ritual as ever existed in any nation." "The sacerdotal order was very numerous; as may be inferred from the statement that five thousand priests were, in some way or other, attached to the principal temple of the capital. The ranks and functions of this multitudinous body were discriminated with great exactness. Those best instructed in music took the management of the choirs. Others arranged the festivals according to the calendar. Some superintended the education of youth, and others had charge of the hieroglyphical paintings and oral traditions; while the dismal rites of sacrifice were reserved for the chief dignitaries of the order. At the head of the whole were two high priests, equal in dignity, and inferior only to the sovereign. Some of the priests were attached to the worship of particular deities; others lived like monks, under the severest conventual discipline. They were called to prayers three times a day, and once at night; were frequent in ablutions and vigils, and in mortifying the flesh by cruel penances of fasting, flagellation, and other austerities. They heard confession and gave absolution as in the Roman Catholic Church, and priestly absolution was received in place of the legal punishment of offenses. As in Europe, ancient Egypt, and India, a vast amount of land was annexed to the temple for the support of the priesthood; so much so as to impoverish the empire. The temples were very numerous. They were called Teocallis, or

Houses of God. They were pyramidal in form, with a square base, each side being sometimes a hundred feet long. They were in terraces, more than one hundred feet high; on the top was a broad area, on which stood one or two towers, the dreadful stone of sacrifice, and altars with the perpetual, inextinguishable fire. Six hundred of these ever-burning altars were within the inclosure of the great temple of Mexico, and during the night illuminated the whole city with their flame. Every month was consecrated to some protecting deity, and almost every day fixed in the calendar for some appropriate celebration. Many of these were of a festive sort, consisting of light songs and dances. Processions of women and children, bearing fruits and garlands, alternated with the procession of the priests, winding round the massive sides of the temples in full view of the people. So in the Pan-Athenaic processions at Athens, they circled the Parthenon behind the colonnades, appearing and disappearing as they passed behind the columns. In the Mexican ceremonies the priests were visible from the furthest parts of the capital, as they circled the pyramid, rising higher and higher, from terrace to terrace, toward the summit and its altar of sacrifice.

Beside a supreme deity, the Aztecs worshipped thirteen others of the first rank, and two hundred or more of a lower rank. One was the God of

War, to whom multitudes of human victims were sacrificed. Another, a more humane being, was God of the Air, patron of agriculture, and giver of happy days.

Exactly as in the Brahmanic and Egyptian systems, there was the conception of one Supreme Being, only partially eclipsed by the later Polytheism; we also find here pure moral teachings, and simple, happy forms of worship, associated with the awful cruelties of human sacrifice. In the formula for confession and remission of sins, the early moral teaching and the later horrors are seen together. The priest said: "O merciful Lord, thou who knowest the secrets of all hearts, let thy forgiveness descend, like pure water, to wash away the stains from the soul. Thou knowest this man has sinned, not from his own free will, but from the influence of the sign under which he was born." After enjoining various penances and mortifications, among which he is commanded especially to procure a slave to be sacrificed to the Deity, the priest concludes by inculcating charity to the poor. "Clothe the naked and feed the hungry," he says, "for remember, *their flesh is thine, and they are men like thee.*" By the confession of the missionaries, the virgins and youth dedicated to God were pure and full of devotion. But with this were combined the bloody sacrifices, which, according to the native traditions, began only about two hundred years before the Spanish conquest. These horrible sacrifices reached an extent unparalleled in the history of any other religion. On those accursed altars the number of human victims has never been estimated at less than twenty thousand every year. The skulls were preserved, and the Spaniards counted in one building 136,000. All this was done as a matter of conscience and religious duty, just as the Inquisitors in Spain burned Jews and heretics, and just as Alva murdered the Protestants in Holland. These horrors are in all cases the sign of a degenerate religion. And such religions, fortunately, must either be reformed, or come to an end. The Inquisition, with its horrors, has been reformed out of the Roman Church; the worship of Moloch in Syria, and the savage cruelties of Mexico, brought about the destruction of both these religions.

CHAPTER IV.

THE IDEA OF GOD IN ALL RELIGIONS. ANIMISM, POLYTHEISM, PANTHEISM.

§ 1. Analysis of the idea of Deity. God as Creator, Supreme Being, Infinite Being, Providence, Justice, Holiness, Unity. § 2. Animism as the lowest form of religious belief. The Idol or Fetich in all religions. § 3. Polytheism in all religions. Origin of Polytheism. § 4. Pantheism in all religions. Evils of Pantheism. § 5. The Truth in Polytheism. Latent Monotheism in Polytheism. § 6. Truth in Pantheism. § 7. The Imperfect Monotheism of the Buddhists. § 8. The conception of God the important matter; the name given to him unimportant.

§ 1. *Analysis of the idea of God.*

BEFORE speaking of the Idea of God as it exists in different religions, we must first inquire what this idea is? and whether it is simple or compound, primitive or derivative, given by intuition or formed by experience.

That the idea of God is not simple but complex appears as soon as we analyze it. Sometimes we call God creator of all things. But that this is no necessary conception of the Deity is evident from the fact that in many religions this notion is absent. Thus it is absent from the vast system of Buddhism, which omits an intelligent will as the author of the universe, and declares that things rise and fall, come and go by nature. It is also absent from the religions of Greece and Rome, according to which the gods themselves, no less than men, were developments from Chaos. Zeus, the supreme God, was not the author of the universe, but was evolved from a lower type of deity. Some of the philosophers taught the creation of the universe by the supreme being as self-revelation; but this conception made no part of the popular religion, as it does in the teaching of Zoroaster and of Moses.

Another part of our own idea of Deity is that of the Supreme Being, the sovereign ruler of all things. This is evidently a different notion from that of Creator, and may exist apart from it. Thus among the Greeks Zeus came to be regarded as the supreme ruler of the world, and appears as such even in Homer, though that poet never suggests that he was the creator of the world. So, likewise, in Buddhism. The Buddha is the supreme ruler of the universe at the present time, though not its creator, since it existed before Buddha himself began to be.[1]

Another form which the idea of Deity takes in

[1] Zeus in the Greek mythology was sometimes regarded as having supreme power, but never as possessing perfect goodness.

our minds, is that of the infinite being; the God who is omnipotent and omniscient, all-wise, and all-mighty. And yet it is possible to conceive of a being infinite in some attributes, and not so in others. The Deity may be regarded as supreme and infinite power, but not as supreme and infinite goodness; or the reverse.[1]

Still another conception of the deity is that of Providence, which always is a part of our own idea of God, but which is not necessarily contained in that of ruler. A deity may govern his creatures, without caring for them; he may reward and punish, without providing for their individual needs. This conception of God as providence, which is expressed so strongly (for example) in the Psalms of David, is wanting in many other religions. The Greek gods took very little interest in human affairs, and when they did, were mostly moved by caprice or personal whim. In most religions the deities might be placated by prayers or sacrifices, and so induced to aid the suppliant whom otherwise they had no intention to help.

[1] Even in our time John Stuart Mill thought it probable, from his consideration of the problem of evil, that though the Deity is perfectly good, he is not all-powerful. So also in the system of Zoroaster, Ormazd is all-good, but limited in his power by Ahriman. In some parts of the Christian Church, the power of Satan has been so intensified, that it has been a limitation to the Divine omnipotence. God has been regarded as ruling over heaven, Satan as absolute over hell, and the sovereignty of the earth as divided between them.

Infinite Justice also forms a part of *our* conception of deity. This is his prominent attribute in the Jewish religion, commonly taking the form of rewarding the good and punishing the wicked. But in Judaism this retributive justice is limited to the present life. In the religion of Egypt, on the other hand, it is limited to the future life. Man is left here free to work out his own will, but must appear hereafter at the judgment-seat of Osiris to be rewarded or punished. A similar imperfect retribution hereafter is to be found in the religions of Greece and Rome. Christianity has usually dropped the Jewish conception of a present retribution, and adopted the Egyptian doctrine of a future judgment and future retribution.

Still another part of *our* idea of Deity is Holiness. This also made an essential element in the Jewish conception, but is hardly to be found elsewhere except in the teachings of Zoroaster. That God is of purer eyes than to behold iniquity, that he loves good and hates evil by his very nature; that is that he is essentially *a moral being,* and that right and wrong are not *made so* by his will, but become so in accordance with *his very essence,* this is a conception of the deity which we chiefly derive from Judaism.

I have emphasized the fact that if the deity is a moral being, and has a moral character, actually loving goodness and alien from evil, then the foundation of duty is not in the arbitrary will, but in the essential nature of God. Right is right, not because God commands it, but he commands it because it is right. Goodness does not consist in obedience to the divine will, but in conformity to the divine character. This is the doctrine of the Old Testament, and is one of its noblest characteristics. In this point of view Mohammedanism is a relapse, and is lower than Judaism; for it makes God only an arbitrary sovereign, whose will is to be obeyed without any reference to its moral character. Ultra Calvinism has sometimes taken a similar ground.

And again, Monotheism, or the divine unity, is still another part of our conception of Deity. A being may be sovereign, holy, wise, good, in the highest possible degree, and yet not be the One Alone. It is certainly possible to conceive of such a being as supreme among others like himself, which was the Greek conception of Zeus presiding on Olympus over a council of deities. The other conception, which we call Monotheism, and which seems to us so natural, is one which the human race has found it hard to attain and difficult to keep. It easily passes into Polytheism on the one side and Pantheism on the other. When we regard the Deity as the infinite substance, filling all in all; as the infinite life in organization and growth; as the motive power or infinite force in nature, as the absolute being on whom everything else depends, we easily go over into that Pantheism which says that everything is God.

The tendency, however, in most religions, has been in the opposite direction, namely, toward Polytheism. Religions based on the worship of natural objects are polytheistic, for the outward world manifests variety more than unity.

One more form assumed by the idea of Deity must be spoken of. Whenever the distinction between right and wrong, good and evil is strongly dwelt upon, it becomes difficult to attribute both principles to one and the same being. Then comes Ditheism, or the doctrine of two gods, hostile to each other: one God, the author of light and good, the other of darkness and evil. This view appears most strongly in the religion of Zoroaster, the essential idea of which is of a perpetual war between the powers of light and of darkness. An evil being, armed with terrible power to create evil and tempt to sin, also appears as Typhon in Egypt, as Siva in India, as Loke in Scandinavia, and as Satan among the Jews, Christians, and Mohammedans.

We therefore see that the fully-developed idea of the Deity is a very complex one, certainly including these elements: —

1. The Supernatural Being, or one above nature.

2. The Creator of all things, or the First Cause.

3. The Supreme Being, or the Ruler of all things.

4. The Infinite Being, regarded as infinite in one or more attributes.

5. The Perfect Being, or infinite in all attributes.

6. As Providence, or a being caring for his creatures, and providing for them.

7. A Holy Being, or one having a moral character, and in whom the distinction between good and evil is in his nature, not merely his will.

8. The Substance which gives reality to the universe.

9. As Law, extending through all things, giving permanence to the order of the universe.

10. As Love, or universal fatherhood, inspiring Hope for unlimited good to all.

11. As Unity, or the One alone.

Now these eleven different ideas enter into the most advanced conception of Deity, to a greater or less degree. The complete idea, therefore, is complex, and not simple.

§ 2. *Animism, as the Lowest Form of Religion.*

The lowest aspect of faith, Mr. Tylor has called Animism, as we said in our last chapter. By this he means the belief in spiritual powers, as opposed to the whole philosophy of materialism. This he holds to be the groundwork of the philosophy of religion in all mankind, from the lowest savage up to civilized man. It implies a universal spiritual sense planted in human nature, and developed by outward influences. In its lowest forms, it attributes all events of which the natural cause is unknown, to supernatural agency; fortunate events to some good power; evils and disaster, to some malignant beings. The good are worshipped; the bad are placated.

This belief in the presence of spiritual beings above and around us, reappears in all religions, from the lowest to the highest. The great ethnic religions of the world suppose this visible human life to be surrounded by a vast shadowy world of invisible superhuman beings: the sun and moon, the stars and planets, the ocean, guided and moved by these demigods. Even the severe Monotheism of Judea accepted from Persia a family of angels and archangels — Michael, Gabriel, Raphael, — beings who were the messengers and mediators between God and man. In Greece, as we know, the air, land, sea, woods, springs, were each the home of some spiritual power.

Christianity, which often assimilates the ideas and practices of other religions, has also had its pantheon of angels and archangels, saints and spirits. Only Protestantism has rejected this vast mythology. But even Milton, the most Protestant of Protestants, makes Adam inform Eve that —

> "Millions of spiritual creatures walk the earth
> Unseen, both when we wake and when we sleep;
> All these with ceaseless praise God's works behold
> Both day and night. How often from the steep
> Of echoing hill or thicket have we heard
> Celestial voices to the midnight air
> Singing their great Creator."

The Idol or Fetich, comes also very easily upon the scene. It is a material object with which some magical power is supposed to be associated. Some supernatural being acts through the fetich and is permanently connected with it. Aladdin's lamp, in the Arabian story, was a fetich, which had genii attached to it. The first man who saw a loadstone attract iron, no doubt considered it to possess magical power. Whoever nails a horseshoe over a stable door, or throws a slipper after a wedding party, practices a sort of Fetichism to-day. But people may believe in fetiches without worshipping them. Father Loyer, a Catholic missionary, who studied the habits of the natives of the Gold Coast, says it is a great mistake to suppose that the negroes regard these things as gods. They are only charms, or amulets. These negroes, Father Loyer says, have a belief in one powerful being, to whom they offer prayers. Every morning they wash in the river, put sand on their head to express their humility, and lifting up their hands ask their God to give them yams and rice and other blessings.

The excellent missionary Oldendorp, who took great pains to become accurately acquainted with the character of the negroes of Africa, assures us that he recognized among them a universal belief in the existence of a God, who made the world, who thunders to show his displeasure, and sends rain when he is pleased. Oldendorp says: "Among all the black nations with whom I became acquainted, even the most ignorant, there is none who does not believe in a God, give him a name, and regard him as maker of the world. Besides this supreme beneficent Deity, whom they all worship, they believe in many inferior gods, whose powers appear in serpents, tigers, rivers, trees, and stones. Some of them are malevolent, but the negroes do not worship the bad or cruel gods; they only try to appease them by presents or sacrifices. They pray to the good gods alone. The daily prayer of a Watja negress was, 'O God, I know thee not; but thou knowest me; I need thy help.'"

Let us not despise the savage and his fetich. We all have our fetiches; some little relics to which we attach a value out of all proportion to the real worth of the article. The British Museum gave £300 for a signature of Shakespeare. Professor Lesley showed to an audience in one of the

Lowell Lectures a nail, from the prison in Virginia, on which John Brown hung his hat. The battle-flags at the State House, borne on many a terrible field, are religiously preserved, and are sacred forever. A little bone, supposed to have belonged to a dead saint, is a present for a Pope to give to an Emperor. Moslems go thousands of miles to see the black stone at Mecca; Christians go as far to see the house where Burns was born, that in which Wordsworth lived, the tomb of Virgil on the Bay of Naples, or the grave at Keats at Rome.

> "Such graves as these are pilgrim shines,
> Shrines to no code or creed confined,
> The Delphian vales, the Palestines,
> The Meccas of the mind."

Thus Fetich-worship has survived, and continues to-day in new forms, in the midst of our highest civilization; the same sentiment in the bosom of the savage and in our own.

And what of Idolatry? The childlike man tries to form his block of stone into something like the figure of a man. He only succeeds in making a hideous and horrible face. But it suggests to his mind some human feeling of authority, power, divine wrath against evil-doers, divine benignity toward docile worshippers. To his dark mind it does the same thing that the Phidian Zeus did for the Pan-Hellenic multitudes at Olympia, or the virgin goddess, who stood in glorious beauty before the Parthenon for the Athenians; or what an altar-piece, by Raffaelle, does for the worshippers in St. Peters. These images help them all to fix their mind on the highest idea they have of a super-human majesty, a celestial benignity. No doubt the savage may worship the idol itself, instead of that which it symbolizes. He then worships the letter which kills, instead of the spirit which gives life. But even so may Christians idolize the letter of their ritual, their creed, their church, their Bible, and sacrifice the end to the means. Idols or images are good or bad, as they are used or abused.

§ 3. *Polytheism in all Religions. Its Origin.*

Some elements of Polytheism are to be found in all religions, but differ in each, both quantitatively and qualitatively. Polytheism is least in the Prophetic Religions; most in the Ethnic Religions.

The Polytheism of Egypt inhered in the nature of things; the Divine elements were seen dwelling in Nature. The Polytheism of Greece had become *detached;* the Greek deities were not personifications, but persons. They were divine men and women, no longer representing Sun, Moon, Stars, Thunder, Clouds, Dawn, Fire, Ocean, though traces of this origin remain. But they sat on

Olympus in gay festivity till the horses of the Sun were unyoked, and then lay down to sleep like mortals. No moral quality attaches to the gods of Egypt; they are too impersonal for that. Nor is there much morality yet in the gods of Greece; they are only full of joyful life. There was a high moral life among the Egyptians, Greeks, and Romans, but not derived from their gods. The gods of Greece were willful creatures, and Plato banished from his republic the poets who described their disreputable proceedings, meaning, no doubt, to say that to worship such gods as those was worse than Atheism.

When we turn to the Polytheism of India we meet with still another quality. In the Vedic Hymns we find no large abstract ideas as in the gods of Egypt, and no pure humanities as in Greece, but the forces of nature spiritualized into objects of reverence and love.

Besides the Supreme Being — dimly or plainly recognized in all Polytheisms — and the gods of the higher order beneath him, there is also a host of inferior gods, or Demi-gods, Spirits, Demons, Angels, Powers, filling the whole interspace between the Gods and men. The vast mythologies of India, Persia, Egypt, Scandinavia, Greece, Rome, testify to the faith in the human soul that between our finite spirit and the Infinite Spirit, there are and must be innumerable moral and intellectual beings extending upward in long gradation. Regarding man either as developed by Natural Law, or created by God, it is impossible to believe him the *only* moral intelligence in the Universe below the Supreme Being. If he was developed by some Law of Evolution, must not that law, working through long ages and æons of time, and through innumerable worlds of space, have succeeded in developing numerous beings higher than he? And if he were created by the Will of God, has God during the whole past eternity only created this one feebly endowed spirit? When we look into ourselves, we find capacities and powers in their germ and beginnings, which we can conceive of as being indefinitely developed. We find intelligence, which reaches upward from the contrivances of a savage to the majestic powers of a Newton or a Shakespeare, which can weigh the sun in its scales, fix the return of a comet, or mark out the path of the planet which moves on its lonely way, in the farthest outer darkness of our solar system. We find moral powers which pass all the way up from the besotted soul of a brutal criminal to the heroes and martyrs, who have counted it all joy to live and die for truth, conscience, and human welfare. Does the long ascent stop here? We can imagine beings, who, though created by God, are yet so vastly above man that our highest intelligence may seem only darkness to their light; our noblest virtue only childlike attempts by the side of their majestic fulfillment. This is one of the possibilities of existence which, as we contemplate it, becomes at last almost a self-evident truth. Polytheism, in all its forms, is the crude aspect which this belief takes in the working of the natural instincts. The great majority of men believe, and have ever believed, in hosts of beings between themselves and the Most High. We have glanced at the gods of the Egyptian and Hindu Pantheon. Those of Greece and of Rome crowded the heavens and the earth, filled the woods as dryads, called from the mountains as oreads, splashed in the fountains as naiads, rolled in the ocean as nereids, or tritons. They sat by the fireside as penates or Vesta, guarded the home as lares. Everything had its tutelar genius; nations, colonies, provinces, the senate, sleep. There were deities of the human soul, Mens, Pudicitia, Pietas, Fides. Agriculture and rural occupations had their deities: Tellus, Saturnus, Ops, Silvanus, Faunus, Terminus, Ceres, Liber, Bona Dea, Magna Mater, Flora, Vertumnus, Pomona, Pales. Thus the human soul put spirit into all things, saw spirit everywhere. This we now call superstition, and consider ourselves wise because we see only matter and motion.

But it is a question whether the old Paganism which filled the world with life, thought, and love, is not, at least, as true as the modern Paganism which makes it only a dead machine.

§ 4. *Pantheism in all Religions. Its evils.*

Polytheism may be absorbed by a Monotheistic religion, as happened to the Polytheisms of Greece, Rome, and Scandinavia, which were taken up into Christianity, and as happened to the semi-polytheistic Christianity of the East, which was absorbed by Mohammedanism; or Polytheism may pass naturally into some form of Pantheism. We will, therefore, look at Pantheism in all religions, for it is to be found more or less prominently in all.

In the most marked form Pantheism appears in the Hindu Religion. The Vedic Hymns, Polytheistic in appearance, were Pantheistic in substance.

This is expressed by a hymn of the Rig-Veda (Mandala x. 90), thus rendered by Monier Williams: —

"The embodied spirit has a thousand heads,
A thousand eyes, a thousand feet; around,
On every side, enveloping the earth;
Yet filling space no larger than a span,
He is himself this very Universe;
He is whatever is, has been, shall be;
He is the Lord of Immortality."

Pantheism, in its extreme development, is the assertion that the Universe is God, and that God is the Universe. It is the opposite pole to Atheism, which says that Nothing is God. Pantheism says, "Everything is God." This is the false Pantheism, equally unphilosophical and immoral. It is unphilosophical because denying the necessary convictions of the Reason and first Laws of Thought. God is infinite Being; but we are compelled to believe in the reality of finite outward existences, which are therefore not God. We are compelled by the ultimate necessity of reason to believe in the reality of our own existence, which we also know to be finite, limited, and dependent, consequently not the infinite and absolute Being. Extreme Pantheism is therefore unphilosophical. It is also immoral, because, if all things are God, then bad actions as well as good are divine, and the distinction between right and wrong disappears. Hence the low morality of the Hindus, on whom this teaching has been at work for so many centuries; hence also the immoral practices reappearing in those Christian sects which claim perfect union with God, and to whom the moral law has ceased to exist.

Buddhism was a moral reaction against Hindu Pantheism; and when Buddhism was expelled from India, the full fruits of this system of Pantheism appeared in luxury, falsehood, cruelty, and slavery. The moral tone of the race seemed almost gone. But not wholly. The better spirit of the earlier Sacred Writings sometimes reappears even in the Puranas, and an imperfect Monotheism, which worships either Vishnu, Siva, or Brahma, contends steadily against this stress of Pantheism. But this remained as the leading tendency of thought, appearing in the Upanishads, the Baghavat-Geeta, and the great systems of philosophy. Thus it is said in a Upanishad, "All this universe is Brahma. From him it proceeds, into him it is dissolved."

There is no Religion in which we do not recognize this element of Pantheistic faith. Even in prosaic China, with its Monotheism and its worship of spirits, appears the impersonal, absolute, all-containing Tao. Of Tao we read, "We look at it and do not see it, listen to it and do not hear it. It cannot be defined; it acts, but without a name. It was chaos before the birth of the worlds; without form, standing alone, unchanging; the mother of all things. It passes on in perpetual flow; it is far off, but close at hand; it is the law which rules all things."

Among the intensely personal Deities of Greece the great Pan was also found, representing the All. The Pantheism of the Orphic theology appears in what remains of that old semi-religious philosophy, as in a poem preserved by Proclus, which says: —

"Zeus is first, last, the head and the middle of all things.
From him all things come. He is man and woman,
The depth of the earth, the height of Heaven,
Sun, Moon, Stars, Fire — Origin of all, King of all,
One Power, God, Ruler."

No system of thought would seem more remote from Pantheism than that of Mohammed; and yet the great Persian sect of Ssufis are mystical Pantheists. One of the chief of these, a saint of the twelfth century, who lived at Balkh, uttered many Pantheistic sentiments. His name was Jelal-ed-deddin. He was the author of the saying, "When we cry in our prayer, 'O my Father,' the answer is in the prayer itself; in the 'My Father' lies hidden 'Here, my child.'"

Bustamius, another of the Ssufis saints, says, "I myself am the sea which has neither bottom nor shore."

Again he said, "While men think they are worshipping God, it is in fact God who adores himself."

Again he cried out, "How long, O my God, art thou pleased that I should thus remain between the Myself and the Thyself. Take away from me the Myself, that I may be absorbed into the Thyself."

§ 5. *The Truth in Polytheism. Latent Monotheism.*

If we ask now, "What is the truth of Polytheism?" it may be said that the doctrine of many

Gods is wholly false to us, because Christianity has given to the word God such a sublime meaning, and associated it with the idea of Infinite and Eternal Being. But to the mind of antiquity, even to that of Judea, the word possessed no such quality. The Gods of the old world were finite beings, scarcely raised above the level of human nature. Jesus himself tells us that in the Old Testament those "were called Gods to whom the word of God came" — that is, inspired men were called Gods. Polytheism peopled the space above our world with superhuman and supernatural beings, all the way up to the realm of the Infinite and Eternal. Judaism, in its strict Monotheism, allowed only angels or divine messengers. It placed God apart from the world and above the world as its sole ruler, in an unapproached majesty. Moses, in a natural reaction of mind against the innumerable deities of the Egyptian Pantheon, based his whole religion on the doctrine declared in the First Commandment, "Thou shalt worship no other God in my Presence."

But which is the most true, the solitary sovereignty sometimes ascribed by the Jewish mind to Jehovah, or that one feature of Polytheism which makes a divine community, a communion of the Most High with his creatures? God, according to Christianity, is essentially Love. This is the very essence of his Being. The most essential attribute is not Power, is not Sovereignty, as Mohammedanism and Calvinism both make it to be, but Love. That means, not loneliness, but communion. It means that God descends into all just as far as they are capable of receiving him. And are men the only moral beings in the universe? Can we doubt that there are innumerable beings higher than man, of such vast intelligence, of such lofty moral nature, so much nearer to the One Above in their knowledge and sympathy that they can receive much more of his fullness than we can? Christianity has attempted to fill the void between our estate and that of the Infinite Father, by creating a heaven of Angels and Archangels, and a whole calendar of Saints. Its litanies unite our prayers with those of the holy company of the apostles, the goodly fellowship of the prophets, and the noble army of martyrs. These are all human like ourselves, but ascended up into a higher world. In the doctrine of the Trinity the Church has endeavored to formulate the communion of God and his creation: regarding the Father as the perpetual fountain of Life; the Word as the perpetual going forth of his truth into the minds and hearts of his intelligent creatures; and the Spirit as the universal Communion of all spirits with each other and with the Most High. Look at it as an attempt to express the Christian idea of Deity as all-embracing Love, and it has great historic value.

In speaking of Polytheism, let us keep in mind this important historical fact: that pure Polytheism never satisfies the mind, and that consequently, in most Polytheistic religions, there are traces of a slightly-veiled Monotheism. The tendency to variety is always accompanied by a tendency to Unity. Among primitive nations it may be a very imperfect and unstable Monotheism, but it occasionally shows itself. Brinton tells us that, not only among the civilized Aztecs, but even among the inhabitants of Hayti, the Lenni Lenape, and other American tribes, we find such names affixed to their deities as "Endless," "Omnipotent," "Invisible," "Maker and Moulder of all things," "Mother and Father of Life," "The one God complete in Perfection and Unity," "The Creator of all that is," and "The Soul of the World." He adds, that in America, among the Peruvians and Mexicans, there were two deliberate attempts to introduce a Monotheistic worship. It is related that about Anno Domini 1440, at a great religious council held in Peru, an Inca rose before the assembled multitude and said: —

"Many tell us that the Sun made all things. But he who makes must remain with what he makes; now many things happen when the Sun is absent, therefore he cannot make all things. It is doubtful if he is alive, since he never seems tired. If he were living he would grow weary, as we do; were he free he would sometimes go elsewhere. He is like an animal in harness, who has to go where he is driven, like an arrow which must go where it is sent by the archer. Therefore he, our Father and Master, the Sun, must have another Master greater than himself, who compels him to go his daily round without peace or rest."

A name was, therefore, invented for this Supreme Power, and a temple built for his worship near Callao, in which were no images nor sacrifices.

In like manner, led by the same profound religious instinct, the King of Tescuco, in Mexico, became tired of the idols of his kingdom, having prayed to them in vain for a son. "What are they," he cried, "but dumb stones, without sense or power! They could not have made this beautiful world; the sun, moon, and stars; the waters and trees; and all the countless creatures which inhabit the world. There must be some invisible and unknown God, the Creator of all things. He alone can console me in my sorrow, and take away my affliction." Therefore he erected a Temple nine stories high, which he dedicated to the Unknown God, the Cause of Causes. He seems to have repeated, without knowing it, the argument of Paul at Athens.

These, however, were in neither case attempts to overthrow Polytheism, or to substitute a Monotheism in its place, but only to add the worship of a supreme God to that of the inferior deities. Yet these facts show that tendency in the soul to Monotheism which appears, more or less distinctly, in the Polytheisms of mankind.

And what is the truth in Pantheism?

§ 6. *The Truth in Pantheism.*

According to Judaism and Mohammedanism there is little of the Divine in Nature. God is regarded as above all; as Creator, Ruler, Sovereign, Providence, and Judge. He is the moral ruler of the universe. The works of the Lord are marvellous, in wisdom has he made them all, but they are marvellous only as indicating the Divine Wisdom which formed them. So a watch or a ship are wonderful works of human intelligence, but we do not regard them as possessing any *human* quality. Nature possessed no divine quality to the Hebrew mind. But the New Testament teaches that God is not only *above* all, as Creator, Ruler, Providence, and Judge, but that He is through all and in all, by perpetually imparting beauty and life. He flows into Nature as the perpetual Creator. This produces the romantic view of Nature, unknown to antiquity, and only gradually developed in very recent times, the view of which Wordsworth is the chief Prophet. Wordsworth is the religious Poet of our century, and his peculiar power consists in his profound feeling of something divine in Nature. He saw in Nature, —

> "The still, sad music of Humanity."

He felt in it, —

> "A sense sublime
> Of something far more deeply interfused,
> Whose dwelling is the light of setting suns,
> And the round ocean, and the living air,
> And the blue sky, and in the mind of man.
> A motion and a spirit, that impels
> All thinking things, all objects of all thought,
> And rolls through all things."

It is this sense of something deeper in Nature than what we see, a plastic life pervading all things, a soul of the world, a perpetual presence of God, as infinite Order, Beauty, Life; it is this which makes the charm of the best of Wordsworth's poems, the "Tintern Abbey," the "Peele Castle," and especially "The Ode to Immortality." This sense of a Divine Presence in sky and earth gives to them a

> "Lustre known to neither sea nor land,"

and gives to "the meanest flower that blows,"

> "Thoughts that do often lie too deep for tears."

This romantic view of Nature, as it has been called, in opposition to the *classic* view, is that which sees a Divine life in all things. The Greeks saw separate divinities in each part. But the modern spirit sees one life pervading all things, and that the life of God himself.

When Jesus said that not a sparrow falls to the

ground without our Father; when he showed with what glory God had dressed each common weed on the plains of Sharon, he gave the idea of this new faith. Paul, in several passages, boldly approaches the very edge of Pantheism, but avoids its dangers, as the comet of 1680 shot down close to the sun, but did not fall into it.

When Paul declares that God is "above all, and through all, and in us all;" when he speaks of the "fullness of Him who filleth all in all;" when he says that in God "we live and move and have our Being," and that "from Him, through Him, and to Him are all things," he avoids the false Pantheism, but teaches the true Pantheism. The false doctrine declares that everything is God. The true doctrine says that God is in everything.

§ 7. *The Imperfect Monotheism of the Buddhists.*

A peculiar form of Monotheism, often improperly called Atheism, is found in the religion of Buddha. It is certainly improper to name a system Atheistic which recognizes one supreme being, lord of Heaven and Earth, above the gods and men. M. Barthélemy St. Hilaire asserts that "there is no trace of the idea of God in the whole of Buddhism, either at the beginning or the end." To this statement Arthur Lillie ("Buddha and Early Buddhism") thus replies: —

"If M. St. Hilaire were to visit any of the Buddhist temples of Tibet, he would hear the *Llamas* chant: —

"'*I adore Ta-tha-gata Amit-batha*,' as the Buddha of Buddhas, the God of Gods.'

"If he should visit a Chinese temple he would there hear the Liturgy, which says: 'One in spirit, we invoke thee. Hail *Amit-abha* of the world.' 'O would that our merciful teacher Sakya-muni, and our great Father Amit-abha, would now descend and be present with us. Would that the perfect compassionate heart would now draw near and receive our offerings. May the omnipotent and omniscient Holy Spirit come to us while we recite these divine sentences.'

"If he goes to Nepaul, he would learn that an intelligent Buddhist there opposed to Mr. Hodgson's charge of Atheism, many quotations from their Scriptures, from ancient Sanskrit works, of which the following are specimens: —

"*Adi-Buddha* is without beginning. He is perfect and pure, the essence of wisdom and truth. He has no second. He is omnipresent. He rejoices in giving joy to all sentient beings. He tenderly loves those who serve him. He heals pain and grief. He has created all the Buddhas. Himself not made, he has made all things. He is the essence of essences, the Infinite, the form of all things yet formless."

It is, however, contended that this doctrine of *Adi-Buddha* is a belief which began in the tenth century, and does not belong to primitive Buddhism. Even if this is so, we may say that a large part of Buddhism now in the world teaches Monotheism, and, secondly, that this Monotheism must be regarded as not inconsistent with original

Buddhism, since it was developed out of it. As a matter of fact, however, Buddha himself, the finite Buddha, is generally worshipped as the Supreme Being, and was so from the beginning, as the shrines in the Rock-cut Temples testify. This is also the doctrine of Southern Buddhism. "I take refuge in Buddha," is the usual prayer. The worshipper asks Buddha to forgive his sins. A Buddhist priest in Ceylon, being asked by one of the Dutch governors of the island if he believed in a Supreme Being, replied, "Although there are many Gods, there is one Supreme above all others."

Spence Hardy, the best authority on the Buddhism of Ceylon, gives us this statement of the belief of Sinhalese Buddhists concerning their Master: —

"Buddha is the joy of the whole world; the helper of the helpless; a mine of mercy; the Brahma of Brahmas; the only deliverer; teacher of the three worlds; Father and helper of the world; universal friend; nearest relative; stronger than the strongest; more merciful than the most merciful; more beautiful than the most beautiful. The eye cannot see, the ear hear, or the mind imagine anything more beautiful than Buddha. He who trusts in Buddha relies on him who is supreme."

§ 8. *The conception of God essential, the name unessential.*

Now, if one worships a being as supreme, lord of all worlds, most merciful, most wise, most powerful, is he not worshipping the true God? Does it matter what name he gives him — Jehovah, Jove, Brahma, or Buddha? Does *any* name fitly describe the infinite being? The Jews had a mysterious name for Jehovah, but Jesus dropped that name, and called God *Father*, showing that it is the character of God and the idea which we have of Him which is essential. When we worship the highest being of whom we can form an idea, we are doing our best to adore the true God.

Retracing our steps, and reviewing the progress made, we see the Idea of God developed gradually from the lowest form to the highest. I do not refer to the historic development, but rather to the logical one. We are not yet able to say whether the whole human race began its upward career with *Animism*, as the Doctrine of Evolution teaches, or whether some purer Monotheistic view may not have existed from the beginning, from which there has been a subsequent relapse. Herbert Spencer grants the probability of such relapses, and considers the religion of many savage tribes as a degraded religion. We have seen the Monotheism of the Vedas degraded into the coarse idolatry of later epochs. But the logical process in the development of religion is an ascent from Animism, through Nature-worship to some form of Monarchic Theism, on to the Absolute Monotheism of Moses, and from that still upwards to the reconciling, all-embracing fullness of Christian Theism.

CHAPTER V.

IDEA OF GOD IN ALL RELIGIONS.—DITHEISM, TRITHEISM, AND MONOTHEISM.

§ 1. Ditheism in all Religions. § 2. The Triads in all Religions. § 3. Monotheism in all Religions. § 4. Origin of our Belief in Spirit, in a First Cause, in an Intelligent Creator, in a Supreme and Infinite Being. § 5. The Christian Idea of God is a combination of all the other conceptions of Deity, with that of Infinite Love.

§ 1. *Ditheism in all Religions.*

CONTINUING our examination into the nature and origin of the Idea of God in all Religions, we now come to the three forms: Ditheism, Tritheism, and Monotheism.

We have seen that all the races of men, from the lowest in civilization to the highest, have believed in a supernatural world of spirits, which faith has been called Animism. We have also seen that a large portion of the human race have believed in numerous divine beings, spirits of a higher order, creators or rulers of this world, a doctrine which we call Polytheism. Another large division of mankind have believed in the Supreme Being, or in Monotheism.

We have seen that all nature religions tend toward Polytheism on one side, or to Pantheism on the other; either to a belief of many spiritual beings outside of nature, or of one spirit immersed in nature.

We have also observed that the prophetic religions take a different course, — all tending toward pure Monotheism. The prophets, founders of these religions, are Zoroaster, Buddha, Confucius, Moses, Mohammed, and Jesus.

But besides this, there are traces, here and there, of a belief in two divine beings, one good and the other evil, which belief may be named Dualism, or, better, Ditheism. The last is the better term, because more specific. Dualism is a word of a larger meaning, including the reception of a two-fold principle in Philosophy, Science, Morals. But Ditheism only signifies the belief in two Divine Beings.

The religion of Zoroaster is usually considered to be a Ditheism, or belief in two hostile powers of equal authority; one good, the other evil; engaged in constant war. No doubt the actual conflict of good and evil which we see around us is more fully emphasized in this religion than in any other. The dual principle, however, is found in all religions. The Ormazd and Ahriman of the Zend-Avesta appear in Hinduism as Brahma and Rudra, the creator and destroyer; in Egypt, as

Osiris and Typhon; in the Scandinavian religion, as Odin and Loke; in Judaism, as Jehovah and Satan. Whether this dualism of good and evil belonged to the original form of these systems of faith I do not stop to ask. Enough to say that in all religions there is a stage of development in which the heart is oppressed, and the mind confused, by the sight of the suffering and sin in the world. In the childlike religions every evil is ascribed to the baleful influence of some particular spirit. In others it seems to denote a struggle for supremacy between two great contending powers, one benign, the other malevolent. The system taught by Zoroaster was arrested in this second stage. It beheld a great warfare forever going on in nature and life; Ormazd and the good angels fighting against Ahriman and the evil angels. It became the duty of every man to fight for good against evil. Every good action was a blow struek on the side of Ormazd; every bad one was delivered in behalf of Ahriman. The same duty of contending for truth against falsehood, for right against wrong, is found in all other systems which have a moral character.

Whenever we fix our attention mainly on the eternal distinction between Right and Wrong, Good and Evil, we are leaning toward Ditheism. Evil seems to us a mighty power in the Universe arrayed against good. In our philosophical mood we may say that all partial evil is universal good; that man can only learn to walk by stumbling and falling; and that evil is only a shadow of which good is the substance. We may go so far as to say that evil is only a stage in the development of good; and so make all evil, and even all sin, purely negative. And in our highest religious mood, we may be satisfied that all things work together for good to those that love God; that where sin abounds, grace doth yet more abound; and thus, that sin itself, by the alchemy of divine love, can be transmuted into the sweetest gratitude; according to the text, that he who is forgiven much, loves much. But in the hour of temptation, of mortal conflict, or when we are forced to look on the actual misery and wrong there is in the world, we find evil an awful reality. Then "the air around us seems thick with universal pain." No moral reform could be carried on; no martyr could die for the truth; no missionary spend his days among savages; no philanthropist struggle to overcome fashionable sins, unless evil, for the time, at least, should seem no negation, but the eternal enemy of goodness and joy. Even in Christianity this conflict of Right with Wrong has taken the form of an eternal Hell of sin and misery by the side of the eternal Heaven. To the Christian imagination Satan and his devils have been as positive presences as God and his angels. The optimistic view which led Paul to foresee a time when the last enemy would be overcome by the power of Christ, and made the author of the Book of Revelation predict the day when death and hell would both be cast into the lake of fire, has retired into the back-ground of the Christian consciousness. The general belief of Christendom has been, that a part of the universe would be always in a state of permanent rebellion against the Almighty.

It was at this stage of the religious development that the system of Zoroaster was crystallized into a permanent form. It was an essentially moral religion. Its prayer, like that of the Christian, is that God's Kingdom may come and his will be done on the earth. Its expectation, like the Christian hope, is that the time will come, in which Ahriman with all his host of evil spirits will be cast into the lake of fire, and be either destroyed, or be purified and redeemed. And the disciple of Zoroaster, like the disciple of Jesus, believes that life is a warfare, and that to fight the good fight of faith, one must put on the whole armor of God. Like the Christian, he wrestles not with flesh and blood, but with the powers of darkness, and with spiritual wickedness in high places.

Thus, there is a dualistic tendency in all religions, and, also, in many systems of philosophy. Anaxagoras distinguished God from Nature, making Nature the dark unintelligent material, out of which God makes beauty and order. Pythagoras and Plato equally regarded all intelligent spirits as free and good; all unintelligent matter as bound by necessity, and forever resisting the power of the divine soul of things.

In modern times many philosophers have sought to solve the problem of evil in the same way. John Stuart Mill is one of the last who takes the same view, regarding God as willing, but not able, to overcome the power of necessity in the universe of matter, and therefore unable to prevent the existence of evil in the universe.

§ 2. *The Triads in all Religions.*

Another fact is the appearance of divine triads in so many religious systems.

The theory of the Hindu theologians, says Colebrook, is this: "There is one supreme unrevealed being — Para-Brahm. By self-contemplation he produced the universe. Then, as Siva, or Mahadeva, he destroyed it; then, as Vishnu, he restored and sustains it. This is the Hindu Trinity — the Trimurti. Its holy inexpressible name is the sacred triliteral word A U M." "This doctrine," say the Hindus, "is so mysterious, that neither man nor angel can understand it."

There is a triad in one of the ancient Chinese religions. The Tau-te-King thus speaks: "You look for the Tao and you see it not. Its name is I.

You listen for it, and do not hear it; its name is Hi. You touch it, and do not feel it; its name is Wei. These three are inscrutable and inexpressible. We combine them into oneness, which has no body, a form without form, an image without image."

Another passage says: "These inscrutable three are but one." "The Tao produced one, one produced two; the two produced three, the three produced all beings."

A series of triad deities were also worshipped in Assyria, and another in Babylon. In Assyria the highest triad was: (1.) Oannes, Chaos; (2.) Bel, He who gives form to Chaos; (3.) A O or Bin, the Son, representing the world as formed.

Another triad represented the sun, moon, and firmament.

The object of worship in Buddhism is also a triad, consisting of: (1.) Buddha, the Supreme Being; (2.) Dharma, the law; and (3.) Sangha, the associated priesthood.

In Egypt the gods were all grouped in triads, and a separate triad was worshipped in each city: at Thebes, Amun, Maut, and Khons; at Memphis, Ptah, Pasht, and their son; elsewhere Osiris, Isis, Horus.

In Greece, as Creuzer believes, there was the notion of a cosmic triad before the time when Homer first humanized the preëxisting Polytheism. This triad, he says, consisted of the heavens above, the earth beneath, and the ocean around all things.

In the Orphic theology there was also a three-formed god, called light, life, and counsel. Some of the Orphic sayings which have been preserved are these: "God is the head and middle of all things. God is the abyss of heaven, the depth of the sea, and the life of all breathing creatures. All these three, abyss, depth, and life, are parts of his vast body."

According to Plato, God is threefold: first as the profound, inscrutable substance and cause of all things; next as manifesting himself in the ideas, which are the roots in the spiritual world of all that exists in the natural world; and thirdly as the life of the universe.

This threefold division was carried out still more fully by the later Platonists, who have a series of trinities, first of beauty, truth, and symmetry, which is the triad of intelligible being; next the vital triad, of the source of life, the power of life, and the existence of life.

Not only Plato, but other Greek philosophers before him, as Parmenides and Pythagoras, conceived of the supreme being as a triad in a monad. The triad of Pythagoras much resembled the Platonic trinity. The first One was above all being; the second One contained the ideas of all being; the third One was the soul of all being. According to

Parmenides, the highest divine being is perfectly and properly one; the second is the one-many, or each and all; the third is the return of the many to the one.

We find, also, that the system of Zoroaster, so long arrested in dualism, finally assumed a triad form by the addition to Ormazd the good principle, and Ahriman the evil, of a third, Mitra or Mithra, the mediator or reconciler.

And even the Jewish mind, when it began to philosophize in Alexandria, took up this conception of the Deity as an imperfect triad. This was especially the work of Philo, who was a contemporary with Christ. He regards the Supreme Being, the cause of all things, as creating the world by his logos or divine mind, which Philo also called the First-Begotten Son of God. So that he conceived of God in a threefold character: as essential being, as the divine ideas which were the archetypes before all things, and as the creative logos, or life which produces all things.

There is no doubt that the Christian doctrine of the Trinity was derived from such forms of thought previously existing in Egypt and elsewhere. It grew out of a philosophical attempt to unite the monotheism of the Jews with the profound tendencies of the Oriental and Grecian mind. Philo had led the way in this attempt; and Alexandria, where he lived and taught, was also the place where the Christian Trinity took its origin. The early Christian thinkers who followed Christ in their faith, took Plato as their master in philosophy. Their object was to see the Divine in the unity of things, and also in their variety. The Supreme Being, One in Himself, is nevertheless the source and author of the infinitely varied world.

The Gnostics also held to a Triad. In some of the Gnostic systems, this Trinity consists of the Spirit in itself, the self-conscious Spirit, and the intelligent Reason.[1] The Gnostics were much occupied with this problem of Creation. Can a finite and imperfect world proceed from an infinite and perfect God? Some of them assumed three first principles of things: the Good God, the Just God, and the world of matter.[2] Others laid stress on the distinction between the Abyss of Being, which is the Supreme but unknown God; the Æons, which emanate from him; and the Demiurg, or Creator of the world.

But even these conceptions of the Deity as a triad, are all evidences of the tendency in the soul to faith in one Supreme and Perfect Deity. They are forms of Monotheism. Everything which we see is finite, yet we believe in an infinite being.

[1] Ferd. Christ. Baur. *Die Christliche Lehre von der Dreieinigkeit*, vol. i., page 140.

[2] Hase, *Kirchengeschichte*.

Everything we see around has more or less of imperfection or evil, yet we must believe in an all-perfect One, to whom no shade of evil can attach itself. These triads are attempts to reconcile such apparent contradictions. They consider God as all-perfect in himself; but therefore as not in immediate contact with the imperfect world. Another being, divine indeed, but of subordinate divinity, is the Demiurg, a creator of all things. The third manifestation of God is in order to recall the world, thus fallen away out of himself, back into himself. Such were the speculative attempts of antiquity, seeking to reconcile Unity and Variety, Monotheism and Polytheism, an All-perfect Deity and this imperfect world which went forth from his mind and hand.

Tritheism, being so universal, must have its source in some necessity of the human mind. This is the attempt, ever foiled, to understand the incomprehensible nature of God. All Trinities are philosophical speculations. They belong to the metaphysics of religion, rather than to religion itself. The first conception of the Deity was of a simple, personal being like ourselves, above all things; and so, like ourselves, outside of the universal order, as its Maker and Ruler; this was simple Monotheism. Then came the sense of the Discord, the imperfection which disturbs this order, the Evil which resists this goodness, and so arrived

Ditheism; and finally men felt the need of a third Being, or Principle, which should mediate between the two antagonist powers, and reconcile them in a higher unity. Thus the Triads were to satisfy the reflecting intellect. But all such attempts prove unsatisfactory. At last the religious nature is contented with the conception of the One God, above all, through all, and in us all.

§ 3. *Monotheism in all Religions.*

Monotheism exists as thought and as life; as philosophy and as religion. The human race has reached, by two distinct and different paths, this high ground where it stands in the presence of one, supreme, all-perfect being. It has arrived at Monotheism by the method of speculative inquiry, and the development of its religious life through conscious intelligent reasoning, and an unconscious unfolding of the spiritual nature. It will be interesting to look for a moment at these two methods, both of which reach at last the same result. By the mouth of two witnesses everything is more firmly established.

Philosophic theism is the belief in a perfect being; self-existent, in whom all things exist; the intelligent cause of all things; above all nature as its cause, yet not outside of it; within all nature as its order and life, yet not shut in by it; beneath all nature as its substance, yet not immersed in it;

around all nature as its providence, yet not separated from it. He is supreme, infinite, eternal; he is absolute, that is, depending only on himself, yet by his infinite goodness is in a perpetual relation of providential care to all his creatures. He is infinite in wisdom, power, and goodness, and thus forever one. Forever one, he is never alone, because bound by his infinite love and perfect wisdom to his creation. The best definition of Deity is this: God is the perfect Being.

Now this idea of God has been held, in a more or less distinct form, by the greatest thinkers in all time. Thus the Ny-ă-ya philosophy in India speaks of the Supreme Soul as infinite, eternal, immutable, omniscient, without form, all-pervading, all-powerful, one only. A writer of this school says: "An omniscient and indestructible being is to be proved from the existence of effects (which require a cause), from the combination of atoms (which imply design), from the sustained order of the universe (which implies an upholder), from the traditional arts among men (which imply an inspiration from above)."

The second system of Hindu philosophy has been called Atheistic. It is the Sankya philosophy. It is rather Agnostic than Atheistic. While it asserts the eternal existence of souls, it denies that the existence of the Supreme Soul is capable of dialectic proof. One branch of this system —

the Yoga — does, however, distinctly acknowledge the Supreme Being, and declares that by ascetic exercises and mortification of the flesh one can come into union with God, and be yoked to him.

The third ancient Hindu system of philosophy, the Vedanta, declares all the universe to be identical with the Supreme Soul, or Brahma. It thus defines him: "Brahma is the all-knowing, all-powerful cause, from which comes the production, continuance, and dissolution of the universe. The Supreme Being is omniscient, for from him proceeded the Veda. Every soul is evolved from him and returns to him. He consists of joy. He, the one God, is light within the sun, and within the eye. He is life, and the breath of life. He is creator and creation, actor and act. He has neither beginning nor end, parts or qualities; he is immutable, and the only real substance."

This doctrine may be called imperfect Theism, because leaning too much to Pantheism. But it is also imperfect Pantheism, because it makes the Supreme Being omniscient, intelligent, and full of joy.

Thus, from the earliest times, philosophic Theism has existed in India, often leaning either toward spiritual Pantheism, or to material Pantheism; but still maintaining the existence of a Supreme Soul, the soul of nature, the origin of all things, the principle of all life.

If we turn to ancient Greece we discover in philosophy, as soon as it emerges there, the existence of philosophic Theism.

Pythagoras considered the monad, or principle of unity, as the source of all things. Xenophanes (born 620 B. C.) first distinctly announced the doctrine of the one all-controlling Godhead. "God," he says, "is all eye, ear, intelligence, — he moves and directs all things by the power of thought." Anaxagoras (born in Asia Minor about 500 B. C.) finds the force which shapes the world, not in the nature of matter, nor in impersonal forces, but in a world-ordering mind. This Supreme Mind is distinguished from matter by simplicity, independence, knowledge, and supreme power. According to Socrates (born 470 B. C.) the world is governed by a Supreme Divine Intelligence, who inspires men to do what is good. He discovered in all the outward world marks of creative design. Plato (born 427 B. C.) makes goodness the supreme idea, and the essence of God. He did not say "God is being," but "God is goodness," just as the apostle says "God is love." One Supreme Being made the world, and made it for good. The highest aim of man and his supreme happiness consists in his becoming like God. So devoted was Plato to the contemplation of Deity that he has been called the Divine Plato, the Christian Theologian before Christ. In passages quoted by Cudworth, Rixner, and Alfred Day, Plato speaks of God as the "Architect of the World," the "Maker and Father of the Universe," "Whom it is hard to find out and impossible to declare," "God over all," "Creator of Nature," "Sole Principle of the Universe," "Cause of all things," "Mind, Supreme King," "The Sovereign Mind which orders all things, and passes through all things," "Governor of the Whole," "Which always is and was never made," "The First God," "The Greatest God," "He who makes earth, heaven, and the gods," "Producing all things and self-existing," "Always good, never evil," "Cause of all blessings," "Who cannot change for the better, and will not change for the worse," "By whose Providence the state is preserved."

Rixner[1] says that Plato is the truly divine philosopher, because he refers all things to God as the ground of their being.

Aristotle, who in his way of thought was the very opposite to Plato, nevertheless speaks of God with a similar grandeur in the Eleventh Book of his "Metaphysics": —

"The principle of life is in God; for energy of mind constitutes life, and God is this energy. He, the first mover, imparts motion, and pursues the work of creation as something to be loved. His course of life resembles ours, but his exists forever, while ours is transient. His

[1] *Handbuch der Geschichte der Philosophie.*

joy is in the exercise of his essential energy. He is eternal and perfect, indivisible, without parts, devoid of passions, and unchanging."

This path of belief has ever since been pursued by the great masters of philosophic thought. However they have differed on other questions, they all, with one consent, agree in this sublime faith. The new Platonists, Plotinus, Proclus, Jamblichus; the medieval philosophers, Erigena, Anselm, Abelard; the great Arabian philosophers, Averroes, Avicenna, and others; the modern thinkers, Spinoza, Descartes, Bacon, Leibnitz, Locke, Kant, Fichte, Schelling, Hegel, — all have conceived of a spiritual, All-perfect Being, as the one ever active cause of all that exists. The consent of thought in this belief is most extraordinary. Read this hymn of Cleanthes, the Stoic, who lived 460 B. C.: —

"O thou who hast various names, but whose essence is one and infinite! O Jupiter! first of immortals, sovereign of nature, who governest all, who subjectest all to one law, I salute thee; for man is permitted to invoke thee. All that lives, all that moves, all that exists as mortal upon the earth, we all are born of thee, we are a feeble image of thee. I address to thee, therefore, my hymn, and will not cease to sing to thee. This universe suspended over our heads, and which seems to roll around the earth, obeys thee alone; it moves and is governed in silence by thy command. Genius of nature! in the heavens, on the earth, in the seas, nothing is made, nothing is produced without thee, except evil, which springs from the heart of the wicked. By happy accord thou so blendest that which is good with that which is not, that general and eternal harmony is everywhere established. Alone, of all beings, the wicked interrupt this grand harmony of the world."

This is essentially the same idea of Deity as in the hymn of Hildebert: —

> "Above all things, below all things;
> Around all things, within all things;
> Within all, but not shut in;
> Around all, but not shut out;
> Above all, as the Ruler;
> Below all, as the Sustainer;
> Around all, as all-embracing Protection;
> Within all, as the Fullness of Life."

The same also as in the lines of Pope, who writes of the Deity that he

> "Lives through all life, extends through all extent;
> Spreads undivided, operates unspent.
> To him, no high, no low, no great nor small;
> He fills, he bounds, connects and equals all."

Or, as in Dr. Johnson's hymn: —

> "From thee, Great God, we spring, to thee we tend;
> Path, Motive, Guide, Original and End."

Having thus seen Monotheism in philosophy, we now come to consider it in all the religions. It may surprise us to learn that Monotheism has existed in all or nearly all religions, and that in the most highly developed Polytheism there still remains, perhaps in an obscure form, a very real Monotheism. This may not mean the conception of one only God, but rather of a Supreme Being, a Most High God. Sometimes this Supreme Being is regarded as the Creator of all things, sometimes not. But in most of these forms, as we shall see, a Monotheistic type is found.

Beginning with the childlike races, we find the Monotheistic idea among some of those who are placed by ethnologists on the lowest plane of human development, such as the Hottentots and Bushmen of South Africa, the negroes of the Gold Coast, the natives of Australia, the islanders of Polynesia, the inhabitants of Terra del Fuego, the Indians of the Amazon River, the North American Indians, the Esquimaux, and the natives of the Andaman Islands in the Bay of Bengal. All of these have been pronounced by different travelers and writers on sociology as destitute of any religion whatever. But later and more careful inquiry has shown that besides the belief in a surrounding world of disembodied spirits (or Animism), common to all races, they believe in a Supreme Being, as is testified to by the traveler Kolben and by missionaries who have lived among them. Of these African tribes generally, Waitz, a distinguished anthropologist, speaks as follows: —

"The religion of the negro is usually considered as a peculiar crude form of Polytheism, and marked with the special name of Fetichism. A closer inspection clearly shows that it is neither very peculiar nor exceptionally crude. A profounder investigation, such as has recently been made with success by several eminent scholars, leads to the surprising result that several negro tribes, who have not been influenced from the outside, have developed their religious ideas so far that if we do not call them Monotheists, we must admit that they have come very near the boundaries of true Monotheism." [1]

There is ample evidence to show (says Max Müller) that the tribes of West Africa believe in a supreme god, a good being. The Ashantis call him by the same name as the sky, but mean by it a personal god, who, they say, created all things, and gives all good things. They believe him to be omniscient and omnipresent. The negroes of the Gold Coast, says the missionary Cruickshank, believe in a supreme god, creator and governor of the world, calling him "Our great friend," or "He who made us." Other missionaries confirm this statement, telling us that these negroes say "God is the old one, he is the greatest, he sees me." Cruickshank adds: "If, besides this faith they also believe in thousands of fetiches, they unfortunately share this fault with many Christians."

In the proceedings of the American Philosophical Society there is an article, by Dr. Brinton, on the ancient gods of Central America. He tells us that he finds in old documents prayers to the Cre-

[1] *Anthropologie der Naturvölker.*

ator of the World, which date back to a time preceding the discovery of America. Some of these he thus translates out of the Maya tongue: —

> "We bring forward the revelation of that which was hidden, the knowledge sent to us by him who creates, who forms creatures. Speak his name; honor your mother and father; call him Hurakan, Soul of the Earth, Soul of the Sky, Creator, Maker, her who makes us, him who creates us; call on him and salute him.
>
> "Hail! O Creator, Maker! thou seest and hearest us. Do not leave us; do not desert us! O Hurakan, Voc, Tepeu, Alom; Grandmother of the Sun, Grandmother of the Light; hear us, help us."

In China, five thousand years ago, as on the western coast of Africa, the idea of a Supreme Being was associated with the visible heavens. In the languages of western Africa, and eastern Asia, one word designated God, and also the visible heavens. The vast, all-surrounding sky, filled with light by day, glittering in the solemn night with uncounted stars, — unfathomable, unbounded, that is, infinite, — this seemed to both races the fittest name for God. That name was Ti, the personal name of heaven. Shang-ti means the Supreme Heaven. Dr. Legge, best authorized to speak on this subject, says: "These characters show us that the religion of the Chinese, five thousand years ago, was a Monotheism;"[1] and he adds, that "these two

[1] *The Religion of China.* By James Legge, 1881.

names have kept the Monotheistic element prominent in the prevailing religion of China down to the present time."

The original Vedic religion was a form of Monotheism, but a very peculiar one. It was not a monarchical Monotheism wherein one Deity is supreme, like that of Greece and Rome. It was a system in which each of the great powers of nature were alternately deified and made supreme. Varuna, the heavens; Surya, the sun; Indra, the atmosphere; Agni, fire; and other beings, were in turn worshipped as the Most High God. Infinite Spirit appeared embodied in every part of nature. The All was seen in each part, and each part included All.

Müller calls it Henotheism; and this word will, probably, be allowed to stand. But that it is really a form of Monotheism appears in this: that whether worshipped as the heavens, the air, the fire, or any other manifestation, it is the same Supreme Being, with the same infinite attributes, who is worshipped.

Thus the hymns of the Rig-Veda address Varuna, or the Heavens, as universal king, divine, of unbounded knowledge, who has made heaven and earth, who embraces in himself the three worlds; who makes the sun to shine; whose breath is the wind; who, by his wonderful skill, makes the rivers to run forever into the sea, but never fill it; whose ordinances are unchangeable; whose messengers go through all worlds; without whom no creature can make the least motion; who sees all that happens; from whom no one can escape, even if he flee beyond the sky; who can drive away evil and purify the soul from sin, prolong life, pardon sin, give eternal happiness to the good. Of Mitra, Indra, Agni, Savitri, the same things are said.[1]

It is evident from such hymns as these, ascribing in turn supreme power to different beings, that these gods, though differently named, are really one. For these hymns are in the same book, and were sung by the same worshippers. Some texts expressly declare this identity; for example, here is one from the Rig-Veda: "They call him Indra, Mitra, Varuna, Agni. Sages name variously that which is but one. Agni becomes Varuna in the evening; rising in the morning he becomes Mitra; as Savitri, he moves through the air; becoming Indra, he glows in the middle of the sky."

Herodotus, — one of the earliest European students of Egyptian civilization, usually as accurate as he was observing, a student filled with infinite curiosity to know and understand all the facts and phases of human nature, — told mankind, twenty-three centuries ago, that the Egyptians of Thebes recognized "one Supreme God, who had no beginning and would have no end." Jamblichus, the

[1] See Muir's *Sanskrit Texts*, Second Edition, vol. i.

new Platonist (A. D. 320), quotes from the old Hermetic books the declaration: "Before all the things that actually exist, and before all beginnings, there is one God, prior even to the first God and King, remaining unmoved in the singleness of his own unity."

One of the first Egyptologists (De Rougé) gave this as his mature judgment: —

> "No one has called in question the fundamental meaning of the principal passages by the help of which we are able to establish what ancient Egypt has taught concerning God, the world and man. I said 'God,' not 'The Gods.' The first characteristic of the Religion is the unity of God, — God, one, sole, and only, no others with him. He is the only being — living in truth. He has made everything." . . .

Among all the local names of Deity "one idea predominates, that of a single and personal God; everywhere and always it is one substance, self-existent and unapproachable." "A hymn of the Leyden Museum calls God 'the One of One.'" "These doctrines were in existence two thousand years before Christ. More than five thousand years ago, in the valley of the Nile, the hymn began to the unity of God and the immortality of the soul. The belief in this unity of the Creator and Law-Giver, are the primitive notions remaining, overlaid by vast mythologies accumulated in subsequent centuries."

Thus a Hymn to Amun — the supreme God of Thebes — says : —

"Hail to thee, Amun-Ra, Lord of the thrones of the earth, the oldest existence, ancient of heaven, support of all things; chief of the gods; lord of truth; father of the gods; maker of men and beasts and herbs; maker of all things above and below; deliverer of the sufferer and oppressed, judging the poor; lord of wisdom, lord of mercy, most loving, opener of every eye, source of joy, in whose goodness the gods rejoice, thou whose name is hidden."

"Thou art the one, maker of all that is, the one; the only one; maker of gods and men; giving food to all."

"Hail to thee, thou one with many heads; sleepless when all others sleep, adoration to thee."

"Hail to thee from all creatures from every land, from the height of heaven, from the depth of the sea. The spirits thou hast made extol thee, saying, 'Welcome to thee, father of the fathers of the gods; we worship thy spirit which is in us.'"

But what is sung and declared about Amun is also said about Osiris.

Osiris is called "lord of eternity; king of the gods; substance of the world; feeder of beings; from whom came the waters, and the winds; master of all the gods; giver of food to men; eldest god and their chief; who made the world and all things therein; who maintains law in the universe; beneficent to gods and men."

That these are one and the same, is evident from this hymn on the walls of a temple in the Oasis of El-Khargeh : —

"The gods salute him as their lord, who reveals himself in all that is, and has many names. It is Amun, persisting in all things. It is Ptah, existing from the beginning. Each god has assumed thy aspect. Thou raisest up, Osiris. As Ptah thou hast made both worlds. As Amun thou art the life of the world. Shu, Tefnut, Nut, Chonsu, are thy forms. Thou art Mentu-Rá. Thou art Sekar. Thou art youth and age. Thou art heaven, earth, fire, water, air, and what is in them all."

We have thus far seen two kinds of Monotheism — both imperfect. The first posits one Supreme Being, presiding over a body of inferior deities. This is the Monotheistic element in the Polytheism of Greece, of Scandinavia, and of all the uncivilized races. The other kind is that of the Vedic hymns and the Egyptian hymns, in which each of the forces of nature becomes in turn a personal and Supreme God, with infinite attributes. There is a singular resemblance between the theology of these two systems of ancient India and ancient Egypt. Both have the conception of a personal being of infinite power, creator and preserver of all things, above nature, before time, flowing through all things. But in both systems this Divine Being is manifested alternately in one power of nature or another; in the heavens, the storms, the sun, the fire; and each of these becomes in turn the Supreme and Infinite Being. This Monotheism resembles a Polytheism struggling with a Pantheism.

By these steps Polytheism and Pantheism pass up, by a steady and sure law of development, into speculative Monotheism in philosophy, and into an included Monotheism in religion. They culminate and combine in the prophetic religion. When the faith of Abraham and Moses became the state religion of the Jewish nation, Monotheism for the first time appeared as the public religion of a people. Down to the time of Christ Judaism was the only pure national Monotheism among men. All of Europe, Asia, and Africa, all except the little land of Palestine, worshipped numerous deities. Judea alone long maintained its inflexible faith in one Supreme, Invisible Spirit, Maker of all things.

§ 4. *Origin of our Belief in Spirit, Cause, Creator, and the Infinite Being.*

We have thus followed the idea of the Deity in all religions, from its lowest form in Animism up through Polytheism, Pantheism, Ditheism, Tritheism, to pure Monotheism. Whence was this belief in God, which we find so universal, derived? We have seen that all men believe in and adore unseen powers, higher than themselves. This worship begins in one great faith, universal and the same,—the belief in the presence and power of invisible spirits. It passes up through various phases of belief, and then at last becomes once more the same faith; namely, belief in one Supreme Spiritual Being. It is one in its lowest form as Animism; one, finally, in its highest form, as Monotheism.

The only source from which man's belief in spirits could have been derived is the consciousness that he is himself a soul, a soul with a body for its present organ, but capable of existing without this organism. Apart from this consciousness, it is difficult to see how his belief in disembodied spirits could have come.

The second step is taken by means of another universal and necessary law of thought — belief in causation. All things around are in perpetual change; but a law of the mind compels us to believe that every event must have a cause, that for every change there must exist a motive force.

This notion of cause is deeply rooted in every human mind. It is a universal idea, for all men have it. It is a necessary idea, for we cannot help having it, even if we deny its existence. It probably arises first in the mind on the occasion of our making an effort and seeing some result follow. Cause is an idea connected intimately with personal action, effort, choice, the exercise of an intelligent will. Childlike races, looking out on the phenomena of nature, the coming of dawn, day and night, storm and sunshine, spring-time and harvest, flowers and fruits, and, seeing that these were caused by the sun, the atmosphere, the spring rains and summer heats, personified these causes as the Sun-god and Rain-god, as Agni, God of Fire, and Indra, God of Storms. Thus the second step in religious belief was taken.

The next idea associated with the gods is that of creation. This belief in a God who has created the heavens and the earth, we have also found to be very widely disseminated among races in every degree of civilization.

What was the origin of this belief? It seems to have risen in the mind by adding to the idea of causation that of finality or design. There is a universal law of thought, by which from the perception of adaptation we infer design. I do not here undertake to decide if this be an original intuition or not, but at present it is a law of thought which works like an instinct. Nearly the whole life of man is spent in adapting means to foreseen and intended ends. From the hunter setting his trap to catch game, up to Shakespeare designing the play of "Hamlet," or the Apostle Paul planning the conversion of Europe, through all human industries, arts, amusements, man is adapting means to ends during all his life. When the Pilgrim Fathers landed on Cape Cod, before they knew whether the region was inhabited, they "came to a tree where a young sprit was bowed down, and some acorns strewed under it. As we were looking at it William Bradford came up, and as he went about, it gave a sudden jerk up, and he was caught by the leg. Stephen Hopkins said, 'It was made to catch some deer.' It is a very pretty device." No one thought it a freak of nature. Adaptation proved design. In a stratum of sand belonging to a geological epoch where the presence of man had not then been suspected, there were found stones rudely shaped into some kind of tools. Their adaptation to cutting and grinding was at once regarded as a sufficient proof of design, therefore as evidence that men had existed on the earth at that remote period. No one can contemplate the myriad adaptations of means to ends in nature without being impressed with the sense of intelligent purpose. We do not stop now to consider the modern metaphysical objections to finality in nature. Such objections certainly never disturbed the primitive reason of mankind. To the common sense of the childlike races, no less than to the penetrating thought of Socrates, it was enough to look at the immense order of the universe, its infinite variety and majestic unity, its thousand-fold adaptations to life, growth, and the progress of the creature, to lead to the conclusion that it was the work of some divine architect, some celestial Demiurg.

One more step was to be taken. If there are supernatural beings above man, yet caring for man, and if among these there is a Supreme Being maintaining the order of the universe, it needs only to proceed a little farther in this process of thought to reach the pure Monotheism of the Greek philosophy and the Egyptian mysteries. A contemplation of the world without shows universal law, fixed and invariable order, the permanence of being; and on this permanence of existing law our whole mind and heart reposes securely. The invariable order of things is the only guarantee of our sanity, and to maintain this order we need infinite power, infinite wisdom, and infinite goodness. This conception of Infinite Being, existing in boundless space and eternal duration, is given us by another law of thought, behind which we cannot go. Given the finite, there is a necessity to believe in the infinite. This is a conception so lofty as to seem above the capacity of a created mind, and yet it is one of the primal truths from which no human reason can escape. It is one of those of which Epictetus says: "He who denies self-evident truths cannot be reasoned with."

§ 5. *The Christian Idea of God combines the other conceptions of Deity with that of Infinite Love.*

The mixture of a hidden and private Monotheism with a public Polytheism was the religion of the civilized world, with the exception of Judea, when Christ came. Now, probably, one half of the human race have a Monotheistic religion. These

Monotheistic religions are the work of two prophets, Moses and Jesus, from whose teachings Mohammed drew his own inspiration. The semi-Monotheism of China and Eastern Asia is also the result of the teaching of two great souls, Buddha and Confucius. The nature of their inspiration we shall consider in another chapter. Christianity teaches the highest form of Monotheism. Jesus gives no personal name to the Deity, as the religions before him had done. He does not call God by the sacred Jewish name of Yahveh, but by a word designating his character of parental care and love, "Father." The peculiarity of Christian Monotheism is that it combines with the conception of one Supreme, All-perfect Being, Maker and Ruler of all things, which is the philosophic Monotheism, and with that of holy Law-giver and Judge, and Beneficent Providence, the faith in an infinite tenderness of love. God in Christ comes near to each soul, as an ever-present friend and helper; as one who forgives and saves; a perpetual inspiration and guide; a friend nearer than any other to every child high or low. Farther than this Monotheism can hardly go, for this combines the two extremes of religious thought in a harmonious whole, that of the Being who is infinitely removed from us by his greatness, and the Being who comes nearest to us by his love. This is the fullness of him who fills all in all.

CHAPTER VI.

THE SOUL AND ITS TRANSMIGRATIONS; IN ALL RELIGIONS.

§ 1. Universal faith in the independent existence and survival of the human soul. The belief in Ghosts a proof of it. § 2. Double souls and a double consciousness. Is there any evidence of this? Soul and Shadow. § 3. Does Buddhism deny the existence of the soul? § 4. The Philosophical basis of belief in a soul. § 5. The objections of Materialism. § 6. Preëxistence and Transmigration. The doctrine of Brahmanism and of the ancient Egyptians. § 7. Transmigration among the Buddhists. § 8. Foundation of this belief. § 9. Human traits in primitive organisms. Chief distinction between the human and animal soul. § 10. The evolution of the soul, as an improvement on the doctrine of Darwin.

§ 1. *Universal faith in the independent existence and survival of the human soul.*

OF all the beliefs of man in regard to the supernatural world, the belief in a human soul as a substantial essence, capable of existing independently of the body, has prevailed most widely. It is found in all parts of the world, in all times, among all classes, however widely separated from each other by physical and moral barriers. The lowest tribes of savages unite with the most sublime philosophers in this conviction. On this point the Hottentot and the Fiji islander agree with Plato and Aristotle.

The evidence of this belief among the lower races, who have no metaphysical theories or language, is to be found in their universal conviction that all men continue to exist after the death of the body, as disembodied spirits, or, as we say, ghosts.

Our word "ghost," it must be remembered, the same as the German "geist," simply means a spirit. Now the belief of the existence of disembodied spirits is well-nigh universal among the primitive races. All believe in apparitions, in unsubstantial appearances of departed friends. The Esquimaux in the Arctic Circle of North America; the natives of Siberia in the same latitudes in Asia; the Australians and Patagonians at the other extreme of the world; the great religions of antiquity — those of Egypt, China, India, Persia, Greece, Rome, Mexico, Peru, the Tartar tribes of Central Asia, the Negroes of Central and Western Africa; the inhabitants of the innumerable islands of the Pacific — have all believed in such a continued spiritual existence of the dead. This belief could only have come from one of two sources — from outward experience or inward consciousness. Either they have all actually seen ghosts, and believe in them for that reason, or else they have not seen them. If they have not seen them, if ghosts have never appeared, this universal belief has prevailed with no facts of outward experience to support it. It must then be based on some profound and universal fact of inward experience. Is there any such fact? There is. We are conscious of a thinking, feeling, and acting self, which has no bodily qualities. This self acts and feels in every part of the body, and yet is not located in any part, for if a part of the body is lost, the thinking and feeling and acting energy remains unimpaired. It seems to go out of the body in dreams, in memory, in imagination, and in thought which makes the past present, the distant near. The soul seems to leave the body in dreams, for then it enters into another world, seemingly as real as this one. It has a marvelous unity, correlating and combining in a central self or ego, imagination, memory, hope and fear, love and hatred, thought and sensation, action, choice, and passive receptivity. It is the one simple ego which has all this experience. Our consciousness does not allow us to suppose that one part of the soul is devoted to thought, another part to feeling, and the like. We say, "I think, I feel, I remember, I am in pain, I like the taste of this fruit, I smell the perfume of that rose, I foresee that some evil may occur, I intend to build a house next year." It is one and the same undivided, indivisible self which does all this. The consciousness of this indivisible unity, a unity of which the body is incapable, is the same in the savage and the philosopher. It is a primitive, universal, and necessary conviction. The body dissolves at death, but the self within the body is indissoluble. It continues one and the same through all the changes of life, and therefore will continue, men believe, after the physical body dies. Primitive man does not argue in this way, and convince himself thus of his immortality; but the belief is the natural outgrowth of his self-consciousness.

§ 2. *Double souls and a double consciousness. Any proof of this?*

Some eminent thinkers, however, take a different view. They tell us that the man who sleeps and dreams thinks he has two individualities, one of which leaves the other in his sleep, and comes back to it again when he wakes.

Schoolcraft reports that "the North American Indians believe in duplicate souls, one of which remains with the body, while the other departs during sleep." But this is surely a misinterpretation of their idea. There is evidence enough that many primitive races believe that the conscious thinking soul leaves the body during sleep. But there is not a second conscious thinking soul left behind. There is no evidence that any human being, on awakening from a dream, ever remembered that he existed simultaneously in two distinct series of conscious thoughts and actions. His thinking self was only one. It seemed to leave his body and go elsewhere. He saw that the body had a principle of life left with it, but not a second principle of thought. This theory, then, of a double soul is a mere misuse of words, and rests on no scientific basis of observation or experience.

There have been instances of persons who, by some strange cerebral conditions, have passed from one state of consciousness into another, and in the second state have forgotten all they knew in the previous condition. They have then passed back, during an interval of sleep, into their original state, instantly remembering all they learned before while in that condition, but forgetting all they knew in the second. But even this extremely rare phenomenon does not justify the assumption of a double soul. The patient in this case had no double consciousness, but simply forgot in one condition what was remembered in another. This was not having two souls, but it was one soul passing into two different states of thought and life.

It is often asserted that the primitive races regard their shadows as their soul, and hence it is argued that the very notion of the soul may have been derived from the sight of the shadow. This is reversing the order of thought. The idea of the soul must have existed before it could have been compared to a shadow. When the Romans called a disembodied spirit an "umbra," or shadow, and the Greeks used the same word, they simply meant that it was unsubstantial, like a shadow.

As a shadow is visible, but not tangible, as it retains the outline of the form, so the ghost was believed to be visible but not tangible, and to have a vague outline of the human form. But how could any human being believe that the shadow which always accompanies the body, and is never seen without it, can be the spirit which has no body, and which leaves the body in dreams? The most striking case on record of such an imagination is in the story of Peter Schlemil, the man who sold his shadow. We ourselves often use the word shadow to express something unsubstantial, as when we say, "What shadows we are, and what shadows we pursue!" No one would infer from this that we considered our souls to be the shadows. We can usually best get at the conceptions of the undeveloped races by recalling our own notions when we were children. We shall remember, I think, that our shadow had a mysterious quality to our infantile mind. It aroused our fancy; we may have tried to run away from it; we have stamped upon it; it was an attendant from which we could not get away. But it never occurred to us for a moment that it was our soul, or self. Similar childish fancies take possession of the childlike races. The natives of Benin call a man's shadow his guide, and believe it will witness if he has done well or ill. The Basutos are careful not to let their shadow fall on the river, lest a crocodile should seize it, and draw them in.

§ 3. *Does Buddhism deny the existence of the soul?*

One remarkable and unaccountable exception, if it is an exception, to the universal belief of mankind in the soul, as a simple substantial principle of feeling, thought, and will, known by consciousness, is the great religion of Buddha. We are positively assured by the best informed writers on this religion, that it persistently denies and rejects the notion of a soul in man. This is stated in the most decided form by Rhys Davids, one of the most recent and learned writers. Buddhism, he says, teaches that man is a flux of emotions, thought, acts, with no abiding principle behind them. He quotes a passage from the "Sutta Pitaka," to the effect that the unlearned and sensual man regards the soul as residing in sensation and matter, and so gets the idea "I am." But the wise man who has escaped both from ignorance and from acquired knowledge does not have this idea, "I am."

Here, however, comes in the necessity of understanding the meaning of words, of entering into the state of mind of the Buddhist thinker. It is of small consequence to have any statement, unless we comprehend the intention of the man who makes it.

Now the whole purpose of original Buddhism was to teach men how to escape the miseries of life by the destruction of desire. Among these desires is the wish for continued existence. This also must be destroyed. Therefore the Pitakas, or oldest religious books, perpetually repeat such statements as this: —

> "I see in the world this trembling race given to desire for existences; they lament in the mouth of death, not being free from the desire for reiterated existences. Look on those men trembling with selfishness; let them be unselfish, not having any attachment to existences."

The object being to produce perfect peace by the destruction of all desire — even the desire for continued existence — the remedy must be found in knowledge, which is the Buddhist way of salvation. Brahmanism in the time of Buddha sought the same end. The Laws of Manu say of the sage: "Let him not seek for death, let him not seek for life." But their method of extinguishing all desire was by ascetic mortifications. Buddha had tried these, and found them insufficient. His great discovery was that salvation came through knowledge, knowledge of the laws of being. He reached that state, not by reasoning or philosophy, which he declares can never produce knowledge, but only fluctuating opinion. To him knowledge came by an interior insight of spiritual, moral, and physical laws. To destroy all desire, the desire for future existence must be destroyed. This is destroyed by seeing that there is no soul, or personal identity, or ego to continue. Thus Buddhism seems to deny the existence of the soul.

On the other hand it teaches transmigration. This is a fundamental doctrine with Buddhism. But how can there be a migration of souls from one body to another, unless there are souls to migrate? The answer is an ingenious one. Here comes in the great law called Karma, which is the law of cause and effect made universal. Every moral or immoral action which a man performs produces its result. If he does right he goes up, if wrong he goes down. When a man dies the whole results of his life are summed up in a new being, who takes his place by the law of Karma. He does not pass into another body, but another being appears as the consequence of his conduct. So the Buddhist metaphysicians say, that what we call transmigration is really metamorphosis.

But this fine-spun doctrine belongs to the metaphysics, not to the religion of Buddhism. Even Hardy himself tells us that "it is almost universally repudiated." "In historical composition, in narrative, and in conversation, the common idea of transmigration is always presented. We meet with innumerable passages like the following: "These four, by the help of Buddha, went after death to the celestial world. 'I myself was the wise merchant of this transaction.'"

This Buddhist doctrine of no soul is, therefore, no exception to the general law. The Buddhists, like the rest of mankind, believe in the personal ego, and its continued existence hereafter. Whatever their metaphysics may demand, their faith is in the continued existence of the individual through many births and deaths till he reach Nirvána. One of the most learned writers on Buddhism, Samuel Beal, takes this view in his introduction to "The Romantic History of Buddha."

§ 4. *The philosophical basis of belief in a soul.*

We have seen how belief in a personal self arises through consciousness. Observation of organized life leads to a like conclusion. We observe in all animals and plants an organization in which matter is governed, moulded, renewed, correlated and brought into unity by some power not perceptible to the senses. There is a cause which operates steadily and constantly on every part of the organization, bringing all under the use of the unit, — a law of growth in the plant, of sensation in the animal, of thought in the man. While the vital vortex is going on, all the physical laws to which the molecules of the body are otherwise subject are neutralized and overcome. The law of gravity is neutralized and overcome in the plant which grows upward. The law of inertia is overcome in animals, who can originate motion. The chemical laws are overcome in plants and animals, which resist change and decay. If the phrase vital principle is objected to, no one can deny the existence of a vital unity, which is unexplained by the senses. We are obliged to suppose some cause of all this, and a common cause of this correlation. Men have decided to call it life or soul.

Not only has the existence of the soul been received in all religions (with the apparent exception of Buddhism), but also it has been the basis of all philosophies which deserve that name.

According to Pythagoras the soul is an emanation of the world-soul, and so partakes of the divine nature. At death it leaves this body to take another, and so goes through the circle of appointed forms. The soul in man is a self-moving principle. Ovid describes this Pythagorean view of transmigration in verses thus translated by Dryden: —

> "Souls cannot die. They leave a former home
> And in new bodies dwell, and from them roam.
> Nothing can perish, all things change below,
> For spirits through all forms may come and go.
> Good beasts shall rise to human forms; and men,
> If bad, shall backward turn to beasts again.

> Thus, through a thousand shapes, the soul shall go,
> And thus fulfill its destiny below."

The human soul, according to Plato, is essentially rational. It is pure mind, but associated with a lower animal soul, composed of energy or active power, and desire or passive affection.

The immortality of the soul is argued in the beautiful dialogue of Phædo, one of the most charming works in all literature. According to Socrates, in this dialogue, the soul is the ego, the mind which thinks, loves, and acts, and when death comes, it is not the mind which dies, but the body. At the close of this long dialogue, one of the disciples of Socrates asks him what he wishes them to do with him after his death. He smiles and says: "Anything you please, if you can catch me."

According to the Stoics, the soul is an emanation of the Deity, an inborn breath of God, extending through the body.

According to Aristotle, all living things have a soul; the plant has a soul which enables it to grow; it is a constructive force. The vital force of the animal adds to this, sensation, desire, locomotion; in man, the faculty of reason is added.

§ 5. *The objections of materialism. Why do some modern thinkers deny the existence of the soul?*

Materialism assumes that what we call soul is

the result of bodily organization. (1.) Because all we know are sensible phenomena. (2.) Because the state of the mind conforms constantly to the condition of the body. All we know, it says, is sensible phenomena, outward facts, and the grouping of these facts into laws. But the simple answer of common sense to this statement is, that we know mind better than we know body; that thought, love, and purpose are not sensible phenomena, and yet we are certain of their existence. All we know of matter we know through the senses; it is that which is hard and soft, extended in space, which has shape, color, and so forth. All we know of mind is different. Moreover, the mind has a unity and identity not found in matter; it is simple, indivisible unity; whereas matter is capable of division. It is one and the same soul which thinks, feels, remembers, hopes, chooses, laments, imagines. It is the same soul which existed last year and exists now. But matter is always changing, never the same. Moreover, there is a principle of life which correlates all parts of a living body, and keeps them working together. Great objection has been made to calling this the vital principle, on the ground that this assumes the existence of the soul before it is proved. But the eminent naturalist, Quatrefages, says he must use some such word to describe the vital vortex, for the fact exists. The equilibrium of life is not maintained by the molecular motion of the atoms, for these act independently of each other. The unity of organic life is maintained by some power not in the material particles themselves. Call it soul, or vital principle, or by any other name, its existence is certain. You cannot explain life in terms of matter and motion. The gulf between an atom of inorganic matter and the lowest form of life has never been passed over by human thought.

The second objection of materialism to the existence of an immaterial soul is that the condition of the body affects the soul, inevitably and always. A little improper food taken into the system affects the mind; a drop of blood extravasated in the brain destroys the power of thought; as the body grows old, the mind weakens; as the brain fibres decay, memory goes; without phosphorus, no thought, — is not then thought the result of the body? To this, however, the answer is conclusive. All these facts only prove that while the soul is in this body, the body is its necessary organ of communication with the outward world. Just as a carpenter cannot work when his tools are dull; as the most accomplished musician cannot charm our souls when the strings of his piano are out of tune, or broken; so the soul cannot communicate with us when the body is disordered. It is highly probable that we could not think if the proper amount of phosphorus was not supplied to the brain. But this is no such great discovery. Not "phosphorus" alone, but a good many other chemical elements have always been known to be necessary. Without oxygen, no thought; without hydrogen and carbon, no thought. All this merely means that while the soul remains in its present environment, it needs a healthy bodily organization with which to do its work.

§ 6. *Preëxistence and Transmigration. The doctrine of Brahmanism.*

We must now pass on to consider the doctrine of metempsychosis, or transmigration of the soul, so alien to our ways of thought, but once so universally believed. It was taught by three great religions, that of Egypt, of Brahmanism, and of Buddhism; by Pythagoras, Empedocles, and Plato, among Greek philosophers; by the Neo-Platonists, the Jewish Cabbala, and the Arab philosophers; by Origen and other church fathers; by the Gnostics, the Manicheans, the Druids; and, in recent times, by Fourier and others.

The soul, Psyche, soul-unit, or vital monad, being assumed, four questions arise: —

1. Did these monads exist before they entered the living bodies of plants, animals, and men, or not?

2. Will they exist after leaving these bodies, or not?

3. If they preëxisted, how?
4. If they continue to exist, how?

The human race, almost universally, as we have seen, has answered the second question in the affirmative as regards the human monad. The conscious thinking, willing, feeling soul will continue to exist after the dissolution of the body.

But, as regards the first question: Have these vital monads existed before their existence here? the answers are not so unanimous.

A vast multitude of men, in former days, and a majority of those now existing, answer Yes. It is curious to see how many have believed in preëxistence because they believed in transmigration.

The doctrine of preëxistence has been very generally held, in one or another form. It has been believed to explain a part of the mystery of evil. If men were born under unfortunate conditions, with depraved organizations, it was assumed that it was in consequence of some sin committed in a former state. When the Jews asked Jesus, "Did this man sin, or his father, that he was born blind?" they asked which of two contending theories of evil was the true one: that of Moses, who taught that the sins of the fathers would descend on the children to the third and fourth generation; or the subsequently adopted theory of transmigration, by which a man's present discomforts were the result of his own misconduct in a former state of existence? Preëxistence and transmigration were both held as a part of a system of penal retribution.

This view of transmigration, as retribution, was held in ancient Brahmanism, as will appear from the following passages from the "Laws of Manu," a Sanskrit work written, some say, eight hundred years before Christ: —

"Be it known that the three qualities of the rational soul are a tendency to goodness, to passion, and to darkness; and, endued with one or more of them, it remains incessantly attached to all these created substances.

"Let the wise consider, as belonging to the quality of darkness, every act which a man is ashamed of having done, of doing, or of going to do.

"Let them consider, as proceeding from the quality of passion, every act by which a man seeks exaltation and celebrity in this world, though he may not be much afflicted if he fail of attaining his object.

"To the quality of goodness belongs every act by which he hopes to acquire divine knowledge, which he is never ashamed of doing, and which brings placid joy to his conscience.

"Of the dark quality, as described, the principal object is pleasure; of the passionate, worldly prosperity; but of the good quality the chief object is virtue, — the last mentioned objects are superior in dignity.

"Such transmigrations as the soul procures in this universe by each of those qualities, I now will declare in order succinctly.

"Souls, endued with goodness, attain always the state

of deities; those filled with ambitious passions, the condition of men; and those immersed in darkness the nature of beasts, — this is the triple order of transmigration.

"What particular bodies the vital spirit enters in this world, and in consequence of what sins here committed, now hear at large and in order.

"A priest who has drunk spirituous liquor shall migrate into the form of a smaller or larger worm or insect, of a moth, or of some ravenous animal.

"If a man steal grain in the husk he shall be born a rat; if a yellow-mixed metal, a gander; if water, a plava, or diver; if honey, a great stinging gnat; if milk, a crow; if expressed juice, a dog; if clarified butter, an ichneumon weasel.

"As far as vital souls, addicted to sensuality, indulge themselves in forbidden pleasures, even to the same degree shall the acuteness of their senses be raised in their future bodies, that they may endure analogous pains.

"Then shall follow separations from kindred and friends, forced residence with the wicked, painful gains and ruinous losses of wealth; friendships hardly acquired, and at length changed into enmities.

"Let every Brahman with fixed attention consider all nature, both visible and invisible, as existing in the divine spirit; for, when he contemplates the boundless universe existing in the divine spirit, he cannot give his heart to iniquity."

The object of the transmigration of the soul after death, according to the ancient religion of Egypt, seems to have been development. It was not punishment, as in Brahmanism, nor purification, as in some other systems. The soul, it is taught, must go through the round of animal existence, apparently to complete its entire education. It must be in sympathy with the Divine Mind in his whole work of creation. It must reach that state of which Wordsworth speaks when he says that —

> "To me the smallest flower that blows can give
> Thoughts which do often lie too deep for tears."

And of which Coleridge speaks when he tells us —

> "He prayeth best, who loveth best
> All things both great and small,
> For the dear God who loveth us,
> He made and loveth all."

In the first rank among the sacred books of Egypt is the "Ritual of the Dead," or the description of the passage of the soul after death into the presence of the judge Osiris. A copy of it either at full length or abridged was deposited in each mummy-case. Many parts were of the highest antiquity.

It opens with a grand dialogue which takes place when the soul leaves the body. The deceased addresses the God of Hades, and asks for admission to his realm. Finally Osiris says, "Fear nothing, but cross the threshold."

Then the soul enters the subterranean region, and is dazzled by the glory of the sun, brighter than noon. He sings a hymn to the sun and goes on. The food which he must take with him is knowledge. Frightful obstacles are in his way; horrid monsters, servants of Typhon, oppose his power. He breaks through at last, and sings another hymn of triumph.

Next comes a period of rest and refreshment. The Goddess Nu gives him water, and at last he reaches the first gate of Heaven. Then there is a dialogue between the soul and the divine light, who instructs him in all the sublimest mysteries of nature.

Having passed the gate, he is transformed into different animals and plants, as a hawk, an eagle, a lotus, a heron, a serpent, and a crocodile.

After this the soul is reunited to its body, for which careful embalment was so important. He reaches the bank of the subterranean river, the Egyptian Styx. A false boatman attempts to deceive him, and induce him to go the wrong way. At last he meets the right boat, but before he can enter he passes a sort of competitive examination to see if he have the right sort and amount of knowledge, the different parts of the boat speaking to him and asking their names. The rudder says: "What is my name?" He replies, "The enemy of Apis." The rope asks the same, and so on for twenty-three questions and answers.

So he enters the boat, crosses the river and arrives at the Elysian fields. Conducted by Anubis, he goes through a difficult labyrinth, and enters the judgment hall of Osiris, where the decisive judgment is to be passed, according to his earthly character and conduct. Each of the forty-two judges questions him in turn, and he must give an account of his whole life. "I have not blasphemed," he says. "I have not stolen, I have not been cruel, not stirred up strife, not been idle, not been a drunkard, shown no improper curiosity, disclosed no man's secrets, slandered no one, not envied others, nor calumniated a slave to his master."

Then he gives an account of his positive good works, among which are: "I have given food to the hungry, drink to the thirsty, and clothes to the naked."

Being justified by Osiris, the deceased man enters heaven. Then comes a third book, containing a mythical description of the higher world and life in heaven.

§ 7. *Transmigration among the Buddhists.*

The Buddhists seem to have taken their doctrine of transmigration directly from the Brahmans, but have developed it according to their own theory. This theory is that by a natural consequence the soul that does right goes up, and the soul which does wrong goes down. Wrong-doing in the present life is the effect and continuation of wrong-doing in a former state. The total result of wrong-doing, and its consequence, perpetual sorrow and perpetual change, is called Sansara; the state of peace and rest opposed to this is Nirvâna. He who is not in Nirvâna is in Sansara, says the old doctrine.

In Sansara there is nothing true or real, nothing fixed and lasting, but only change and deception. All is vanity and vexation of spirit; life is uneasy and empty. All things revolve in a circle, without meaning or purpose. Birth leads to death, youth to age; grace is deceitful, and beauty vain. This emptiness of existence here below is the perpetual theme of the Buddhist teachers.

What, then, is the Buddhist doctrine of transmigration, and how far does it go?

St. Hilaire replies that it goes as far as possible; everything migrates below the Buddha down to inert matter; and this also was taught in the Sankya philosophy in which Buddhism originated.

The Buddha himself migrated many times. Hardy tells us that he was born as an ascetic eighty-three times, as a monarch fifty-eight times, as the soul of a tree forty-three times, and many times also as ape, deer, lion, snipe, chicken, eagle, serpent, pig, frog, and so forth, being born four hnndred times in all. According to a Chinese authority he is made to say, "The number of my births and deaths can only be compared to those of all the plants in the universe."

The Buddhists believe, therefore, in hereditary depravity, and that this is the chief source of transmigration. Buddha is reported to have said that a man who has lived a good life here may yet be punished after death by being sent down into a lower form because he has not atoned for evil committed in a former state. On the other hand, a person who has done wrong here may go up hereafter, not yet having exhausted the power of good actions done in a former state of existence.

Karma, or the law of merit and demerit, governs all existence. It is the reason for the varieties in human fortunes, for differences of condition and character. Thus it is shown that all things depend on Karma, and that perfect justice presides over the universe. As a man sows, so he reaps, or shall reap hereafter. As he has sowed in former states of existence so he reaps in this world.

It is also a doctrine of this system that the law of merit is more powerful than that of demerit; that is, that the consequences of doing right are much more extensive than those of doing wrong. This they admit is contrary to appearances, for evil seems to prevail over good, and punishment comes much sooner than reward. But they answer that the best things ripen most slowly; as the chicken is able to get its food as soon as it chips its shell, but a human child is helpless for many months. Moreover they say merit increases, because it is in harmony with all truth; but demerit decreases, for all things oppose it.

§ 8. *Foundation of the Belief in Transmigration.*

Such a widespread belief as this of transmigration must rest on some reasonable foundation; we can hardly believe that it is unmixed error. What basis of probability can be found in it?

Many of the reasons for believing that man has a soul, which can exist independently of his body, would induce the conviction that animals have souls of a similar character, though in a lower state of development. Animals can think, feel, will, remember, imagine, reason, love, just as man does. Beside what we call instinct in animals, there is distinctly present the power of reflection, of adapting means to ends, of meeting new exigencies with new contrivances. What love, what devotion, what fidelity there is in the dog! The elephants in Ceylon are taught to build stone walls, and an elephant will bring a stone, lay it in its place, push it with his trunk until it is plumb, just as a mason would do. I have seen in my own horse unmistakable evidence of pride and shame, the sense of fun, the memory of Sunday when it came, and, above all, the sense of the supernatural. He was once put into a tip-cart to draw water, and he evidently felt degraded by that occupation. He hung his head and looked so mournful that we had him at once taken out of the cart. I often tried his memory by laying the reins on his back and letting him choose which way to go. On Sunday he would turn to the right, going out of the gate, and take every turn correctly till he reached the church in Boston. On other days he invariably turned to the left, and went in the opposite direction to the village. Once, when driving him on the road near my house, we met, coming down the hill toward us, a horse-car which had been allowed to run down without horses, simply by the power of gravitation. My horse was dreadfully alarmed at this phenomenon, which seemed to him a sort of miracle, and he very nearly overturned me in the gutter. To see the car coming without horses to draw it, frightened him. It was an effect produced without any visible cause. He felt as a man would if he should see his dining-table suddenly float up to the top of the room.

Observing in animals so many elements in common with man, and seeing man with so many traits which are very marked in animals, it was natural to suppose that the human soul has passed through these lower forms of animal life. One man is cunning like a fox, another has the qualities of a good, honest Newfoundland dog, another the stealthy ways of a cat, and so on. We say, "She is as proud as a peacock," "Sly as a snake." Some men are like tigers in ferocity, others like sheep in blindly following their leaders; others, again, like the hog, the parrot, the vulture, the monkey. Seeing such traits, it was not a very absurd theory to suppose that the mind of man had reached its present state of development by passing through these lower forms. It was also natural to believe that souls which had misused their opportunities might have to go back and pass through their preliminary exercises again; also, that one who had behaved like a hog, or a fox, or a tiger while he was a man might be fitly punished by being made to pass into those bodies after death. Transmigration, therefore, was for development and for retribution.

§ 9. *Human traits in primitive organisms.*

I was once walking in the British Museum through the rooms which contain, in a systematic and progressive arrangement, specimens of the classes, orders, and genera of animal life; and I became quite interested in imagining the transmigration of a soul passing up through this long series of bodily organizations. In the room of the Radiata I imagined the soul to have once inhabited a star-fish, and by stretching out in every direction to have learned the existence of an outward world. As a mollusk, rolled up in a shell, I supposed the soul occupied in digesting these experiences, and becoming acquainted with itself. As a fish the soul learned the joy of easy motion, supported on all sides by the buoyant but yielding element. Alacrity, vivacity, the energy to act is developed in some forms of insect life. In bivalves the soul may have learned how to grasp and hold. The crocodiles, all mouth, give us the devouring element, that rapacity, that irresistible appetite, which may have any and all things for its object. Who knows but that the insatiate appetite for knowledge in a Casaubon or Scaliger may have been cultivated when, in some previous state of existence, they roamed about as sharks. The form of birds with all their varied attitudes and quick bright expression, seemed to represent the airy, ready, quick perception, the rapid analysis, which can penetrate the entanglements of life, as a bird darts through the bushes.

Animals, as we have seen, can reason, remember, imagine ; they have conscience and are capable of the feeling of wrong-doing ; they have the love of approbation and are pleased with praise ; contrivance, and can adapt means to ends ; pride, which can be wounded ; a sense of reverence for man, as a higher power, in which is the germ of religion ; and a sense of the supernatural. If the animal soul has these faculties, wherein, it may be asked, does it differ from the human. How far has the human soul gone above it ?

Many distinctions have been pointed out between men and animals. The human hand has been said to make an essential physiological distinction between man and all the animals. The perfection of its structure consists in the size and strength of the thumb, which can be brought into exact and powerful opposition to the extremities of the fingers, each of which is also separately movable. This enables the human hand to perform with dexterity a variety of movements, of which the highest order of monkeys is incapable.

Another distinction between man and animals is in the human power of using articulate speech and verbal language. Animals have no verbal language; if they had we could learn it and talk with them.

The real and chief distinction between the soul of all other animals and that of man, is, that the human soul is capable of conceiving abstract ideas, and the animal has no such power. The dog can understand a general or generic name, but not an abstract name. Tell him to go and get an apple, he understands you; but not if you speak of truth, beauty, justice, right and wrong, good and evil, cause and effect. He is incapable of adopting an aim apart from what is given in his organization. Man can say: "It shall be the object of my life to attain knowledge, to form my character, to obtain rank, fame, fortune, popularity, to please God, to serve my fellow-creatures." There is no evidence that any animal can thus adopt an abstract idea as his purpose in life, and pursue it. This power gives man his immense superiority over all other creatures, and makes him capable of high moral and intellectual development.

§ 10. *The Evolution of the Soul, as an improvement on the doctrine of Darwin.*

That man has come up to his present state of development by passing through lower forms is the popular doctrine of science to-day. What is called evolution teaches that we have reached our present state by a very long and gradual ascent from the lowest animal organizations. It is true that the Darwinian theory takes no notice of the evolution of the soul, but only of the body. But it appears to me that a combination of the two views would remove many difficulties which still attach to the theory of natural selection and the survival of the fittest. If we are to believe in evolution, let us have the assistance of the soul itself in this development of new species.

> "For of the soul the body form doth take:
> For soul is form, and doth the body make."

Thus science and philosophy will coöperate, nor will poetry hesitate to lend her aid. For have not two great poets in our time intimated their belief in some such law of preëxistence and transmigration? Wordsworth long ago declared that —

"Our birth is but a sleep and a forgetting;
The soul that rises with us, our life's star,
Has had elsewhere its setting,
And cometh from afar."

And Tennyson also suggests, —

"For how should I for certain hold,
Because my memory is so cold,
That I *first* was in human mould?

"It may be that no life is found,
Which only to one engine bound
Falls off, but cycles always round.

"But, if I lapsed from nobler place,
Some legend of a fallen race
Alone might hint of my disgrace.

"Or if thro' lower lives I came —
Tho' all experience past became
Consolidate in mind and frame —

"I might forget my weaker lot;
For is not our first year forgot?
The haunts of memory echo not.

"Moreover, something is or seems,
That touches me with mystic gleams,
Like glimpses of forgotten dreams —

"Of something felt, like something here;
Of something done, I know not where;
Such as no language may declare."

It would be curious if we should find science and philosophy taking up again this old theory of metempsychosis, remodeling it to suit our present modes of religious and scientific thought, and launching it again on the wide ocean of human belief. But stranger things have happened in the history of human opinion.

CHAPTER VII.

THE ORIGIN OF THE WORLD; IN ALL RELIGIONS. EVOLUTION, EMANATION, AND CREATION.

§ 1. Different theories concerning the origin of the Cosmos. All races of men believe it had a beginning, and has not existed always. The primeval chaos. § 2. Doctrine of Evolution. Its antiquity. The World-egg. Orphic poets. Laws of Manu. Aristophanes. Hesiod. Ovid. American Indians. Eddas. The Polynesian theology. § 3. Doctrine of Emanation. Source of this view. The Vedas. The Gnostics. Their problem. § 4. Doctrine of Creation. Different forms of this doctrine. The Hebrew Bible, the Zend-Avesta, the Assyrian tablets, the philosophers. Objection to the doctrine of Creation by modern thinkers. § 5. Darwin and Natural Selection. § 6. Theory of Creation by beings above man, but below God. This theory would harmonize the doctrines of Evolution, Emanation, and Creation.

§ 1. *Different theories concerning the origin of the Cosmos. All races of men believe it had a beginning, and has not existed always. The primeval chaos.*

WE all recollect the old gentleman in the "Vicar of Wakefield," who astonished Dr. Primrose by his profound learning in regard to the origin of the universe. "The cosmogony, or creation of the world," said he, "has puzzled philosophers of all ages. Sanconiathon, Manetho, Berosus, and Ocellus Lucanus have all attempted it in vain." This venerable man, with his jargon about cosmogony, turned out in the end to be a venerable humbug. But notwithstanding this warning, we are obliged to follow his steps and show how largely the origin of the world has occupied the human mind.

All possible theories about the origin of the universe may be reduced to these: —

1. It had no origin, but has always existed as it is now, a Cosmos of order.
2. It came by a process of evolution.
3. It came by a process of emanation.
4. It was created by some intelligent Being.

The first of these theories, that the world has always been as it is now, has never been the belief of mankind. All races of men, in all times, have agreed in a remarkable way in assuming a beginning of the universe, and a gradual process of development or of creation. We may add that these different theories commonly suppose the world at first to have been in a chaotic state. Chaos was first in almost every system.

One is much struck by this fact, which reappears continually in the most opposite quarters. We recollect how the account of the creation begins in the Book of Genesis: "The earth was without form, and void, and darkness was on the face of the deep." Hesiod, the theologian of Greek thought, says: "In the beginning was chaos." The tenth book of the Rig-Veda, eleventh chapter, says: "Then there was neither nothing, nor something; no world, no sky; nothing involving, nothing involved; no water, no death nor life; only One alone breathing calmly with nature. The universe was shrouded in darkness, a mass of indistinguishable waters."

So the Laws of Manu say: "The universe existed in darkness, imperceptible, undefinable, as if immersed in sleep."

The Phœnicians said: "The beginning of all things was a dark, condensed air, a chaos turbid and black."

The Scandinavian Edda says the same, making all things begin in darkness and unformed matter. We also find this doctrine of chaos in the myths of America and Polynesia.[1]

It is an unquestionable fact, and a very curious one, that the human race should thus have held

[1] The Quichés said: "There were neither men nor brutes; neither birds, fish, crabs, sticks, nor stones; valley nor mountain; stubble nor forest; nothing but the sky. The face of the land was hidden. There was naught but the silent sea and sky. There was nothing joined, nor any sound, nor anything that stirred; . . . nothing but stillness, and rest, and darkness, and night."

So, too, the picture-writing of the Aztecs says: "In the year and day of clouds, before years and days, the world lay in darkness; all things were without order; a water covered the slime and the ooze." See Brinton: "*Myths of the New World.*"

to a beginning. They never seem to have thought for a moment that things have always been as they are now. They have believed in the existence at first of formless matter which afterward took form under the influence of some superhuman intelligence. Every religion and every mythology has held to the same formula, "From Chaos to Cosmos."

This belief of the earliest races was a dim prophecy of what modern science has revealed as the actual fact. Geology turns over the stone leaves of the planet, and shows how our present order emerged from vast cataclysms and catastrophes, from epochs when the globe was a mass of fire, or submerged below the waters, or covered with an armor of ice. Finally, the doctrine of evolution once more teaches that all began in chaos, in a homogeneous nebula, without form, and void.

§ 2. *Doctrine of Evolution. Its antiquity. The World-egg. Orphic poets. Laws of Manu. Aristophanes. Hesiod. Ovid. American Indians. Eddas. The Polynesian theology.*

The doctrine of evolution is not, therefore, a recent discovery, but is found among most of the primitive races and in many ancient religions, often indeed combined with that of creation. It is suggested most naturally to the childlike races by the phenomena of the seed and egg. They see the seed under telluric and atmospheric influences developing into plant and root, producing flower, and fruit, and seed again, by a cycle of perpetual change. In all this there is nothing abrupt, but regular growth. There is no visible interference of any Creator from without; all steadily unfolds by some mysterious principle of life within. This is the law for the world of living things, the whole vegetable and animal kingdom. Consequently the origin of the world by evolution has been a very common belief. The notion of a world-egg or world-seed, from which all things have come by a process of development, and this often connected with a Creator, is to be seen among many races.

The Orphic writings have a cosmogony in which time is the first principle of things. From time came chaos and ether. From these were formed the primitive egg, from which issued Phanes, or manifestation.

In the account of creation given in the "Laws of Manu," the ideas of creation, emanation, and evolution are united. The following extracts are from the first book:—

"The universe existed in darkness, — imperceptible, undefinable, undiscoverable, and undiscovered, — as if immersed in sleep.

"Then the self-existing Power, undiscoverable himself, but making the world discoverable, with the five elements and other principles, appeared in undiminished glory, dispelling the gloom.

"He whom the mind alone can perceive, whose essence eludes the external organs, who has no parts, who exists from eternity; even he, the soul of all beings, shone forth.

"He, having willed to produce various beings from his own divine substance, first with a thought created the waters and placed in them a productive seed.

"The seed became an egg, bright as gold, blazing like a luminary with a thousand beams, and in that egg he himself was born as Brahma, the Father of all Spirits.

"In that egg sat the great power, inactive for a whole year of the creator, at the close of which by a thought he caused the egg to divide itself.

"And from its two divisions he framed the heavens above and the earth below.

"From the supreme soul he drew forth mind, then consciousness, an inward ruler.

"Then pervading, with emanations from the supreme spirit, the minutest atoms of existing things, he formed all creatures."

In one of the Choruses of Aristophanes we read this: —

"Dark chaos and night existed, and in the beginning dark Erebus and Tartarus; but neither earth nor air, nor sky was then. Before all, in the infinite circle of Erebus, the black-winged night produced an egg, not brooded on, whence in time sprang love, parent of desire, beating its back with its gilded wings like the whirl of a tempest. Love, joined with dark, unresting chaos, produced heaven, earth, sea, and the deathless race of the Immortal Gods."

In like manner Hesiod says: —

"In the beginning was chaos, next the earth with its broad bosom, the immovable foundation of all beings, the vast Tartarus, in the depth of its abyss; and love, the most beautiful of the Immortal Gods."

So Ovid sings: —

"Before the sea and land and all-covering heaven appeared, there was one aspect over the whole of nature. All was rude, unelaborated — a mass, which was called chaos. It was inert weight, the seeds of things in disorder and confusedly intermingled — no sun, no moon, no earth hanging balanced in the air, no ocean embracing continents with its mighty arms. This conflict of the elements God and benign Nature pacified, distinguishing each from each, solid from fluid, earth from air. Whoever that God was, he distributed all things, sending each to its place."

But directly after, when speaking of the origin of man, Ovid hesitates whether man was the work of that divine artificer, or whether the earth, retaining in it some seeds of heaven, brought him forth and Prometheus gave him form.

An Orphic poet also deduces all things from primeval chaos and the inspiration of love: —

"We will first sing a delightful song concerning the ancient chaos; how heaven, earth, and seas were framed out of it, as also concerning that much-wise and sagacious love, oldest of all and self-perfect, which produced all these things, separating one from another."

The idea of the evolution of all living creatures out of the earth appears in the often-repeated phrase, "Mother Earth," which is found in many ancient writers. Æschylus makes Prometheus call, "O divine æther, and ye many-winged blasts, ye fountains of the rivers, thou multitudinous smile of the ocean, and thou earth, the universal mother, I call on you all!" So the Comanche Indians call on the earth as their mother, and the Great Spirit as their father. The Mexicans called the sun and earth "the father and mother of us all."

The Indians of Guatemala, the Quichés, who are very rich in their mythology, had this account of creation, singularly like those we have been considering. It almost reads like a translation of Ovid, and yet is given by Bancroft[1] in the original Quiché language:[2] —

"The heaven was formed, and its boundaries fixed toward the four winds by the Creator and Former, — the Mother and Father of all living things, — he by whom all move, the father and cherisher of the peace of men, whose wisdom has planned all things."

"There was as yet no man, nor any animal, nor bird, nor fish, nor green herb, nor any tree. The face of the earth was not yet seen, only the peaceful sea and the space of heaven. Nothing was joined together, nothing

[1] *Native Races.*

[2] This differs a little from the translation from Ximenes, by Brinton, given in a previous note.

clung to anything else, nothing balanced itself, there was no sound. Nothing existed but the sea, calm and alone, immobility and silence, darkness and night.

"Alone was the Creator, the former, and the feathered serpent, enveloped in green and blue, their name Gu-cu-matz, or Feathered Serpent. They are the heart of heaven. They spake together and consulted, mingling their thoughts. They said 'Earth,' and earth came, like a cloud or fog. Then the mountains arose, and the trees appeared, and Gu-cu-matz was filled with joy, saying, 'Blessed be thy coming, O Heart of Heaven! our work is done!'"

There is much more, but this is a specimen.

Cross the Atlantic, and return to Europe, and visit the Scandinavian peninsula. There, a thousand years ago, the Eddas, sacred books of the Teutonic race, thus described the origin of things: —

"In the day-spring of the ages there was neither sea, nor shore, nor refreshing breeze, neither earth below nor heaven above, but one vast abyss. Then arose a shining world of flame in the South, and another, cloudy and dark, in the North. Torrents of venom flowed from the North into the abyss, and filled it with ice. But from the South a warm breath came, and melted it into living drops, from whence came the giant Yimer, and afterward from these drops, as from seeds, came the Mundane cow, and Ror, the father of Odin, who made heaven and earth from the body of the giant Yimer, and then created a man and woman, Ask and Embla. Chaos having disappeared, Odin became the All Father, maker of gods and men, having Hertha, the earth, for his wife."

This is creation by evolution, with a grain of theism in it.

In the islands of the Pacific a curious series of myths exist, belonging to this circle of thought. According to this Polynesian theology, all things began at a single immovable point, which they call "the root of all existence." There are three worlds: the highest the abode of spirits, divided into seven heavens, above the circuit of the sun and moon. The second world consists of the islands where the Polynesians live. Each island has its spirit or essence, called "The Well Poised." It is surrounded by the ocean, the name of which is "The vast outspread plantain leaf." The third world is below the island, and is called *a-via-ki*. This under-world is hollow, like the inside shell of a cocoa-nut. Beneath its lowest region is a thick stem, tapering down to a point which supports everything, and is called "the root-of-all existence." This point supports the universe; and from this, by a peculiar process of development, all existence has proceeded. This point, though stationary, has a kind of demonic life. From it we rise to a second point or demon, in the stem, called "breathing," or "life." Above this demon of sentient life resides a third, still fixed forever in the basis of all things, and called "The long-lived," or perhaps "Time." Above him, at the bottom of the under-world, lives "the great mother."

She made the first man, and, being apparently pleased with the result, repeated the experiment till she had created five more, all residing in different spheres of the vast under-world. The upper floor, inhabited by Avatea, communicates with the upper-world by two apertures on the east and west, through which the sun and moon come up and go down at their rising and setting. Below "the Thin-land," the home of Avatea, who became the father of gods and men, is a second place, belonging to a second son, named "The innumerable," a sea-god, the father and maker of all fishes.

Further down in the hollow cocoa-nut under-world is the residence of the bird-god, the author of that which inhabits the air. A fourth child of the great mother is Echo, who inhabits a region of hollow rocks. Lower still is the home of the goddess Raka, or Trouble, who rules the winds, and keeps the storms shut up in a basket, till she sees fit to set them free. Lowest of all, by the side of the great mother, is her sixth child, called "Stick-by-her-Parent," living with her in the "Land of Silence," where no voice is heard.

According to this remarkably elaborate system (only a part of which I have here related), all existence begins with one unchanging point or substance of being, then passes into the stage of pulsating or breathing life, then into everlasting time, then into the stage of production, or the beginning of continued development by growth. Thus conscious being comes up into the world of light, from the dark, unconscious abyss below.

§ 3. *Doctrine of Emanation. Source of this View. The Vedas. The Gnostics. Their Problem.*

The second form which the origin of the world takes is that of Emanation. Primitive man saw in nature a tendency to growth; and, beginning with this, some nations deduced the world from a process of evolution. These were the races most immersed in nature. Other races, with an opposite tendency of thought, living more in self-consciousness than in observation, found in themselves the notions of cause, purpose, plan, choice, will, effort, adaptation of means to ends, the sense of spiritual substance, the ideas of the infinite and eternal. With these conceptions they formed their theory of the origin of the world. They began at the summit and went down, inferring the finite from the infinite. The other races began below and went up, rising toward the infinite from the finite. The one began with the dark abyss of chaos, and went upward to intelligence. The other began with the dark abyss of infinite being, and by means of a series of emanations or fallings away from this inconceivable first essence, gradually reached an intelligent Creator and an intelligent creation.

This system of emanation appears more or less developed in different theologies, mythologies, and philosophies.

It is essentially Oriental in its origin, coming first in the cosmogony of the Hindus.

The Veda thus speaks of the beginning of things:[1] —

"Nothing then existed, neither being nor non-being; no world, no air, no firmament. Where was then the covering of the universe? Where the receptacle of the water? Where the impenetrable depths of air? Death was not, nor immortality, nor anything that marked the boundaries of day and night. But That breathed in solitude without afflation, absorbed in his own thought. Besides That nought existed. The universe was at first enveloped in darkness; the water was devoid of movement; and everything was gathered up and blended together in That. The being reposed on the bosom of this void; and the universe was at last produced by the strength of his devotion. In the beginning desire was formed in his spirit and this was the first productive principle. It is thus that the wise men, pondering in their heart, have explained the union of being and non-being."

Another Vedic hymn thus speaks: —

"Originally this universe was indeed soul only; nothing else whatsoever existed, active or inactive. He thought, "I will create worlds;" thus He created these various worlds: water, light, mortal beings, and the waters.

"He thought, 'These are indeed worlds; I will create guardians of worlds.' Thus He drew from the waters

[1] *Rig-Veda*, Book X., chap. xi.

and framed an embodied being. He viewed him; and of that being, so contemplated, the mouth opened as an egg; from the mouth speech issued; from speech, fire proceeded. The nostrils spread; from the nostrils, breath passed; from breath, air was propagated. The eyes opened; from the eyes a glance sprang; from that glance the sun was produced. The ears dilated; from the ears came hearkening; and from that the regions of space. The skin expanded; from the skin, hair rose; from that grew herbs and trees. The breast opened; from the breast mind issued.

"These deities being thus framed, fell into this vast ocean; and to Him they came with thirst and hunger; and Him they thus addressed: 'Grant us a smaller size, wherein abiding we may eat food.' He offered to them a cow; they said, 'That is not sufficient for us.' He exhibited to them a horse; they said, 'Neither is that sufficient for us.' He showed them the human form; they exclaimed, 'Well done! ah! wonderful!'"

The most detailed and systematized theories of emanation are to be found among the Gnostics. The Gnostic element of thought was in the air before the coming of Christ. It pervaded Asia Minor, Syria, Egypt. It appears in the writings of Philo. It was an effort of the human reason to unite the most important religions into one universal religion. After Christianity began its career the various schools of Gnosticism appeared as large and imposing bodies of religious thinkers. They sought to combine Christianity with the system of Zoroaster, of Moses, and the Brahmanism and Buddhism of the East, all harmonized by the philosophy of Plato.

These philosophies begin with the conception of God as the infinite, unknown, unapproachable Spirit, the abyss of being, from whom all things proceed. They consider existence as coming from this unfathomable essence by a series of emanations.

This doctrine of emanation, of dropping away of the world out of God, by successive lapses, is one of the methods of meeting the great Asiatic problem, "How can an infinite being create a finite world?" Asiatic pantheism answered the question easily. It simply said: "The finite world has no existence. It is a mere appearance without reality. Only the infinite is real." European materialism also had no difficulty about this problem. It said: "The infinite does not exist. All we know is the finite." But as the large majority of men believe in the reality both of a finite world and an infinite author of the world, the speculative problem became this: "How can the finite proceed from the infinite?" One of the attempts to answer this question was given by the doctrine of emanation.

The most complete working out, in a systematic way, of this theory, appears among those Gnostics who came into the Christian Church during the second century. They occupied themselves greatly with the problem of the beginning of things. One of them, Basilides, taught that there proceeded from the First Cause (the Unnamed Being) seven Æons whom he called "Reason," "The Word," "Intelligence," "Wisdom," "Power," "Righteousness," "Peace." From these seven there emanated 365 heavens, denoted by the mystic word, Peace. By seven angels of the lowest of the heavens, the world was made, under the superintendence of the God of the Jews, whom he called "The Ruler."

The system of Valentine (who died about 160) is still more elaborate. With him the fountain of all being is the vast Abyss, with whom dwells Silence. From this abyss emanated thirty male and female Æons, whom Valentine calls the "First Begotten," "Wisdom," "Truth," "Life," etc. These thirty constitute the Pleroma, or fullness of being. The lowest of these, Sophia, or Wisdom, passionately strives to return to the infinite source of all, the Divine Abyss. From her longing there comes another being, Sophia Achamoth, who wanders through the universe, outside of the Pleroma, imparting life to matter, and at last forming the Demiurg, by whom the world is created. The world consists of three elements: Spirit, which came from Sophia Achamoth, and which she derived from the Pleroma; the soul of all things, which is the animating life; and the lower world of matter. Two new Æons now appear, Christ and the Holy Spirit, who come into being to restore the harmony of the Pleroma, interrupted by the falling from it of Sophia. From the Pleroma, thus enlarged, proceeded Jesus the Savior, who united himself with the man Jesus at his baptism, in order to redeem the world thus fallen away from God, and bring it back into a perfect unity.

These doctrines, strange as they seem to us, had a wide influence in the Christian Church, and form, as I have said, the most marked example of the doctrine of emanation.

§ 4. *Doctrine of Creation. Different forms of this doctrine. The Hebrew Bible, the Zend-Avesta, the Assyrian Tablets, the Philosophers. Objection to the doctrine of Creation by modern thinkers.*

We now come to the third view of the origin of things, namely, creation by intelligent will; that is, by the deliberate purpose and act of supernatural intelligence. This view includes several different kinds of creation. According to the Jewish view, as expressed in the Old Testament, it is the creation of the universe by the Supreme Being alone, excluding the agency of inferior beings. According to the doctrine of Zoroaster, as contained in the Zend-Avesta and in later books, the world was created by the Supreme Being, but through the agency of inferior powers. In these two ancient religions, together with those of Christ and Mohammed, the doctrine of a creative intelligence appears in the most distinct form.

A very curious discovery was made by Mr. George Smith, of the British Museum, of Assyrian clay tablets, on which were found written accounts of the creation, the fall of man, the deluge, and the tower of Babel, much resembling those in the Book of Genesis.

In a mound on the Tigris, opened by Mr. Layard, were found thousands of fragments of tablets, making a part of the Royal Assyrian Library. They were covered with cuneiform inscriptions. Some of these were deposited in the British Museum; and Mr. Smith, an accomplished scholar, found in these fragments partial accounts of the creation. These tablets state that a watery chaos preceded creation, when as yet there was not a tree nor flower. They go on to say that all the great God made was beautiful; that God fixed the stars in the sky in twelve months, to govern the year; and the moon to give light in the night till the day dawns.

Just as the mythical theories have been those of emanation or evolution, so, too, have the philosophic theories. The German philosophy from Descartes, Spinoza, and Leibnitz down, through

Kant, Schelling, and Hegel, begins with God, or the absolute, and endeavors to make some kind of passage to the relative, or finite. It assumes being, and tries to deduce phenomena. Its idea of creation is of God extending himself outward as the universe, and developing himself onward as history. Creation is the unfolding of God.

On the other side, we have the English school of philosophy, which has usually tended toward materialism. It begins with the outward world, and often fails of finding the Creator. The best representative of this school is Herbert Spencer, who distinctly declares the impossibility of thinking creation. He tells us in the "First Principles" that the doctrine of creation assumes that the heavens and the earth were created as a workman shapes a piece of furniture. He says that "Equally in the writings of Plato and of living men of science, we find it taken for granted that there is an analogy between the process of creation and that of manufacture." He objects to this on the ground that it does not show us whence the material came which the Great Artificer thus formed. He also holds that a self-existent Creator is inconceivable; and so, by a few logical arguments, extending through less than three pages, dismisses the belief in creation as an impossible idea.

The answer to one who tells us that the idea of creation is unthinkable, is that the majority of mankind have always thought it. When we have logic on one side and fact on the other, it is not necessary to take much time in replying to the logician.

Modern philosophers have strongly objected to the argument to prove a Creator from the adaptations of means to ends in nature. Their objections seemed for a time to discredit this belief. But when the objections are more carefully analyzed, their importance is found to have been exaggerated. The latest and most careful thinkers have been led to accept again this finality argument, or proof from final causes in nature. In fact, the more recent discoveries in biology give it an almost irresistible power. How is it possible to see the marvelous organizations in microscopic life, the wonderful instincts of animals, the innumerable correlations of part to part, of organ to function, of each to all, of prenatal organs to future external conditions, and explain them, as the ancient materialists did, as arising from the fortuitous concourse of senseless atoms, driven by blind forces, during innumerable ages? Suppose that by a long succession of happy accidents, the beginning of an organized universe has come. Even this beginning would imply a run of luck in favor of a Cosmos, which would exceed any of the possibilities of a gamester's good fortune. But what blind forces create, they are equally likely to destroy. A single revolution of the wheel of fortune would reduce again to chaos the half-formed universe.

Hence modern scientific thinkers have abandoned the notion of chance as untenable. Accident has given way to law. Those who deny creation by intelligence, substitute for it origin by law. But then the question immediately returns: Did these laws come by chance or by design? If they have no intelligence behind them, it is still chance which continues to be the source of a wonderful order. Laws mean nothing but regularity of action. Laws are not creative forces, but only the rules by which such forces work. But regularity, rules, methods, according to which forces accomplish admirable results, are themselves indications of intelligence. So that the argument for design remains in its full force, after we have fully admitted that all things come according to immutable and eternal laws. The universe created by law and method, and not merely by an arbitrary will, does not imply less intelligence at its source, but more.

§ 5. *Darwin and Natural Selection.*

It is believed by many that the theory of natural selection, as enunciated by Mr. Darwin, disposes finally of the argument from adaptation to design. Mr. Darwin himself is too careful a thinker to commit himself to this statement, but some of his more incautious followers imagine that the chief argument for design in nature is forever set aside. Mr. Morley, for example, says: "In the face of the Darwinian hypothesis, with the immense mass of evidence already accumulated in its favor, the inference from contrivance" (to an intelligent will) "exists, to say the best of it, in a state of suspended animation."

Granting, for the sake of this argument, the scientific truth of the Darwinian theory, in what way does it affect the argument from design? The theory consists of three parts: First, the law of descent, by which the seed or egg reproduces the specific character of the plant or animal from which it came. This law of heredity we are all familiar with. Secondly, the fact of occasional variations from this law. Thirdly, the hypothesis that an accumulation of favorable variations gives an advantage in "the struggle for existence" which leads to "the survival of the fittest." It is supposed that this last hypothesis, taken in connection with the foregoing fact and law will explain the origin of the most complex organism, the most marvelous instinct. But when we say "law of descent" or "heredity," have we explained anything? We have merely given a name to the marvelous fact that some potency lies in each seed or egg, which causes it to produce a plant or an animal like that from which the seed or egg came. No explanation is given of this power; there is no physical explanation possible. Nothing we can discover by our finest instrument shows why an acorn will inevitably develop into an oak, and not into an elm; why it will produce the wood, bark, leaves, flower, and fruit of an oak. Neither the Darwinian theory, nor any other purely physical theory, throws the least light on that fact. Some unseen force is there, some masterful and spiritual potency.

But suppose that we can explain it. What then? Is the instinct less marvelous when it arrives, because its origin is understood? Is there a less wonderful adaptation and balance of organs in the human body, by which the nerve forces of the brain and ganglionic centres carry to and fro life forces, by which the heart pours its stream of life during seventy years, night and day, to supply every part of the body with its appropriate nourishment; by which the lungs continually supply oxygen to the blood, and maintain the vital heat; by which the nutritive system works on; and by which all these organs are kept in balance and equipoise, each doing its own work in perfect harmony with the rest, maintaining thus the vital vortex, and all serving the uses of the mind, the heart, the will? This is the evident end which this infinitely complicated apparatus serves. Let us grant that this wonderful home of the soul has come by the Darwinian process, is it any the less a marvelous display of means adapted to an end, and that end one of supreme importance?

You show a man a Waltham watch. He cries out: "I know how that watch was made. I was at the factory yesterday, and saw all the machinery at work." Does that explain away the adaptation of the parts to each other, and their co-relation to an end?

You read to another man the play of "Hamlet." He informs you that he can tell you precisely how the play came into being, where the paper and ink and pens came from, the mechanical process by which the ink was absorbed, and the chemical law by which its blackness was produced. All very well, but what is behind it all? A common objection to creation by intelligent purpose is to call it contriving how to avoid difficulties. Paley is quoted, who admits that "contrivance by its very definition is the refuge of imperfection. Why resort to contrivance when the power is omnipotent?" But the adaptation of means to ends does not necessarily imply overcoming a difficulty by contrivance. In reading I turn over the leaf of the book. This is adapting means to an end. But it implies no contrivance to avoid a difficulty. When the poet sings, the saint adores, the lover utters his affection, they all adapt means to ends;

they exercise no contrivance, but accomplish their purpose through universal law. An Infinite Intelligence would act on the world in accordance with its own everlasting laws. The law of the universe involves everywhere the adaptation of means to ends, and so design is written on the whole face of nature, on the heavens above and the earth beneath and the waters under the earth. And, if the doctrine of universal evolution be at last accepted, instead of destroying the argument for design, it will, as Professor Asa Gray argues, establish it on immutable foundations. The whole physical life of nature proceeds by this method. But did it ever occur to those who saw God in the growth of trees, flowers, animals, that there was less of a divine presence because the whole vegetable kingdom is evolved by the law of insensible gradations from seeds, and the whole animal kingdom by the same law from eggs?

§ 6. *Theory of Creation by beings above man, but below God. This theory would harmonize the doctrines of Evolution, Emanation, and Creation.*

The countless adaptations of the world show to us all-pervading intelligence. But we may grant that the argument of design in nature was pushed too far when it was inferred that these wonderful adaptations demonstrated a Supreme Mind. They prove conclusively that the world we see has come from an intelligent purpose. But they do not tell us whether that intelligence was infinite or finite, subordinate or supreme. Our faith in a Supreme and Infinite Intelligence does not come to us from these methods of creation, but from the sight of universal order. We know there must be one Supreme Being, above all, through all, and in all; from whom, through whom, and to whom are all things; because we see in nature all parts coöperating together into a Cosmos, or whole. The universe is a majestic unity, the result of innumerable varieties.

Some of the difficulties which we find in the actual constitution of things would be removed if we accept another theory. This is the view, that while God is the Creator and Preserver of the universe as a whole, he has permitted beings inferior to himself, but vastly superior to man, to carry on the work of creation in subordination to his own universal laws. In a previous chapter we have seen how probable it is, that there is an immense hierarchy of intelligences, extending upward from man toward God. Some of these may possess such large wisdom, such resources of reason and insight, as to be able by making use of God's laws, to create races of plants and animals, such as we see on the earth. They would be creators under God, just as man is a creator under God. Man's inventions are creations. Man has invented the plow, the pump, the carriage, the ship, by making himself acquainted with what we call the laws of nature. But these laws are only the ever-present agency of God. He fills all in all. He holds the universe in its every atom by the mysterious power of gravitation. He balances this power by another, by which all things are prevented from rushing together in ruin. But within the operation of these laws he allows man to combine and create. Why may he not have allowed other beings superior to man to combine and create higher works than man can accomplish. When we read in historic geology of the vast tribes of creatures, radiata, mollusks, reptiles, birds, fishes, mammals, which have inhabited the earth during enormous periods before man came, we are led to think it possible that these creatures may have been the invention of great intelligences by the permission of the Most High. And though man, in his higher nature, derives his being directly from God, — as the idea of right and wrong, cause and effect, and the reason which contains the light of the infinite and eternal, testify, — yet his lower bodily nature, by which he is allied to other animals, may have been gradually developed by the inventive powers of subordinate beings.

All this is only a theory, a mere suggestion. But I see in it nothing irrational, and nothing opposed to faith in God as the Supreme Creator.

Indeed, it tends to exalt our conceptions of him, to imagine this great hierarchy of powers, ascending upward in long gradation, the highest and greatest still far below the ineffable majesty of the Supreme Being. And with this conception of his greatness, there is an increased strength of filial trust and love, in knowing that he reaches down, through this vast range of being, to hold every human soul to himself, by his indwelling spirit, and his perpetual providence.

If such a theory as I have suggested be tenable, it would combine in one belief the essential doctrines of evolution, emanation, and creation. All things would be from God, but would come by the mediation of inferior spirits who have emanated from him; and these, as finite spirits, would proceed by finite and tentative methods, creating one after another the varieties of life. The whole flora and fauna of the world would then speak to us, not only of Him in whom all things live and move and have their being, but also of the great multitude of benign intelligences employed by God in these offices of creation. In every flower, every tree, every organ of the humblest animal, we should see, not only the divine presence and providence, but the loving, patient work of spirits akin to ourselves.

What an immense gain it would be to substitute for the cold, mechanical theories of evolution by dead force and blind law, a higher doctrine of evolution which, retaining every fact of science, should fill the world with spiritual life and energy. If, beside the Supreme Creator, there are also subordinate creators, we may conceive of them as still present in nature, still helping to reproduce its beauty and life, still visible in the tender coloring of the sky and the graceful sweep of the elm, still audible in "the melodies of woods, and winds, and waters." Gracious and fair were the divinities of the Greeks by the side of their fountains, and in the depths of their forests, but how much higher the conception which, while filling all space with spiritual ever-active powers, still believes in God as the Alpha and Omega, first and last, whose fullness fills all in all, whose light inspires all intelligence, whose life is the animating principle of all being.

CHAPTER VIII.

PRAYER AND WORSHIP IN ALL RELIGIONS.

§ 1. Prayer and worship to invisible powers universal. § 2. Prayer among the primitive races. Zulus. North American Indians. Races of Asia. Islands of the Pacific. The principal element of this prayer is supplication for outward good. § 3. Prayer in Ethnic Religions. Adoration the principal element in these prayers. The Vedic Hymns. China. The Greeks. Mexicans. § 4. Prayer in the Catholic Religions. Desire for moral goodness now appears. The Zend-Avesta. Buddhism. Mohammedanism. § 5. The universality of Sacrifices. Their origin. § 6. Jewish Prayers. The Book of Psalms. God spoken to as a friend. Christian Prayer. No liturgy in the New Testament. The prayer of love. § 7. Imprecatory prayer in all religions. Improvement in the spirit and method of prayer. § 8. Decay of prayer at the present time. Divine personality doubted. The Future of Prayer.

§ 1. *Prayer and worship to invisible powers universal.*

ONE of the universal facts in the history of man is the custom of prayer and worship addressed to invisible powers. All that man does must derive its motive from without or from within, from his outward experience or his inward tendencies. Therefore, when we find this custom of worship in all races, barbarous and civilized; in all times, the most ancient and most recent; in all religions, from the lowest superstition to the highest spirituality; one of two things must be true. Either men have found that their prayers are answered, and that they actually receive blessings in consequence of prayer which they could not obtain without it; or else, though there is no answer to prayer, and they get no good by it, they continue to pray from the necessity of their own nature. Prayer either brings divine aid, or it does not bring it. If it brings aid, then there are unseen personal beings who hear and answer prayer; and so Materialism and Atheism and Agnostic theories are confuted. If prayer does not bring aid, then, in addition to man's other endowments, he must have been created with such instincts of the heart, intuitions of the mind, and aspirations of the soul as to maintain a communion with powers unperceived by the senses. He talks forever to a silent world from which comes no response. Then he must have a religious organization, which has survived through all the long processes of development. If we accept the doctrine of the "survival of the fittest," we must grant that the fittest man is the man who prays, and that prayer in some way or other has been helpful, and continues to be so. The Evolutionist, at any rate, must believe that he is made to pray, and that it does him good to pray.

§ 2. *Prayer among the primitive races. Zulus. North American Indians. Races of Asia. Islands of the Pacific. The principal element of this prayer supplication for outward good.*

Beginning with the primitive or tribal religions, we find prayer as universal there as elsewhere.

We have seen among the primitive races the beginnings of religious faith in things unseen, in their strong conviction of the continued existence of human souls after death. To these disembodied spirits it is natural to speak. This conversation with the unseen world is the rudimentary form of prayer. The Sioux Indians say, "Spirits of the dead, have mercy on us." The Zulus of Africa call on the spirits of their ancestors, without specifying their wants, thinking these spirits can know without being told. They simply cry aloud, "People of our house!" Sometimes they say, "People of our house; cattle!" "People of our house, good luck and health!" On more solemn occasions, after the cattle-feast and sacrifices are over, the head-man of the tribe speaks thus, amid a profound silence: "Our people! I pray to you. I sacrifice these cattle to you. I pray for more cattle and more corn, and many children; then this your home will prosper, and many will praise and thank you."

From such conversation with departed friends

and appeals to souls of ancestors, the steps are simple to the worship of higher powers. This also is found among primitive nations. In the Papuan island of Tanna, a prayer is offered by the chiefs, with the first-fruits. They say, "Compassionate father, here is some food for you. Eat it, and be kind to us on account of it." In the Samoan Islands, at the evening meal, a libation is poured out, and the head of the household prays thus: "Here is ava for you, O gods! Look kindly on this family; let it prosper, let us be kept in health, let our food grow, let us be a strong people."

The Osage Indians prayed to the Master of Life, Woh-konda, "Pity me, Woh-konda! I am very poor. Give me success against my enemies. Let me avenge the death of my friends. Let me take many scalps, many horses." When the Algonquin Indians set out to cross Lake Superior, the canoes stopped close together, and the chief, in a loud voice, offered a prayer to the Great Spirit, entreating him to give them a good passage. "You have made this lake," said he, "and made us, your children. Cause this water to be smooth while we pass over." Thus he prayed for some minutes, and then they all threw a little tobacco into the lake as a propitiatory offering. A Nootka Indian, preparing for war, says, "Great Qua-hoot-zee! let me live, not be sick, find the enemy, not be afraid of him, find him asleep, and kill many of him."

To these people there was nothing wrong in such a prayer, for to them war was a duty. The moment a war seems right, to pray for victory seems right also. Christian nations in their churches still pray for victory over their enemies. But there are more tender prayers to be found among these childlike tribes. A Delaware Indian prayed thus: "O Great Spirit above! Have pity on my children and on my wife. Let them not mourn for me. Let me succeed in this enterprise, slay my enemy, return in safety to my dear family and friends, that we may rejoice together. Have pity on me, and protect my life." The negro on the Gold Coast prayed, "God, give me to-day rice and yams; give me slaves, riches, and health. Let me be brisk and swift." Sometimes, when taking medicine, they would say, "Father Heaven! bless this medicine which I take." The negro on Lake Nyassa, offering to his Supreme Deity a basket-full of meal and a pot of native beer, will cry out, "Hear thou, O God, and send rain," and the people, softly clapping their hands, will respond, intoning their prayer, as they always do, "Hear thou, O God."

Passing over to Asia, as we have passed from America to Africa, the Kárens of Burmah pray to the harvest-goddess thus: "Grandmother! thou guardest my field, look out sharp for thieves. If they come, bind them with this rope." The

Khonds of Orissa cry out, "O Boora-Penner, who created us and made us to be hungry, who gave us corn, and taught us to plow. Remembering this, grant our prayers. When we go out in the early morning to sow, save us from the tiger and the snake. Let not the birds eat the seed. Let our plows go easily through the earth. Let the corn be so plentiful that we shall drop it on the way. Let our cattle be so many that there shall be no room for them in the stalls. You know what is good for us. Give it to us."

In the islands of the Pacific similar prayers abound. I quote one, which is offered before a thieving expedition: —

"O thou divine Outre-reter!
We go out for plunder.
Cause all things to sleep in the house.
Owner of the house, sleep on!
Threshold of the house, sleep on!
Little insects of the house, sleep on!
Central-post, ridge-pole, rafters, thatch of the house, sleep on.
O Rongo, grant us success."

Such are the prayers of the childlike races. They are prayers for temporal success and outward blessings only. There is in them little or no petition for moral improvement.

But let us not fail to observe, that even in its lowest forms, prayer exercises an influence to ennoble human nature. The man who prays belongs to two worlds; the prayerless man to only one.

The man who prays looks up to something higher than himself, and so is made better. Lord Bacon remarks that a dog who looks up to his master and relies on his superior wisdom, has in him the germ of religion, and gathers strength out of that reliance. The praying-troopers of Cromwell were more than a match for the light-hearted Cavaliers who laughed at their prayers. "We must recognize," says Tylor, "even in savage religion, that prayer is a means of strengthening emotion, sustaining courage, and exciting hope; while in higher faiths it becomes a great motive power of the ethical system."

§ 3. *Prayer in ethnic Religions. Adoration the principal element in these prayers. The Vedic Hymns. China. The Greeks. Mexicans.*

The ethnic, race, or national religions which we are now to examine in reference to their prayers and worship, are those of China, India, Egypt, Assyria, Greece, and Rome. None of these race-religions have a prophet for their founder, for Confucius did not found the religion of China, but only edited and systematized its existing religion. It is unnecessary to say that we trace in them the same supplications for outward good that constitute the substance of worship in the primitive or tribal forms of prayer. This runs through all religions, and is the beginning of the tie which binds the soul to God.

Another element which now enters prayer and becomes very prominent is that of adoration. The worshipper exhausts the resources of language in expressing his sense of the greatness, the excellence, the wisdom, the power, the goodness of his God. He heaps upon him titles of reverence.

The Vedic hymns, for example, are filled with this strain of adoring homage. The following are specimens from Muir's "Sanskrit Texts."

"Of which god now, of which of the immortals, shall we invoke the amiable name? Let us invoke the amiable name of Aditi; of the divine Agni, first of the immortals; of Varuna, the thousand-eyed, skillful-handed, possessed of all resources, embracing the three worlds, whose breath is the wind, who knows the flights of the birds, the course of the far-traveling wind, and is a witness of human truth and falsehood."

Of Agni, god of fire, it is said that he is "The divine monarch;" "who spread out heaven and earth;" "who has made all that stands, flies, walks, and moves;" "who is the summit of the sky, the centre of the earth;" "at whose mighty deeds men tremble;" "who knows men's secrets, and hears their prayers."

Here is a hymn to the dawn: —

"The light has arrived, the greatest of all lights, the glorious and brilliant illumination has been born. The shining Ushas, fair and bright, have opened the doors of the sky, setting in motion all living things. Usha [the

Dawn] has awakened all creatures. Daughter of the sky, youthful, clad in shining attire, auspicious, shine on us to-day! O best of all dawns, arise! Magnificent Goddess, protecting right, imparting joy, undecaying, immortal, arise! our life, our breath!"

These are specimens of the Vedic hymns, which adore and worship in turn one or another of the powers of nature, fire, air, the sun, the dawn, the soma plant; yama, god of immortality; rivers, waters, and the like. Language is exhausted in finding terms of adoration, reverence, love for these deities, each of which represents in turn the Infinite Power behind them all. But there is something vague in this worship. Each deity lacks substance, reality. These prayers gratify the sentiment of devotion, but, strictly speaking, are not offered to any personal being.

In China we see that the dominant form of religion is the piety which reverences the parent and the ancestors. Ancestral worship was early introduced and was encouraged by the teaching of Confucius. Then followed the worship of higher spirits, as intercessors and mediators with the Supreme Being, the abstract and far-removed heaven of heavens. The Shi-King and the Shu-King, books composed from about eighteen centuries to six centuries before Christ, speak of Shang-Ti as the true God, ruler of the world, giver of all things. Dr. Legge gives an account of a special series of prayers offered to Shang-Ti by the Emperor of China in the year 1538. A slight change was to be made in the name of the Supreme Being, and all the spirits in the skies were invoked to intercede with him on behalf of his worshippers. The service begins, —

"I, the Emperor, have respectfully prepared this paper to inform the spirit of the sun, the spirit of the moon, the spirits of the five planets, of the stars, of the clouds, of the four seas, of the great rivers, of the present year, etc., that on the first of next month we shall reverently lead our officers and people to honor the great name of Shang-Ti. We inform you beforehand, O ye celestial and terrestial spirits, and will trouble you, on our behalf, to exert your spiritual power, and display your vigorous efficacy, communicating our poor desire to Shang-Ti, praying him to accept our worship, and be pleased with the new title which we shall reverently present to him."

When the day came the Emperor and his court assembled around the circular altar. First, they prostrated themselves eleven times, and then addressed the great being as he who dissipated chaos, and formed the heavens, earth, and man : —

"Thou, O Ti, didst open the way for the forces of matter to operate ; thou, O Spirit, didst produce the beautiful light of the sun and moon, that all thy creatures might be happy.

"Thou hast vouchsafed to hear us, O Ti, for thou regardest us as thy children. I, thy child, dull and ignorant, can poorly express my feelings. Honorable is thy great name."

Then food was placed on the altar, first boiled meat, then cups of wine, and Ti was requested to receive them, with these words: —

"The Sovereign Spirit deigns to accept our offering. Give thy people happiness. Send down thy favor. All creatures are upheld by thy love. Thou alone art the true parent of all things.

"The service of song is now completed, but our poor sincerity cannot be expressed aright. The sense of thy goodness is in our heart. We have adored thee, and would unite with all spirits in honoring thy name. We place it on this sacred sheet of paper, and now put it in the fire, with precious silks, that the smoke may go up with our prayers to the distant blue heavens. Let all the ends of the earth rejoice in thy name."

These Chinese prayers are of adoration and reverence, for the whole mind of that nation has been steeped in reverence from the beginning.

As regards prayer among the Greeks, this is what the learned Döllinger wrote while still an orthodox Roman Catholic: —

"As the life of the Greeks was penetrated with religion, and all things were related to the gods; therefore, prayer was woven into their whole public and private life. As a rule they prayed in short formulas; and a certain magical or compulsory power was ascribed to these formulas, binding the gods, and compelling them to assist their worshippers, as was still more the case among the Romans. Plato says, 'Every man of sense, before beginning any important work, will ask help of the gods.'

Therefore, he himself, before commencing the Timæus, says, 'Since I am about to speak of the nature of the Universe, I must first invoke the gods, that I may say what is reasonable and true.' "

Plutarch tells that the great orator Pericles, before he began to speak, always prayed to the gods for power to do a good work by his oration.

In Homer, Nestor is represented as praying for success for the ambassadors to Achilles, and Ulysses prays before going to the Trojan camp. Priam also prays before going to ask for the body of Héctor. Lucian speaks of Demosthenes praying, with his hand on his mouth, before beginning his speeches in the Greek Courts. Xenophon, during the retreat of the Ten Thousand, prays before each day's march. Plato, in "The Laws," speaks of children who, every day, hear their mothers eagerly talking with the gods in the most earnest manner, beseeching them for blessings.

Seneca, the philosopher, says: —

"We worship and adore the framer and former of the universe; governor, disposer, keeper; him on whom all things depend; mind and spirit of the world; from whom all things spring; by whose spirit we live; the divine spirit diffused through all; God all-powerful; God always present; God above all other gods; thee we worship and adore."

Epictetus says: —

"Dare to lift thine eyes to God and to say, use me for

what thou wilt. I agree, and am of the same mind with thee. I refuse nothing that seems good to thee. Lead me where thou wilt, and I will go."

The cuneiform writings on the tablets show us that the Assyrians also prayed. On an unpublished tablet in the British Museum, is this prayer of King Asshur-da-ni-pal, B. C. 650: —

"May the look of pity that shines in thine eternal face dispel my griefs.

"May I never feel the anger and wrath of the God.

"May my omissions and my sins be wiped out.

"May I find reconciliation with Him, for I am the servant of his power, the adorer of the great gods.

"May thy powerful face come to my help; may it shine like heaven, and bless me with happiness and abundance of riches.

"May it bring forth in abundance, like the earth, happiness and every sort of good."

The ancient Mexicans recognized a Supreme Being, and addressed him as "the God by whom we live;" "thou Omnipresent, who knoweth all our thoughts, and giveth all gifts;" "without whom man is nothing;" "invisible, without body, one God, of perfection and purity;" "under whose wings we find repose and sure defense."

They had regular forms of prayer; and what is a very curious coincidence, they baptized children with this formula: "Let these holy drops wash away the sin that it received before the foundation of the world; so that the child may be new born."

§ 4. *Prayer in the Catholic Religions. Desire for moral goodness now appears. The Zend-Avesta. Buddhism. Mohammedanism.*

We now pass to prayer and worship in the monotheistic or prophetic religions, in which we include the systems of Zoroaster, Buddha, Moses, Mohammed, and Christ. Here at once comes in a new element. In addition to the prayer for pardon in the past is the desire for improvement in the future. It is a supplication for goodness; to be made morally better. The Zend-Avesta is full of such expressions as these: "May we, by means of good thoughts, good words, and good actions, resist evil thoughts, evil words, and evil actions." "O Lord of good things, who givest to us the purity by which we live, announce it to us, O Mazda, that we may know it, and teach it to all living." "Let me know fullness of life, purity, and immortality." "May power and strength come to me, that I may maintain purity in thought, in word, and in action."

Buddhism, we know, is often said to have no God. But if Buddhism is without a God, how can it have any prayers? If the Buddha has entered Nirvâna, and if Nirvâna means cessation of existence, how can he be an object of worship? According to this theory, then, the Buddhist ought not to pray. But we are assured by travelers in Buddhist countries that prayer is universal. In Thibet prayer-meetings are held at evening in the streets, and Father Huc was much edified by those he saw in Lassa, and wished that similar meetings might be held in Paris. Mr. Malcolm one day visited a pagoda in Burmah, and was impressed by the sight of an old man who came reverently in, leading a little boy by the hand, and both knelt in worship before the image of Buddha. Koeppen says that some of the Buddhist prayers might, with a few alterations, be suitable for Christian churches. As an example, he gives a part of a Buddhist prayer recorded by Pallas: —

> "Thou in whom innumerable creatures believe!
> Thou, Buddha, Victor over the hosts of evil!
> Thou, all-wise Being, come down to our world!
> Made perfect and glorified by innumerable by-gone revolutions; always pitiful, always gracious toward all creatures!
> Look down upon us; for the time has come to pour out blessings on all creatures.
> Be gracious to us from thy throne built in thy heavenly world.
> Thou art the eternal redemption of all creatures, therefore bow down to us with all thy unstained heavenly societies."

Among Mohammedans prayer is universal. The Koran calls prayer the pillar of religion and the key of Paradise. The pious Moslem prays five times a day: (1) Before sunrise, (2) at noon, (3) before sunset, (4) after sunset, (5) when night has shut in. Wherever he may be, in the street, in his shop, he steps aside, spreads out his carpet or cloak, takes off his shoes, and, with his face toward Mecca, goes through his picturesque devotions. The call to prayer is intoned from the minarets in the cities; rosaries with ninety-nine beads for the names of Allah are carried in the hands, wherewith to count the prayers of ejaculation. Great solemnity and decorum is maintained in the worship of the mosques, and travelers have said that, when crowded with worshippers, you might shut your eyes and think you were alone.

One of the Persian Mohammedans, called Ssufis, thus speaks: —

> "Unceasingly a divine influence flows down from the unknown world into our souls. The voice of God comes into our heart, and this is the root of all language. If God speaks, man answers. Nay! if God should speak to dead matter and ask, 'Art not thou also my creature?' it would reply, 'O Lord! I am.'"

The same Mohammedan writer speaks thus of prayer: —

> "There are three degrees of prayer. The first is when it is only spoken by the lips. The second kind is when, with difficulty and by a resolute effort, the soul succeeds in fixing its thought on divine things. The third is when

it finds it hard to turn away from God. But it is the very marrow of prayer when God takes possession of the soul of the suppliant, and he is absorbed into the Divine Being and ceases from all thought, so that the prayer seems like a veil between himself and God."

Here are some examples of Mohammedan prayers of this mystical sect called Ssufis.

Prayer of Attac, twelfth century: —

"Soul of the Soul! Neither thought nor reason comprehend thy essence, and no one knows thy attributes. Souls have no idea of thy being. The prophets themselves sink in the dust of thy road. Although intellect exists by thee, has it ever yet found the path of thy existence? O thou, who art in the interior and in the exterior of the soul! thou art and thou art not that which I say. In thy presence reason grows dizzy; it loses the thread that would direct it in thy way. I perceive clearly the universe in thee, and yet discover thee not in the world. All beings are marked with thy impress, but thyself hast no impress visible; thou reservest the secret of thine existence."

Prayer of Abulfazl, A. D. 1595: —

"O Lord, whose secrets are forever veiled,
And whose perfection knows not a beginning!
End and beginning both are lost in Thee;
No trace of them is found in thy eternal realm.
My words are lame; my tongue, a stony tract;
Slow wings my foot, and wide is the expanse.
Confused are my thoughts; but this is thy best praise.
In ecstasy alone I see Thee face to face."

§ 5. *The universality of Sacrifices. Their origin.*

In all parts of the world, and in all religions, from the lowest upward till we reach Christianity, sacrifices have been common. Men have offered to their gods the best things they had, the fruits of the earth, the flocks and herds which made up their wealth. Sacrifices are visible prayers, prayers in act. The sincerity of the worshipper appears in his offering. Some sacrifices are thank-offerings, given as an expression of gratitude for benefits received. Other sacrifices are offered as supplications for help desired, as when before a military expedition a hundred victims were sacrificed for success in war. Thus a valuable present is offered to the gods to induce them to be propitious, just as it would be offered to an Eastern king, or to a Prime Minister to obtain his favor. Other sacrifices are sin-offerings, given in expiation of some crime, to turn away the indignation of the Deity. Others again were offered to confirm a vow, or make fast a covenant between the worshipper and his God. Thus every part of prayer is represented by these visible orisons: thanksgiving, confession, supplication, adoration, self-dedication.

Sacrifices, being so universal, are evidently the natural methods taken by men to express their religious feelings, and show their religious sincerity.

But the sacrifices which always became most prominent were those in expiation of sin. These we find in all nations and all religions, testifying that conscience is universal in man. These sacrifices show that man has the sense of wrong-doing. He believes that he needs to do something to obtain pardon. Such ideas spring up naturally in the soul.

While some inward instinct of the soul leads man to adore and worship these invisible presences, and to supplicate help from the heavenly powers, an opposite tendency drifts him away from such spiritual communion, and subjects him to the rule of sense. Outward things distract his attention, and make him forget his prayers. Therefore he seeks for help in those very outward things themselves. To keep his mind fixed on God, he makes an image and calls it God, and by this means fixes his attention. This is the origin of idolatry. The Roman Catholic kneeling before a picture of the Madonna does not mean to pray to the picture, but by means of the picture to keep his mind fixed on the invisible mother of Christ. Just so the savages use their idols as helps, and pray to the God behind them. Such is the legitimate origin of idolatry. After awhile the religious associations which connect the idol itself with the divinity it represents grow so strong that the image becomes sacred, and the God appears to be fixed to it, to dwell in it. All idolatry runs into this extreme, and worships the means of religion as if they were the end. The Sabbath was a means of shutting out the world, it was "made for man." But at last the Sabbath was considered as holy in itself, apart from its uses; then man seemed made for the Sabbath. So the church and the temple were made as places where the worshipper could be surrounded with sacred associations, and helped to fix his attention on things unseen. The use of the Liturgy, of the Rosary, of the Bible, are for the same end. All are meant as helps to prayer, and as such are good. But when we talk of the Holy Sabbath, the Holy Church, God's day, God's house, we are drifting toward the same sort of mechanism in religion which led to the prayer-mills of the Buddhists.

§ 6. *Jewish Prayers. The Book of Psalms. God spoken to as a friend. Christian Prayer. No liturgy in the New Testament. The prayer of love.*

When we turn from these ethnic and prophetic religions, and read the Book of Psalms in the Old Testament, we seem to enter into a new atmosphere. In the Vedic hymns, in the hymns on the Egyptian monuments, and in the other religions we find adoration, reverence, profound sincerity, and a longing for help from on high. But the element which comes into prayer with the Psalms of

David is one of happy trust, the freedom of child-like intercourse. God, who in the other religions was far away, has now come near and walks with man as a friend. Therefore this Jewish psalter continues to be the best prayer-book for Christians down to this hour. With much in it that is not Christian, and which we cannot believe in or rightly use, there is in it so much of inspiration, comfort, and joy, so much to purify and strengthen the soul, that we feel it often reached the very spirit of Christ before Christ came.

The New Testament contains no liturgy, no hymnal, no forms of prayer except the Lord's Prayer. This could not have been accidental. The disciples asked for some such help for their devotions. Jesus gave only this brief summary of worship. He feared routine; he warned them against endless repetitions, like those of the Vedas and Zend-Avesta. He preferred private to public prayer, as being more sincere and real. "Be not like the heathen," he said, using "vain repetitions." The worshippers of Baal called to their god the whole morning, crying, "O Baal! hear us!" The Ephesians cried for two hours, "Great is Diana of the Ephesians!" Terence makes one of his characters say: "Wife, cease deafening the gods with your prayers. You seem to think them like yourself, unable to understand a thing till it has been said a hundred times." Martin Luther says: "Few words and much meaning is Christian; many words and little meaning is heathen."

Jesus teaches us to pray in spirit and truth, to ask in faith, to ask especially for the Holy Spirit, to "ask in his name," that is in his spirit.[1]

Thus we see the ascent of prayer; first of all it is a magical charm, an incantation, a mere means of gaining power, wealth, pleasure, victory; then it rises higher and becomes adoration, and a form of sacrifice. Then we see it helping itself with outward aids; with images and idols; with sacrifices and incense; with holy places, holy persons, holy altars and holy books; with liturgies and litanies. At last, in the teaching of Jesus, it reaches the highest form, as a life of communion with the all-loving, ever-present father and friend.

As man ascends, his prayer also becomes more elevated. The element of fear is first partially eliminated. It is not true, as Lucretius asserted, that all religion rests on fear. But in many religions the gods were regarded as capricious, revengeful and cruel. And this view is the source of human sacrifices, of ascetic mortifications, and of a thousand devices for appeasing an angry Deity.

[1] The Concordance will show how often in the Jewish books, "name" stands for the character, nature, or spirit of the person or thing.

§ 7. *Imprecatory prayer in all religions. Improvement in the spirit and method of prayer.*

As prayer continues to ascend, the imprecatory element drops out of it.

The imprecations of Greeks (says Potter), were very terrible, and so powerful, when duly pronounced, as to occasion the destruction, not only of many persons, but of whole cities. The imprecations of Myrtilus on Pelops brought all the dreadful sufferings which Atreus, Agamemnon, and Orestes endured. The most dreadful imprecations were those by parents, priests, kings, and prophets. Criminals were publicly cursed by the priests. Alcibiades was banished and cursed by all the priests of Athens. A single priestess (we are glad to hear) refused. Theano said her office was to bless and not to curse. Pliny says, "All men fear imprecations."

Among the Jews we read of the curse of Saul on Jonathan, and of Balaam sent for to curse the Israelites. The imprecatory Psalms are still read in many churches. And this element of imprecation survives in the Church of England; soon, let us hope, to be removed. There is a commination service still ordered to be read on the first day of Lent, in which to each of a long series of curses the people are to say Amen. But Jesus has explicitly forbidden all this. "Bless your enemies," he says: "bless and curse not." He tells us to be like God, who sends blessing and not cursing on his enemies.

As prayer ascends, supplications for outward blessings greatly decrease, and prayer for inward spiritual blessings takes their place; and finally, formal prayer, the prayer of place, time, routine, gives way to the prayer of the spirit, of life, of love.

We do not always notice what a step forward was taken by Christianity when it dropped the ritual of the Jewish and Pagan religions. The whole system of sacrifices disappeared; the magnificent temple worship came to an end; the priesthood was abolished; fasts and festivals were no more; there were no processions, no sacred temples, no altars or shrines; no holy mysteries; no augurs, nor auspices, nor divination; no public worship of any kind. Every Christian was a priest, having direct access to God; the rest of the soul was the true Sabbath; the true prayers were not at Gerizim or at Jerusalem, but were to be made in spirit and truth, by going into the closet of the heart and shutting the door. It is true that Ritualism afterward reappeared in the Christian Church; the old Roman calendar of sacred days was reproduced in a Christian calendar of saints' days; new festivals and fasts took the place of the old. But for three hundred years Christianity was a religion without a ritual, or a priesthood, or temples, or altars, or public worship. And when these returned they came back in a purer form and a better type. Jesus did not put his new wine of the soul into the old bottles of Jewish or Roman ritual.

§ 8. *Decay of prayer at the present time. Divine personality doubted. The Future of Prayer.*

There have been times when all men prayed, from a sense of duty, a feeling of need, or as a long-established form, an unquestioned custom. We have passed into another period, when faith in prayer has been much diminished. Men no longer pray as they once did, as a matter of duty or as a form; and large numbers do not pray as a matter of conviction. They have ceased to believe in prayer, either as a duty or as a source of strength and comfort. They do not pray for outward blessings, for they believe that these come or do not come in accordance with inexorable natural law. They do not pray for inward strength and comfort, doubting whether these also may not be under the same rigorous domain of unchanging law. "Why ask for outward or inward blessings?" they say. "If it be right that we shall have them, they will be given without our asking; if wrong, they will not be given, no matter how much we pray." They do not see that this simple logic may be met by other arguments as intelligible, that the prayer itself may enter into the nexus of things as a new element, to make that right which otherwise would not have been so. But a deeper objection still operates in our time to palsy the spirit of prayer. It is doubt concerning the personality of God, — a kind of Pantheistic view of the Deity as the unconscious soul of the universe, — as the vast plastic power of nature, with no eye to see, ear to hear, or heart to pity the needs of mankind; and without a belief in the personality of God, no prayer is possible.

But what precisely is meant by denying the personality of God? Personality in man is the highest spiritual fact of which we have knowledge. We mean by it that wonderful unity of thought, love, and will, out of which centre influence radiates in all directions. The glorious distinction of the human soul is that its action is combined with its knowledge and desire, that it puts forth its power deliberately, sustained by all its knowledge, and all its hope.

If we have any distinct meaning when we use the word God, we mean the highest being of whom we are capable of conceiving. Make him impersonal, and he is not the highest; we have omitted the chief perfection. An infinitely mighty power, working blindly, chained by law, would be lower than man. Man's conscious, deliberate purpose would make him superior to such a God. Man, as a person, is essentially higher in the scale of being than an impersonal deity.

But these difficulties and doubts, which at present prevent so many from having the strength, light, and peace which come from a habit of prayer, can be only temporary in their influence. We are on our way to a higher conception of Christian prayer than those which have hitherto prevailed. The prayer of mere form and ceremony is passing away, never to return. The prayer of the Spirit, the sense of God's presence in the soul, the child-like prayer taught and exemplified by Jesus, will be found an indispensable element of human progress. The full development of man will only be reached when he is in constant communion with God, according to the favorite formula of Jesus, who said of the Father: "I in him, and he in me." Thus work and prayer, though not the same, will be each for the other. Work will lead to prayer and prayer to work, and human life will be full of God. Until this fullness of God comes to us, we have not reached the object of our existence. Toward this great end the human race is tending, when religion shall fill all of life, when it shall inspire all work, gladden all labor, be comfort and strength at all hours, and promote the highest development of which the human race is capable.

The saying quoted by Christ, "My house shall be called the house of prayer for all nations," may be applied to our globe. It, also, is a house of prayer for all nations. Jeremy Taylor, in one of his picturesque paragraphs, supposes one looking down from the battlements of heaven, and seeing all the woes of earth spread out beneath him in one great panorama of misery. But this supposed spectator would also behold another more consoling spectacle: that of mankind lifting up its heart out of those miseries to the God of all consolation. The world is always at prayer. This uninterrupted worship is continually going on around the globe. As the sun rises on the eastern shores of Asia it looks down on the prayer of the Buddhists in Japan; as going westward it continues to unseal the eyelids of the morning, it beholds the Chinese praying in the shrines of their ancestors or in the pagodas of Pekin; it sees the monks in the Buddhist monasteries of Tartary at their early matins, the Brahmins of India reciting the Vedic hymns, the Mohammedans, called by the voice of the muezzin to early worship. And as the line of coming day moves on into Europe, it lights up the Christian churches of the East, the minsters of Central and Western Europe, and so crosses the Atlantic to find other thousands of churches, raised for prayer and praise by the Christians of America. It looks in turn on pagoda and mosque, Roman

Catholic cathedral and Protestant meeting-house, the costly temples of New York and the camp-meetings in Western woods, where men worship

> "In that fane, most catholic and solemn,
> Which God has planned."

Thus the hour cometh, and now is, when the world shall be full of the knowledge of God, and when the whole wide earth shall be the temple of the Deity, in

> "A cathedral, boundless as our wonder;
> Whose quenchless lamps the sun and moon supply;
> Its choir the winds and waves; its organ thunder;
> Its dome the sky."

CHAPTER IX.

INSPIRATION AND ART IN ALL RELIGIONS.

§ 1. Inspiration in its most general form. § 2. Different kinds of Inspiration. § 3. Religious Inspiration. § 4. Inspiration of the Bible. In lower Religions. Inspiration as Frenzy. Possession and Self-possession. § 5. The Bible compared with the Vedas and Koran. § 6. Peculiarity of the Inspiration of the New Testament. § 7. Art the child of Religion. Egyptian Architecture. § 8. Buddhist Architecture. § 9. Jewish and Christian Architecture. § 10. Mohammedan Art. § 11. Greek Art. § 12. Religion in Painting and Poetry.

§ 1. *Inspiration in its most general form.*

WE begin by considering inspiration in general. Man must have a capacity for inspiration, otherwise he could not be inspired. This is a human faculty, therefore common to all. There is more of it in some men than in others; those who have the most of the faculty are prophets, seers, or men of genius. Men are inspired in regard to other kinds of truth, as well as in regard to religious truth. Thus we speak familiarly of an inspired poet or an inspired artist. Inspiration in general is an order, of which religious inspiration is a genus.

Inspiration, considered in the largest sense, is the sight of inward truth, a truth which is seen within the mind, in distinction from the truth which comes to us from without through the senses. All our knowledge is of three kinds: that which we perceive outwardly through the senses; that which we perceive inwardly in the mind itself through consciousness; and that which being thus taken in, is worked up by the reflective faculties. The substance of all truth comes to us from without or from within; we can only by thinking give it more distinct form. We all know that ideas come to us from within the mind, without any effort of ours. The poet, the artist, the inventor, when the course of his thoughts is checked by some obstacle, stops, waits, looks in, looks up, for an inspiration. Many of our best thoughts visit us in this way unexpectedly, and take us by surprise. John Locke, certainly no enthusiast, invented a Common-place Book, and advised all students to keep such a book. He said that they ought to write down in it the ideas which came to them thus, when they were walking or conversing, as these were often the best, a kind of seed corn which would unfold into the most valuable results. If you read the biographies of great inventors, discoverers, poets, artists, you will often find it recorded that the germinal ideas of their whole life-work fell into their minds in this way. Thus we may say that not only Isaiah and Paul were inspired to teach religious truth, but that Newton was inspired to discover the law of gravitation, Phidias to carve the Olympian Jupiter, Columbus to discover America, Champollion to decipher Greek hieroglyphics, Milton to write the "Paradise Lost," and Mrs. Stowe to write "Uncle Tom's Cabin;" for "every good gift and every perfect gift cometh down from above, from the Father of lights." The truths seen by such thinkers were not inventions of theirs, but were realities shown them by God.

§ 2. *Different Kinds of Inspiration.*

What then is the difference between these different kinds of inspiration? It is qualitative and quantitative. It is a difference of kind and of degree. It differs in kind according to the subject which occupies a man's thought and in which he is interested. The artist is interested in beauty; the poet and musician in poetry and music; the inventor in his invention, and each finds what he is looking for. The religious man is interested in religious truth, and to him that truth is inwardly revealed. The poet is haunted by some ideal beauty which he struggles to seize and embody in suitable forms. Columbus is haunted by the vision of a continent beyond the Western ocean. Newton sees dawning before his mind the approaching sun, which when it rises is to reveal the fundamental law of the outward universe. Neither of them can verify his vision, or convince others of its reality, until it is fully made known. They are all counted as visionaries till then. But when, by faithful work, the law of gravitation is found, the play of "Hamlet" written, the "Divine Comedy" finished, the Parthenon built, the electric telegraph discovered, when the Vedas take shape, when the prophecy is fulfilled, then the visionary suddenly appears before men as a genius, a seer, a great discoverer, a divine poet.

§ 3. *Religious Inspiration.*

Among these inspirations religious inspiration is the highest, the most far-reaching, the most widely influential. Such inspirations embody themselves in the sacred books of the human race, the Vedas, the Zend-Avesta, the Koran. These constitute an order or a kingdom by themselves, and they all seem to possess an immortal life. They may greatly differ as to the quality and quantity of their inspiration, as we shall directly attempt to show. They are not preserved from error by a miracle. Sacred books are not necessarily infallible. But they live, they last, because they hold some truth which God has sent, and which man needs.

> "One accent of the Holy Ghost
> The heedless world has never lost."

Consider that the Rig-Veda, one among five Vedas, contains 1017 hymns, composed from 1000 to 1500 years before Christ, and preserved during hundreds of years by being committed to memory. Writing seems not to have been known in the Vedic times. It was the regular work of many men to commit to memory every line of the Vedas and recite them day by day. This habit has been maintained to the present time; and there are to-day boys in India from twelve to fifteen years old who can repeat from memory the whole Veda. These hymns have been handed down by tradition in India during three thousand years. Such is the power over the human soul of religious inspiration. Wherever it comes it gives perpetuity to the speech of man. The Bible does not differ from other sacred books in its method of production. All sacred Scriptures are written from within, from the soul moved inwardly by a sacred spirit. The poet truly says: —

> "Out from the heart of nature rolled
> The burdens of the Bible old;
> The litanies of nations came
> Like the volcano's tongue of flame,
> Up from the burning core below, —
> The canticles of love and woe."

There is no impropriety in placing in the same class all the works which are thus created by an inward illumination. The architecture, music, and poetry, which last, which have in them the element of immortality, came from souls inwardly open to some heavenly influence.

> "Earth proudly wears the Parthenon
> As the best gem upon her zone,
> And morning opes with haste her lids
> To gaze upon the Pyramids.
> O'er England's abbeys bends the sky
> As on its friends with kindred eye —
> For out of thought's interior sphere,
> These wonders rose to upper air."

§ 4. *Inspiration of the Bible. In lower Religions. Inspiration as Frenzy. Possession and Self-possession.*

It is no degradation to the Bible to classify it thus, in a broad way, with the Parthenon and the Zend-Avesta. There is still a wide gulf between them. There is a wide gulf between man and the highest inferior animals, and yet we put man among the mammalia, in the same class with whales and elephants, and into a larger division with fishes. He is not degraded by being thus classified, for he constitutes a distinct order in this class. So we may classify inspired works. The same class includes inspired poems, inventions, discoveries; the Parthenon, Pyramids, the works of Michael Angelo, of Dante, of Raffaelle, and the sacred books of all nations. One order in that class includes all the works of religious inspiration, the Vedas, the Koran, the Suttas, the Kings of China, and the Bible. One genus of that order contains the Old and New Testament, each of which again may constitute a separate species.

Something which was thought to be religious inspiration has appeared in a low and crude form among primitive religions. Its chief characteristic there is the loss of self-consciousness and self-possession. Thus the Samoieds of Siberia have diviners who work themselves into a state of wild frenzy before delivering their oracles. The same notion of an inspired madness appeared in the insanity of the Pythian priestess, and in the Greek diviners who fell into trances in which they lay without sense or motion. Plato speaks of one Pamphilus who lay ten days for dead on the field of battle, then revived when about to be put on the funeral pile and related what he had seen in the three worlds.

This same notion of inspiration as a kind of possession or frenzy, found its way into the religion of Greece, where it is seen as an alien element. It appears in the mad dances of the Bacchantes, and the shrieks and self-laceration of the Corybantes. In the Hindu religion we find it in the Yoga, or one who seeks union with God by wholly withdrawing himself from outward things. The Yoga assumes painful positions and contortions of the limbs, he suppresses his breath, and performs other incredible mortifications.

So the Greenlander, in his freezing climate, has

his prophets, whom he calls Angekoks. These also abandon the converse of men, fast and torture their body, and remain in a fixed intensity of thought, till they believe that they see and hear spirits. The Flatheads of Oregon, the Indians of Brazil, the Zulus of Africa, have a similar belief in an inspiration which comes from fasting, loneliness, and self-torture. We read in the Bible of the priests of Baal who cut themselves with knives to bring down an answer from their god. We know how Balaam was compelled to utter an involuntary prophecy.

It is curious to see in our time, and in Christian countries, the revival of this lowest claim to inspiration, a belief in a blind, helpless possession of the soul by some supernatural power, good or evil. Of this sort are the effects often seen in the West and South in revival meetings, where the convicted sinner falls senseless on the ground, or is seized with convulsions. In the great revivals at the beginning of this century in Kentucky and Tennessee these phenomena took the name of "the jerks." The limbs of persons who were present and indisposed toward the revival would often jerk violently against their will, and this was supposed to be the influence of the spirit. The dancing of the Shakers and the whirling of the Mohammedan dervishes belong to the same class of bodily exercises, which, according to St. Paul, profit little.

But the typical inspiration of the prophetic religions is of a higher kind. The Jewish prophets controlled and directed their inspiration. They were inspired from on high, and yet self-possessed. The intellect was lifted to greater clearness, armed with a more powerful logic, concentrated on the important argument, and enriched with lofty and tender images of beauty.

§ 5. *The Bible compared with the Vedas and Koran.*

The sacred books of all nations are full of high thoughts and noble utterances. Such are the Vedic hymns, the liturgies of the Zend-Avesta, the moral teachings of the Buddhist Pitakas, the ballads of the Eddas, the Suras of the Koran, the Psalms of David, and the Epistles of Paul. All of them have the same qualities of clearness, coherence, and practical purpose. They differ greatly from each other in many ways. The Vedic hymns are somewhat monotonous repetitions of praise and adoration to the deified power of nature. It was seriously proposed, at one time, by some of the members of the transcendental school, to read these Vedic hymns instead of the Bible. Probably those who made the suggestion never tried the experiment themselves. Here and there are beautiful passages, like the Hymn to Varuna so often quoted, but the majority of these thousand hymns consist of endless repetitions, and the same images applied first to one and then to another of the objects of adoration. The Zend-Avesta differs from this wearisome monotony in some respects. Although there is also a vast deal of repetition in these very ancient litanies, they come nearer to life, to men, to human duty. They have a pure moral inspiration which is invigorating. The Buddhist scriptures are rather ethical essays, and consist of a multitude of directions for conduct, and for the formation of character.

The Mohammedans consider the Koran to have a beauty which is of itself a sufficient proof of the divine authority of Mohammed. But it is not very interesting reading to the Western mind. It is badly arranged, obscure in some parts, trivial in others. "To us," says Renan, "the Koran appears declamatory, monotonous, tedious." Its merit is in its intense earnestness, reflecting the various experiences of its author. It certainly has exercised a great fascination over the mind of the East. Comparing it with the Bible it may be said that the Koran lays claim to a verbal mechanical inspiration, alike in every part; the Bible, as is now generally recognized, makes no such claim. The Koran is incapable of being translated and retaining its beauty; the Bible loses little in this process. The Bible is the work of a great number of authors, poets, prophets, statesmen; the Koran comes from the brain of a single man. The strength of the Koran is in its unity, intolerance, and narrowness; that of the Bible in its variety, breadth, and liberality. One of the Suras of the Koran declares that, "If men and genii should try together to produce a book like the Koran, they would fail." To which Dean Stanley replies by asking whether any single passage in the book can be compared with Paul's description of charity in the Epistle to the Corinthians.

But let us do what justice we can to Mohammed by selecting some of his best sayings. Here is one called "The folding up:" —

> "When the sun shall be folded up, and the stars shall fall, and the mountains be put in motion, and the seas boil, and the leaves of the book be unrolled, and the heavens be stripped off like a skin, and hell begin to blaze, and Paradise draw near, then shall every soul know what it has done."

Or this description of the infidel: —

> "As darkness over a deep sea, billows riding on billows, billows below and clouds above, — one darkness on another darkness, — so that if a man stretches out his hand he cannot behold it, thus is he to whom the light of God doth not come."

The very intensity of the Koran, however, shows a survival of that lower order of inspiration in which a man is possessed by his idea, and does not fully possess it. The peculiarity of the New Testament inspiration is that the spirit of the prophet is entirely subject to the prophet. In one particular alone was early Christianity a kind of spiritual possession; I mean what was called the gift of tongues. Paul, in writing to the Corinthians, describes and strongly condemns a state of things resembling the excitement at the revival meetings to which we have before referred. "If when the church come together you all speak with tongues and there comes in an unbeliever, will he not say you are mad?" "I had rather speak five words with my understanding than ten thousand in a tongue," "for God is not the God of confusion but of peace." But this peculiar ecstatic state soon passed away, and passed away so entirely that no one can now say exactly what it was.

§ 6. *Peculiarity of the Inspiration of the New Testament.*

The calm clearness of the New Testament, its union of profound spiritual insight with perfect simplicity of expression, almost disguises its inspiration. It is only when we see how deep, rich, full are its utterances; see how they satisfy us always and never tire, that we begin to recognize from what a deep place in the soul they must have come. Take the letters of Paul, written from time to time, to one and another church, as occasion prompted. They were written with no notion of publicity; once read he probably thought they would never be heard of again. And yet what wealth of thought is in them, what affluent originality of language, what condensed fire, what charm of imagination. They have the careless abandon and absence of method which belongs to letter-writing. There is no plan; one thought suggests another. It occurred to him as he wrote that several persons in the church at Corinth did not believe in any resurrection, therefore he gives his view, his reasons, and his explanation of the mysterious hereafter, as he saw it in the depths of his soul. Little did he suppose that those hasty words would be read century after century by the side of thousands of open graves, and would comfort the hearts of such a vast multitude of mourners. Sometimes he seems almost carried away by the rush of thought, but no touch of obscurity comes in consequence. It is fire without smoke. Thus he describes the work of his life: —

"Approving ourselves in all things as God's servants; in much patience, in afflictions, in necessities, in distresses, in strifes, in imprisonments, in tumults, in labors, in watchings, in fastings; by pureness, by knowledge, by long-suffering, by kindness, by the Holy Ghost, by love unfeigned, by the word of truth, by the power of God, by the armor of righteousness on the right hand and the left, by honor and dishonor, by evil report and good report; as deceivers, and yet true; as unknown, and yet well-known; as dying, and behold we live; as chastened, and not killed; as sorrowful, yet always rejoicing; as poor, yet making many rich; as having nothing, and yet possessing all things."

Paul seems a little surprised himself at this rapid flow of his thoughts and feelings. He adds: "O Corinthians, my mouth is open to you, my heart is enlarged." But I have quoted this passage, not for its unsurpassed eloquence, but as illustrating the peculiar inspiration of the New Testament, by which every human faculty seems sharpened, thought quickened, language exalted. Every one of these clauses might be analyzed and expanded into a chapter, each is so compact with meaning.

The result of this comparison is that the inspiration of the Vedas is the expression of the Divine element in nature, its glory, beauty, power, beneficence. The inspiration of the Avesta is the perception of the Divine strength of a righteous cause in conflict with evil, or "the power not ourselves which makes for righteousness." The inspiration of the Buddhist sacred books is the contemplation of the law of cause and effect, by which every tree must bear its own fruit, and by which virtue is carried up higher and wickedness sent down lower, according to inflexible natural laws. The inspiration of the Old Testament is the vision of an Omnipotent, Omniscient, and All-good Ruler, whose providence guides all men and all things, and in whom every good man is safe, and every good life sure to be blessed. Here the personal relation between God and his child begins to come in. This gives its heavenly charm to the Book of Psalms, their sublime majesty to the strains of the prophets. And the inspiration of the New Testament is in the consciousness of a Divine life in the soul, of intimate and constant union with the Perfect Love, which unites the highest being in the universe with the humblest child. Higher than this it cannot go, for this is the fullness of Him who fills all in all.

§ 7. *Art the child of Religion. Egyptian architecture.*

We will now pass on to consider Art in all religions. Art itself, in all its methods, is the child of religion. The highest and best works in architecture, sculpture, and painting, poetry and music, have been born out of the religious nature. The most sublime structures in all times and in all lands have been temples to the unseen powers.

Some four or five thousand years have passed since the Pyramids were erected, and they are still the grandest architectural work ever accomplished by the genius of man. Through all these centuries they have declared his faith in an invisible world; they stand as records of his belief in immortality and in a resurrection. As they now rise, rude and disjointed, stripped of their casing, they still give the impression of indestructible solidity.

These artificial mountains, in the midst of the vast sandy African plains, have a mountainous grandeur. What must they have been, when their sides were covered from base to summit with polished blocks of granite fitted so exactly that the blade of a penknife could not penetrate the lines of juncture, and their polished surfaces wholly covered with inscriptions and carved with sculpture. Loftier than the highest spire of Europe, the Great Pyramid widened out into a still more enormous base, containing ten millions of cubic yards of stone, enough to build a wall two feet thick and six feet high from Boston to San Francisco. The interior is equally astonishing from the mechanical skill displayed in its construction. An eminent architect, Mr. Fergusson, says: —

> "Nothing can be more wonderful than the knowledge displayed in the discharging chambers over the rooms of the principal apartment, to throw off the crushing weight of stone above; in the exact slopes of the galleries; the provision of ventilating shafts; all so precisely arranged that notwithstanding the immense superincumbent weight, no settlement can anywhere be detected to the extent of an appreciable fraction of an inch."

By the side of the Pyramids stands the colossal Sphinx, of the same period, carved of solid rock, an enormous statue ninety feet long and seventy-four high, image of a funereal god, the genius of the setting sun. "It seems," says Ampère, "like an eternal spectre. This stone phantom appears attentive; one would say it hears and sees. Its great ear collects the sounds of the past; its eyes, directed to the East, gaze into the future; an image of perfect calm, contemplating the unchangeable in the midst of all change."

The Labyrinth, described by Herodotus, and fifteen hundred years after by Lepsius, was as enormous a work as the Pyramids. It contained three thousand chambers of stone, with vast courts and ranges of columns, and was a vast catacomb for dead princes and priests.

The ruins of the sacred city of Thebes are still so imposing that the French army under Desaix, pursuing the Mamelukes, in want of everything, without food, fainting with the heat, no sooner got sight of the ruins of Thebes, than they forgot their sufferings and their dangerous enemy, and began to clap their hands with delight. "Imagination," says Champollion, "sinks with awe before the one hundred and forty colossal columns of the Temple of Karnak." "Conceive," says Ampère, "a forest of towers, each as large as that in the centre of the Place Vendôme, eleven feet in diameter, the capitals sixty-five feet in circumference, seventy feet high, each as large as the trunk of an enormous tree, in a hall three hundred and nineteen feet long, and one hundred and fifty wide, entirely roofed over with stone, and all the surface carved with sculpture." And this vast interior is only one building in a city of temples, arcades, avenues of sphinxes, and colossal statues. The Temple of Karnak itself is twelve hundred feet long, and three hundred and sixty wide, twice the area of St. Peter's at Rome, "one of the largest," says Fergusson, "as well as the most beautiful in the world." He goes on to say that in its beauty, its massiveness of form, wonderful lights and shadows, and brilliancy of decoration, it is the greatest architectural work of man.

§ 8. *Buddhist Architecture.*

If we pass from Egypt to Asia we find the most extraordinary and beautiful works of architecture, as the direct product of the Buddhist religion. Though described as atheism, it has built some of the grandest temples for the worship of God; though said to have no belief in a future life, its dagobas, or shrines of saints, are innumerable, and covered with exquisite carvings; though accused of denying the existence of the soul, its monasteries for the devotional life of anchorites, carved out of solid rock, are older than the coming of Christ.

One Buddhist temple in Java, that of Boro Buddor, is a pyramid, rising in nine terraces, covered with carved spires and cupolas of various forms, the chief of which cover four hundred and thirty-six niches, occupied by as many statues of Buddha, as large as life. Between these are numerous bas-reliefs, and below them, on the lower story, is an immense bas-relief, sixteen hundred feet long, running round the whole building, and representing scenes from the life of Buddha. All these are on the outside, but the inner faces of the five ranges of buildings are still more profusely and minutely ornamented with figures and carvings, to an extent (says Fergusson, from whom this account is taken) unrivaled by any other buildings in any part of the world. Not far off is a group of two hundred and forty temples, all richly ornamented, in every one of which was a seated carved figure.

This Buddhist architecture extends over all of eastern Asia. It early assumed the three forms of topes or pagodas, which are lofty buildings containing the relics of Buddhist saints; monasteries, some of which are so large as to contain ten thousand or twenty thousand monks; and temples, for worship. These buildings are found in India, Ceylon, Burmah, Thibet, Tartary, China, Japan, and every other Buddhist country, and go back for their beginning to two or three centuries before Christ. As soon as the religion was well established, its peculiar architecture sprang up. Every great religion has produced its own special type of architecture. The style of ancient Egypt is massive; its idea is undecaying immortality. The idea of the Buddhist is of sacred shrines, tombs lifted into the air, so that the worshippers might look up at the pagoda, in which were contained the holy relics. The Greek temples were for a worship of display: visible pageants, not dark interiors for hidden mysteries as in Egypt; but lovely façades, where the spirit of intellectual beauty is made manifest, where every apparently straight line is tenderly curved to satisfy the fastidious Hellenic eye; where proportion, measure, restraint, unity, show to us art at the highest point ever reached on earth, — the glory of Greece, and the despair of the rest of mankind. But the Greek temples took their form from the nature of the religion, which was one of festivals and out-door ceremonies. The exterior was everything, the interior a mere cell to contain the priestly apparatus, or at most a chamber for an image. The colonnades around the Parthenon were for the purpose of an ambulatory, where on festivals the processions marched round and round between the columns, appearing and disappearing to the eyes of the people gazing up from below. Such was the Parthenon and the Temple of Jupiter at Athens, the latter having two rows of columns and two aisles along its sides, three rows of columns on the back and four rows in front.

§ 9. *Jewish and Christian Architecture.*

The object of the Jewish temple was entirely different, and consequently its magnificent architecture was wholly opposed in style to that of Greece. The Hellenic worship was visible worship, to be seen by all; so its decorations were on the outside of the temple.

The Jewish worship was exclusive; therefore, thick and high walls of stone surrounded the temple, with gates so massive that it took twenty men to open and close them every morning and evening. The beautiful colonnades and gates were all inclosed within this wall, so that the building was in fact a fortress, and so defensible that it resisted the assaults of the Roman engines long after the rest of the city was taken. Even the outer court of the Gentiles, further than which they might not penetrate under pain of death, was thus shut in; and the courts of the Jews, of the women, of the priests, and the holy place itself, were surrounded by other walls. An exclusive holiness was the type of this style of architecture.

The pointed or Gothic architecture of the middle ages sprang up in like manner out of the character of Christian worship. The Greek temples were beautiful without, to be seen by all men. The Jewish were glorious within, for the exclusive worship of a chosen people. Those of Egypt were significant of mysteries, and to their dark interiors only the initiated were admitted. But Christianity, whose nature it was to fulfill in itself all forms of righteousness, built its cathedrals beautiful both without and within. The exterior, in which the perpendicular line predominates, indicated the aspiration of all human souls to heaven. The interior, whose lofty aisles and domes sheltered with protecting roof the worshippers, spoke of the divine love which bends around every trusting heart to comfort and bless. The stained glass admitted the common light of day, but made it speak, as it passed in through saintly forms, of a Christian holiness, given to lighten every man who comes into the world. Thus Christian ideas created a new style of art, before unknown, and which no one could have predicted before it arrived. In one or two centuries it covered Europe with the marvelous beauty of its cathedrals, as in Antwerp, Cologne, Strasburg, Friburg in Belgium and Germany; at Pisa and Milan in Italy; Salisbury, Canterbury, and York in England; and in many other like examples.

§ 10. *Mohammedan Art.*

Perhaps, however, there is no more striking example of the power of a new faith to create a wholly new style of art than in the case of Mohammedanism. The sudden rise and rapid spread of Islam is one of the most startling events in the history of mankind. In one or two centuries this great wave swept from Arabia westward across Africa to the Atlantic, rolling on in a flood of conquest into Spain, and to the east pushing over Syria and Persia into India and Turkistan. And out of this movement came a new form of civilization, new inventions and discoveries, a new literature, and finally new forms of art. Especially the Saracenic architecture extended itself from India on the east to western Spain, carrying all its peculiarities, its delicate forms, exquisite tracery, lofty minarets, egg-shaped or bulb-shaped domes, and long arcades. Being as exclusive a religion as that of the Jews, it usually confined its ornaments to the interior, and had vast courts within for its worshippers. The numerous domes of this style seem to symbolize the protecting dome of sky, type of the unity of God in its vast, undivided expanse, its infinite depth and all-surrounding presence. The minarets express the perpetual declaration of faith in one God and his prophet, and its call on all people to receive his teaching. The whole architecture shows the combined activity, poetic tendency, and quick, light movements of the Saracenic races.

Thus is art the child of religion, every form of religion producing its own form of art, for

"Out of thought's interior sphere
These wonders rose to upper air."

So sculpture, appearing first on the walls of Egyptian temples, passed into Greece, and in that human religion, where all the gods were men and women, created its marvelous statues. At Athens rose the colossal form of the divine virgin Pallas-Athené, carved of gold and ivory. Tranquil serenity, serious purpose, self-conscious power and clear-sighted intellect were the characteristics of this goddess, and it is to the credit of the Athenians that they chose such a pure being for the guardian of their city. Still more wonderful was the Phidian Jupiter at Olympia, whose majesty was such that it was an event in life to have seen it, and not to have seen it before death one of the greatest of calamities.

§ 11. *Greek Art.*

It has hardly been noticed that the elevated character of the Greek religion is due, not to the poets, but to the sculptors and philosophers. Homer and Hesiod were severely blamed by the more serious Greeks, for presenting the deities as often frivolous and sometimes immoral. Such gods as they described, were hardly objects of reverence. The Greeks had no sacred books and no prophets; instead of sacred books they had their wonderful statues; instead of prophets, such teachers as Socrates and Plato. The dialogues of Plato were the real Bible of the Athenians. But how elevating must have been the impression made by the noble statues of the gods, in which there is nothing trivial, nothing impure; which are calm, wise, serene, benignant. Each of the gods seems to have a typical expression of face and form, significant of mental and moral elevation. The Olympian Zeus took its highest form in the soul of Phidias. All succeeding artists followed the type which he created, the leonine masses of hair, falling grandly on either side of the face, the calm brow, the wide-open eyes full of contemplation and authority, the delicate gentleness of the cheek and lip, the full beard with wavy tresses, the large chest, dignified and expressing at once power and benignant will. How much higher is this than Homer's Zeus who vaunts himself strong enough to lift the gods and the world by mere physical force. Heré, Demeter, Pallas, and Artemis were types of the same kind, all indicating noble purity of soul. Heré, or Juno, is a queen and mother, uniting majesty and unfading bloom, a matron always young, to whom all kinds of evil are abhorrent. The best expression of this may be seen in the colossal head in the Ludovisi villa. The Greeks must have learned from her that it is the business of the mothers to keep the state pure. Demeter, whom the Romans called Ceres, shows the kind womanly heart which goes out in sympathy with the children of men. She is the goddess softened by suffering, who seeks her lost daughter through the earth. This was a type of character very interesting to the mind of antiquity, shown also in the sad Isis searching for the remains of the dead Osiris. The sculptors gave still another variation of this theme of womanly purity in Artemis (or Diana), the goddess living in the depths of shady woods, vowed to chaste seclusion. This conception was developed by the sculptors Scopas and Praxiteles. Hers is one of the few Greek statues representing rapid motion. She seems like moonlight flashing among the leaves, an untouched, inaccessible goddess, separated from human passions or worldly desires. Her brother Phœbus resembles her, in the light, youthful form of the limbs. He is god of the joyful spring-time, type of health and order, who purifies the soul by music, who represents genius and inspiration, as Dionusos stands for geniality and excitement.

Another celestial form, the creation of these inspired artists, was that of Pallas-Athené, the noble virgin, a defender against evil, the guardian of her well-beloved city. In her form and face purity was confirmed by wisdom. Clear intelligence looked out of her eyes; and she was the wise protector of all who carry on useful arts with discretion. In Heré, the Greeks expressed woman's natural hostility to vice; in Pallas they showed her natural love of peaceful and useful activity. Thus we may say that these inspired artists created the highest form of Greek religion, and kept always before the eyes of a worshipping people the divine attributes of purity, wisdom, serene benignity, and noble elevation of soul. What the philosophers did to lead upward the minds of the thoughtful, the sculptors accomplished for the mass of the Greek people.

Of Greek painting we know very little. The names only of such artists as Zeuxis and Apelles have come down to us, with some little description of their peculiar styles. Apelles claimed for himself grace as his special merit, and hence must have been the Raffaelle of antiquity. The earlier painters, Polygnotus and his contemporaries, had more religious depth and simplicity, and so must have resembled Fra Angelico and the Pre-Raffaelites, but like these were ignorant of the technicalities of art. What the Greeks called skiagraphy, and the moderns chiaro-oscuro, came later. But in Zeuxis and the later artists, who had all these secrets of shade and color, Aristotle missed the "ethos" or moral tone of the earlier school, just as we miss it in the successors of Fra Angelico.

§ 12. *Religion in Painting and Poetry.*

We know well how much the painters of Italy and Germany have done for religion, and how much it has done for them. The best inspiration of Michael Angelo and Raffaelle are seen in their great religious subjects. The sublimity of the Old Testament was the inspiration of the one, the tenderness of the Gospels gave spiritual life to the work of the other. Who that has seen the wonders of the Sistine Chapel, or has studied the fine engravings from the Prophets and Sibyls in our art museums, but has better understood the solemn souls of Isaiah and Jeremiah? Michael Angelo has brought together, side by side, the two kinds of heavenly insight, as shown in man and woman. Study the Prophets and the Sibyls; and you find in one more of fire, in the other more of calm; in the Prophets majestic energy of will, in the Sibyls a greater depth of human sympathy; insight in one turns to wisdom in the other. And passing from these to Raffaelle, beside the angelic grace of his forms, we see in the unfathomable eyes of the infant Jesus a vision of a higher world than this, — a Kingdom of Heaven above us and yet near.

Poetry also received at first its inspiration from religion. It soared upward to Heaven in the Vedic hymns, the litanies of the Avesta, the poems to the gods carved on the Egyptian temples, the Psalms of David, and the sublime strains of the book of Job. In Greece nearly all the poetry was connected with religion, as the hymns of Hesiod and Homer, the odes of Pindar, and the great Dramas. In modern times two of the greatest poets, Dante and Milton, have been controlled by a religious inspiration. And how powerful to move, to soften, to uplift the soul, has been the hymnal of Christendom. It has accompanied Christianity from the beginning, from the time when Paul told the disciples to sing together in psalms and hymns and spiritual songs, down through the hymns of the middle ages, the "Dies iræ, Dies illa," hymns to the Virgin, hymns to the Spirit, those of Luther, Watts, Wesley, and all the others whose strains constitute so large a part of our worship, making the true church catholic and universal.

Thus in all times the highest inspiration is born out of religion. It works by a half-unconscious power, creating a new heaven of beauty and a new earth of sweetness and charm. In all ages, entering into holy souls, it has made of them prophets of beauty and sublimity to their race. Not confined to Christianity, religion has had prophets since the world began, and has not been without its witness in every land on which God smiles. One interior light, it enters every waiting soul, and enables it to do some good work; something to help or bless the human race.

CHAPTER X.

ETHICS IN ALL RELIGIONS.

§ 1. The moral sentiment in man. First element; the idea of Right and Wrong. § 2. Second element; knowledge of what is right and wrong. Third element: Habits of virtue. § 3. The basis of Ethics immutable. Primal convictions. Truth and Love. The place of utility in ethics. § 4. Manly and womanly virtues. § 5. Morality among primitive races. § 6. The races of Africa. § 7. Development of moral impulse in character. Romans and Greeks. Socrates. The Stoics. § 8. Ethics of Buddhism. § 9. Ethics in ancient Egypt. The oldest book of the world. § 10. Influence of Religion on Morality.

§ 1. *The moral sentiment in man. First element; the Idea of Right and Wrong.*

MY purpose in the present chapter is to speak of morality and ethics in all religions. I shall treat, first, of the ideas of right and wrong among the primitive races. Secondly, of the same ideas as taught in the ethnic religions. Thirdly, as they are taught in the monotheistic religions, and notably in Christianity.

But before entering on this discussion, we must understand what morality is. Man is a moral being because he possesses a moral sentiment, moral ideas, and a moral power. The moral sentiment is the sense of right and wrong, producing the feeling of duty and obligation. Moral ideas consist in the belief that certain acts are right, and others wrong. Moral power is the ability to do what is right, and to refuse to do what is wrong.

Let us consider any moral act, and see how these three elements enter into it. A poor and hungry boy sees a loaf of bread in an open window. He is strongly urged by hunger to take it. But he knows that it is wrong to take what does not belong to him; he feels that he ought not to do what he knows or believes to be wrong; he, therefore, puts forth an effort and goes away, resisting the temptation.

This example will stand as a type of every moral act of which men or angels are capable. Into every such action these three elements of feeling, thought, and will must enter. Omit either, and there would be no morality.

In the case just cited there was a strong temptation, and a strong effort of the will to resist the temptation. This, however, is not essential to a moral action. The highest form of morality is that in which no effort is required to do right; when right-doing has become a part of the nature. It requires a great effort in a miser to give a small sum to a starving child. It requires no effort in a benevolent man to give his whole income to good objects, for he finds his best pleasure in so doing. There is more merit in the first instance, but there is a higher goodness in the other. The latter possesses what in the striking language of the Bible is called "The Beauty of Holiness." So long as the effort to do right is visible, this beauty has not arrived.

The sense of right and wrong is a primitive element in the soul. It cannot be analyzed or resolved into anything more simple. All such attempts lead only to mental and moral confusion. To trace it back to a sensation of pleasure is to confound things wholly different. The desire for pleasure is one thing, the sense of obligation an entirely different thing. They are not only different, but often opposed, as in the instance of the hungry boy above mentioned. The desire for pleasure would have induced him at once to take the bread, if he could have done so without being seen. The sentiment of duty forbade his doing it; the two then were in exact opposition.

This first element of morality is not only primal, but also universal. It is one and the same thing, wherever it exists. The sense of an eternal distinction between right and wrong and of the eternal obligation to do what is right and to refuse to do what is wrong, must be the same in the child and the archangel. Kant found in it the proof of the being of God, since it goes down so deep, and goes up so high, and speaks with the absolute authority which belongs to God alone. The desire for pleasure speaks with no such voice of command. We are not bound by any obligation to seek enjoyment. But the awful voice of conscience listens to no excuse, allows of no apology. It says, "Do right, though the heavens fall."

§ 2. *Second element. Knowledge of what is right and wrong. Third element. Habits of virtue.*

The second element in morality is that of knowledge. In order to do right, we must know what right is. This is the domain of ethics, of instruction, of education. What some people think right, others believe to be wrong. Where some see a duty to be done, others find an error to be avoided. This is the part of morality which can be taught. The world advances in virtue, by seeing more clearly what its duty is.

The third element in morality is the habit of doing what we believe to be right. Many persons see their duty but fail to do it.

> "Video meliora, proboque — deteriora sequor."

> "I know what 's right, and I approve it too —
> Condemn the wrong, and yet the wrong pursue."

It would not be necessary to give this analysis of morality, were it not that so many theories are put forth which prevent all clear thought on these questions. For example, Buckle tells us that there is no change, and no progress in moral systems; that the rules of morality are as well understood in one age as in another. His words are these: "To do good to others; to sacrifice for their benefit your own wishes; to love your neighbor as yourself; to forgive your enemies; to restrain your passions; to respect those who are set over you, — these, and a few others, are the sole essentials of morals; but they have been known for thousands of years, and not one jot or tittle has been added to them by all the sermons and text-books of moralists and theologians."[1] Hence Buckle argues that there is no such thing as improvement in morality.

On the other hand, the utilitarian school of moralists assert that there is nothing fixed; no foundation of moral truth; that all is in progress. Paley expresses this doctrine most forcibly. He says that there is hardly a vice or crime which has not been considered right in some country or some period; that theft was rewarded in Sparta; that to put to death little children, or aged parents, has been thought proper in some places; that the Indians approve of cruelty; that Paul thought it his duty to persecute the Christians.

[1] Mr. Buckle has omitted, in this list, truth, honesty, and temperance.

If we recur to the positions we have taken in regard to the three elements of morality, we shall find that Buckle's view is true as regards one element of virtue, and Paley's as regards another.

§ 3. *The basis of Ethics immutable. Primal convictions. Truth and Love. The place of utility in ethics.*

There is an immutable basis to ethics, though not exactly what Buckle assumes. The sentiment of right is always the same. It may be stronger or weaker, greater in quantity in some periods, less in others, but its quality is unchangeable.

There are also two moral convictions which are to be found in all races, from the lowest to the highest. These are of justice and mercy, or truth and love. Everywhere it has been accounted a duty to be just to others, not to take what belongs to them, to pay one's debts, to tell the truth, to keep one's promises, to be faithful to one's engagements. This is radical in morality. And again it has always been considered morally beautiful to do actions of kindness, of charity, to be benevolent to the poor, to be hospitable to strangers, to return good for evil. There is, therefore, not only a fundamental sentiment of right, but these two fundamental ideas of right.

But these ideas of justice and mercy are often found in apparent conflict. Justice requires one course, mercy another. Which ought we to follow? Truth demands this action, love that; what ought we to do? All the cases of conscience, all practical problems of morals, arise from this antagonism of two fundamental ideas. When we have a real difficulty in knowing what we ought to do, we shall usually find that truth requires one course of action and love another.

It is at this point of conflict that the doctrine of utility comes in; and here comes in also the possibility of progress in morality. We find out, more and more, what course of action is, on the whole, for the best, and how we can do what is right without sacrificing either justice or mercy. This constitutes the ethical education of mankind; and the moral progress of the world consists in the gradual lifting up of the moral ideal, as well as in an increasing moral enthusiasm for goodness. Better knowledge of what is right, and a stronger impulse to do it, marks the history of the growth of mankind in virtue.

The two types of morality which I have designated as rooted, one in the idea of justice, the other in that of mercy, are to be found among all people; in a rudimentary condition among the primitive races, more developed in the more civilized. Assuming that most of our moral actions have justice and mercy at their foundation, we shall find them constituting two families, or groups of qualities. The justice-group includes honesty, truthfulness, obedience to law, courage to do, fortitude to endure, and the love of individual freedom. The mercy-group of virtues includes sympathy with suffering, hospitality to strangers, domestic affection, loyalty to one's chief, the love of fame or glory, kindly manners, civility, and the desire for equality.

Some races by a natural instinct or by acquired habit, lean more to one of these classes of virtues; and other races to its opposite. Take for example the English and French. The English virtues are those belonging to the group of which justice is the root. The French qualities to those of mercy. The English are truthful, the French, civil. The English believe in honesty, in keeping one's word, in faithfulness to all contracts, obedience to law. The French are more kindly, more sympathetic, are remarkable for the strength of their domestic affections, have a great love of glory, are fond of approbation. The English care greatly for freedom, demand their individual rights, wish to be governed as little as possible, but do not care much for equality. They rather prefer to have an aristocracy to look up to. The French love equality, dislike aristocrats, are democratic in every fibre of their being, but are willing to be governed by any Louis XIV. or Napoleon who will give them national glory. They will die for their chief, but wish him to speak to them as a comrade or equal.

These distinctions may be traced throughout the Teutonic races on one side, and the Keltic races on the other.

§ 4. *Manly and Womanly Virtues.*

All the virtues may be distributed in a large way into these two classes, the manly and the womanly virtues.

The manly virtues include conscientiousness, courage, justice, love of truth, independence, reverence for right, and love of freedom. The womanly virtues include benevolence, prudence, sympathy with suffering, reverence, hospitality, domestic affection, loyalty to one's chief, desire of approbation, love of beauty, kindly manners, universal charity, and love of equality. The manly and womanly virtues are both necessary to make a good moral character; both should be united in every man and every woman. Not only is neither class by itself adequate, but any one of them, unless united with the opposite, loses its own quality and becomes a vice instead of a virtue. Thus the virtue of courage, unless joined with the virtue of prudence and caution, ceases to be courage, and becomes rashness. So the virtue of benevolence or sympathy, unless joined with the virtues of conscientiousness and independence, will degenerate into a transient emotion of weak sentimentalism. These cannot exist as virtues unless united with their antagonist qualities. Independence unbalanced by humility becomes pride; firmness without reverence for others turns into obstinacy. The desire to be approved and esteemed, unless joined with the love of truth and right, runs into vanity.

What we mean then by distinguishing these as manly and womanly virtues is only this: That the natural man, without culture, tends more to one, and the woman more to the other. The most courageous and heroic among men have been those who added to their courage, tenderness; to their independence, reverence. This union constituted the chivalric character of a Bayard, who was not only without fear, but without reproach; of a Douglas, who was not merely true, but also tender; of Jeanne d' Arc, whose unflinching courage enhances her womanly sweetness and purity. Each grace can only attain its own perfection when it has the opposite for its companion. The manly virtues culminate in truth, and the womanly in love. But truth without love is not fully truth, and love without truth is not love. In God both are perfectly one, and man approaches the divine perfection only as he unites both in himself.

§ 5. *Morality among Primitive Races.*

It is extremely difficult to ascertain the moral character of the primitive races. The reports concerning them have come from travelers who usually were only a short time in the country; who did not, perhaps, understand the language; who were suspected and avoided and, perhaps, regarded as enemies by those who had been ill-treated by previous visitors; and who judged of the character of a people by their own personal experience. So English travelers visiting America pronounce a judgment on our national life derived from their experiences in railroad stations, Western hotels, or among the hackmen at Niagara. So too Americans, after a few weeks in France or Italy, decide *ex cathedrâ* on French or Italian civilization by judgments derived from their observations among *commissionaires* and couriers.

Many travelers show by their self-contradictory statements concerning them their inability to observe the people they visit. Thus Mariner reports that the Tongans, or Friendly Islanders, are loyal, pious, obedient children, affectionate parents, kind husbands, modest and faithful wives, and true friends; and are at the same time without any words for justice and injustice, and do not regard theft, revenge, and murder as crimes; that they see no harm in seizing a ship and murdering the crew; that the men are cruel, treacherous, and treat their wives badly, but live happily with them; and that domestic quarrels are seldom known. Other writers say that the Tongans unite a remarkable mildness with great courage. They are brave, but do not boast of their valor. Mariner himself tells us of a young warrior who was called up and praised by the king for an act in which courage and generosity were united. The youth blushed, and went modestly back to his place, and never boasted of what he had done.

The inhabitants of the Navigators' Islands are described as being "hospitable, affectionate, honest, and courteous." They are very warm-hearted, and "their honesty is really wonderful." On one occasion a European vessel went ashore on the rocks, and the whole of its cargo was at the mercy of the Samoans, but not a man stole anything, and the property was taken charge of for its owners. In how many Christian countries would not the wreckers have carried off the whole cargo!

Courtesy among the Samoans is regarded as one of the duties of life. The early voyagers were struck by the gentle demeanor, perfect honesty, scrupulous cleanliness, graceful costume, and polished manners of this people. One of the chiefs had a large number of presents given to him by the captain of an English vessel, such as knives, scissors, needles. He took each one separately, laid it on his head, and returned thanks for it, and then returned thanks for the whole. Then he turned to his people and said: "The English chiefs have given us all these presents, now let us give them in return something to eat, for there are no pigs running about on the sea, nor any bread-fruit growing there." On hearing this the whole company ran away, and returned bringing a large quantity of pigs, bread-fruit, and yams, and presented them to the English. We have dwelt on the good morals of this particular people because the description is unquestionably correct; because it shows us a race in whom good morals and manners have grown up without any influence from without, they having lived for thousands of years alone on their islands, and because they united the two classes of virtues, viz., that of courage and honesty with that of kindness and courtesy, and both in a high degree. We certainly ought not to call such a people savages.

§ 6. *The Races of Africa.*

The negroes of Africa have been charged with all sorts of vices and crimes, theft, cruelty, treachery, disregard of life. But it must be remembered that the negroes of whom we have usually heard, have been for centuries corrupted by the slave-traders, both on the eastern and western shores of the continent. Foreigners have come among them to steal men and women, and have murdered thousands and tens of thousands in the operation. What wonder that the Africans should retaliate on foreigners in the same way. But the travelers who have penetrated the interior, like Du Chaillu,

Livingstone, and Stanley, and who have convinced the natives that they came as friends, have met with warm hospitality; have found them true to their engagements; have left them in charge of what to them was untold wealth, and have had it taken care of and faithfully restored again. They have, in short, found the rudimentary forms of the kingly and queenly virtues of truth and love, justice and mercy, united in the hearts of these benighted heathens.

Du Chaillu says that the Aponos, a merry race, who live near the equator, were an honest people, and stole nothing from him, and that some of them always took his part in any dispute which arose.

Livingstone, whose rule in going among the negro tribes was to make them feel that he was one of themselves, and that he loved them, was met everywhere by a responsive good will. When he died, hundreds of miles from the coast, and with no white man near, his faithful negro servants carried his body, his papers, and other valuables, all the way to the sea. His biographer says, —

"If anything is needed to commend the African race, and prove it to be fitted to make a noble nation, the courage, affection, and persevering loyalty shown by his attendants after his death is sufficient. It was a great, difficult, and dangerous work to carry his body to Zanzibar. It took nine long months of toil to do this. They dried the body in the sun, wrapt it in calico, inclosed it in a bark cylinder, sewed a piece of sailcloth round all, and set out. They were not themselves well; they had to make their way through hostile tribes, and though a white party who met them urged them to bury the remains, and not run the risk of carrying them further, they were inflexible, and persevered."

Such are the virtues which already appear in primitive man, rudimentary virtues, indeed, but partaking of the qualities of both the types described above. In courage, in loyalty to friends and tribe, in fidelity to engagements, honest dealings, we find the truth-cycle in its early forms; in hospitality, kindness to those in need, and domestic affection, we see the beginning of the love-cycle.

Proceeding onward from the primitive races and religions to national life and the ethnic religions, let us see what progress there is in morals.

§ 7. *Development of moral impulse in character. Romans and Greeks. Socrates. The Stoics.*

This important fact we immediately discover: that what is moral impulse in the child-like races grows up into principle and character in the higher forms of human life. We find this eminently among the ancient Greeks and Romans. In the national life of both races there are numerous and well-known examples of high moral character.

The Greeks were to the Romans as the French to the English. In both instances the nation nearer the rising sun was more vivacious, alert, active; had more tact and ardor, a greater love of fame and glory; that to the West was more strong, solid, fixed in principles, practical, believing in justice and law. Their virtues shared these characteristics. The morality of the Roman, like that of the English, belonged to the cycle of justice; the Greek morality to the cycle of kindness, mercy, and sympathy.

Of the Roman virtues in their sterner form such men as Coriolanus, Brutus, and the two Catos are examples. The sense of justice appears developed to the utmost degree of strength in the character of the younger Cato. We read, in our Plutarch, that from his youth he displayed, even in his look and in his amusements, solidity and inflexible purpose. When he was fourteen years old, during the tyranny of Sylla, whose house was like a place of execution, seeing the heads of many citizens carried out whom Sylla had murdered, he said: "Why does not some one kill that man?" "Because," said his preceptor, "they fear him more than they hate him." "Give me a sword," said Cato, "that I may kill him and deliver my country." Though rich, he lived with extreme simplicity. "He carried," his biographer says, "an impulse like inspiration into every virtue; but his greatest attachment was to justice, and justice of that severe kind that is not to be wrought upon by compassion."

When asked why he did not speak in public, he said: "I am willing men shall blame my silence, provided they do not blame my life. I will speak when I have anything that is worth saying." He showed so much coolness and capacity as a soldier in the servile war that the general in command offered to reward him by promotion, but he peremptorily refused the honor, saying: "I have done nothing which deserves such notice." But there was a tender side to Cato's nature, as was shown by his devoted love for his brother, Cæpio. The shrewd observer, Plutarch, does not fail to remark this trait of tenderness in his character, and tells us that the affection which was universally felt for Cato by his soldiers is a proof of it; and adds that the virtue which only inspires respect and not love seldom influences the lives of others. Cato also gained great popularity by refusing the presents offered him, especially by the king of Galatia, who besought him to accept many valuable gifts, and if he would not take them himself to allow his friends to do so. Cato, who knew that these were bribes to secure his influence, sent back the presents, saying to his friends: "If I give them to you I am taking them myself. Corruption will never want a pretense. Never mind. I will share with you whatever I can gain honorably."

In these days, when the reform of the Civil Service occupies so many minds, the example of Cato is worth remembering. When he became Quæstor,—which was the same office as Secretary of the Treasury among ourselves,—he found that many abuses had crept in. Previous Quæstors had usually been young, and ignorant of the business, and thus had naturally left the direction of the Treasury to the under-officers, who had been there long, and were experienced in office. But Cato, before he became a candidate for this office, had made a thorough study of the whole subject, and took the reins into his own hands, putting an end to all such corruptions. In this way he made the Treasury as respectable as the Senate, and the office of Quæstor equal to that of Consul.

Cato's truthfulness was so well known that it became a proverb. "I would not believe that, even if Cato said it." All this severity made him, of course, obnoxious to those who had jobs, for they knew they could do nothing while Cato was in the way. One of these men he charged with bribery; the man was defended by Cicero, who undertook to ridicule the austere virtue of Cato, as of a man who was righteous overmuch. Cato merely remarked, "We have a very amusing Consul."

We find the same type of virtue in Greece in such men as Aristides, Phocion, and Timoleon, but less austere, less stern. You could not apply to them the phrase of Horace, "the atrocious soul of

Cato." But what a charming story is that of the proposal of Themistocles, showing the profound confidence inspired in the hearts of the people by the lofty virtues of Aristides. Themistocles told the people that he had a plan which would bring a great good to Athens, but it must be kept secret. The Assembly directed him to communicate it to Aristides alone, and they would abide by his decision. The plan of Themistocles was to seize the armed ships of all the Confederate Greeks, and so to make Athens the ruling power in Hellas. Aristides returned to the Assembly, and said: "Nothing could be of more advantage to Athens than the proposed scheme; but nothing could be more unjust." The democracy of Athens immediately commanded Themistocles to abandon all thought of this action.

And yet Themistocles seems a better representative of the Greek character than Aristides. Themistocles was consumed by the love of glory; he was intrepid, keen-witted, bright. He was a man who stood by his friends, right or wrong. His longing for renown was such that he said: "The trophies of Miltiades will not suffer me to sleep." Brave, full of resource in war, a great general, one of the saviors of Greece, by the force of his genius compelling his rivals to follow his ideas, he was still a dangerous man in times of peace. He was one of those who are possessed by the demon of ambition; he must be doing something extraordinary, good or bad. He was full of wit. But he sometimes met with a keen retort. Attempting to levy a large contribution from the Greeks of Andria, he told them: "I have brought with me two gods, Persuasion and Force," to which they replied: "We also have two still more powerful gods on our side, Poverty and Despair."

Phocion was an Athenian who resembled Cato in self-control and self-denial. Ridiculed for his sternness by some triflers, he said: "My black looks never gave any of you an hour of sorrow; but the laughter of my critics has cost many a tear." Being asked, before speaking in public, what he was thinking of, he answered: "I am thinking how I can shorten what I have to say." He never hesitated to resist the clamor of the multitude and the tumult of the citizens demanding wrong things. When the people were in a difficulty, and charged him with being the cause of it, he simply said: "Let us first escape from this danger, afterwards you may banish me, if you like." He would not allow them to rejoice at the death of their enemy, Philip, saying: "It would show that we were afraid of him, to express any satisfaction at his death." Alexander, who had a great respect for him, sent him a hundred talents. He refused the gift. The ambassador urged him to accept it, saying that Alexander offered it to him because he believed him to be the one honest man in Athens. "Then," said Phocion, "let him allow me to remain so."

Such are the anecdotes which the greatest of biographers has preserved for us concerning the nobility of character among the Greeks and Romans. What we see is this. We have ascended to the elevation where moral sensibilities, moral ideas, and moral actions have become organized into moral character. As far as we can see, the external influences which helped this development were the social life of Greece, and the political life of Rome. In Rome, devotion to the state, to the public good, was the atmosphere which men breathed. To serve the Roman people, to have the honor of becoming one of the chief citizens, to win the respect and gratitude and influence which came to him who deserved well of the republic, this was the ambition and pride of the noblest Romans. In Greece it was different. It was not so much power and respect, as fame and love which impelled the soul of the great Athenians. There were men of Roman fibre, no doubt, among the Greeks, like those we have mentioned; and men with Greek souls among the Romans, like the Gracchi and Cicero; but the religion of Rome was the state, the religion of Greece was glory.

One character, however, among the Greeks carried the moral element to a still higher degree.

Socrates does not seem to have cared for fame nor for power, except the power of reason with which to mould the hearts of the young and educate them to virtue. His religion was moral culture. He taught the art of self-culture in the streets of Athens. In one respect his method singularly resembles that of Christianity. In Christianity goodness springs from the two roots of humility and faith, self-distrust and trust in God, repentance and hope. And so Socrates always sought; first, to bring the young man whose soul was capable of culture to a sense of his moral and mental needs; and secondly, to animate him by the sight of the supreme beauty of goodness. He first brought him under conviction, by convincing him of his ignorance, and then inspired him with the hope of an insight like that of his master. Thus he taught the youth temperance, sobriety, the love of knowledge, the love of goodness, the worth of friendship, courage, and wisdom. He sought to take out of them their vanity, self-indulgence, and love of wealth, fame, and power, unless when these were deserved by great qualities. The conversation of Socrates with Euthydemus, as reported by Xenophon, is one of the best examples of his method. Euthydemus was an ambitious youth, who had collected many books, and read them, and imagined himself a superior person on that account. But he did not think it necessary to take any instruction, or to frequent the teaching of the wise.

Socrates meeting him one day said: —

"I hear, O Euthydemus, that you have many books, and that you read them diligently; that is a very good thing, much better than to spend one's money on pleasure. I suppose that you are studying some art or science. What is it? Do you propose to be a physician? An architect? An astronomer or geometrician?"

Euthydemus answered "No," to these questions.

"Then," said Socrates, "you mean perhaps to become a statesman and public man?"

Euthydemus admitted that he did.

"That," said Socrates, "is a noble pursuit. I suppose you will agree with me that a man who wishes to govern justly should know what justice is."

"Certainly, Socrates, and I think I know that very well."

"Suppose then," said Socrates, "that we make a list of just and unjust actions. We will put an A over the first, and B over the second."

"You may," said Euthydemus, "if you think it necessary."

"Begin then with lying. Is it just or unjust to lie?"

"Certainly," answered the youth, "it is unjust. Put that under B."

"But suppose, my Euthydemus, that you are a general, in command of the Athenian army. Would it be just in you to deceive your enemy, and so get an advantage over him?"

"In that case," said Euthydemus, "lying would be just."

"Is it wrong or right, O Euthydemus, to take property which does not belong to you?"

"It is wrong."

"The general then has no right to take the property of the enemy?"

"Of course he has a right," said Euthydemus; "in war everything is right against our enemies."

"Then we will take these cases from B and put them under A?"

"We may," said the disciple.

"I suppose," said Socrates, "you mean that in war, for a general to speak falsehood to the enemy is just, but to speak it to his friends is unjust?"

"That is what I mean."

"Suppose then," continued Socrates, "that the general, perceiving the courage of his troops to falter, should make them believe that new succor was at hand. Would that be just or unjust?"

"I think that would be just."

"Is it right to use violence to our friends against their will, and prevent them by force from doing what they wish, or is that unjust?"

"It is unjust."

"Then if your friend, in a fit of despair or insanity, should try to kill himself, you ought not to take the sword away by force; for that is what you just said?"

"I take back that opinion," said Euthydemus, "if I may be allowed to do so."

"Certainly," responded Socrates, "it is always far better to change our opinion than to persevere in a wrong one."

And so the dialogue goes on, till the poor youth is quite mortified at his own ignorance, and declares that he begins to believe that he does not know anything, and had better be silent altogether. But being of a generous temper, he did not suffer this mortification to estrange him from Socrates, but became one of his most devoted disciples.

In considering this character of Socrates, we perceive that he has led us up to a still higher region of ethics. To him goodness is something sacred in itself. The best Romans and Greeks had in their heart a desire for superiority over others, they wished the respect, or esteem, or affection, or praise, of the state and of their fellow-citizens. This was certainly not a wrong motive. But Socrates saw what the Bible calls the beauty of holiness, the divine quality of virtue, the infinite superiority of this to all other possessions. This was the faith that upheld him when he made his memorable defense, which one cannot read without being made better. This is what gave him the calm, sweet wisdom shown in the long day's discourse, of which his death was to be the end, which almost brings tears to our eyes after twenty-five centuries. Our only conclusion must be that of Elihu, "There is a spirit in man, and the inspiration of the Almighty giveth him understanding." That is all we can say. The noble qualities in the soul of

Socrates were given him by God. He was raised up to be a prophet to the whole civilized world, and by his lofty wisdom he was a Greek John the Baptist, preparing the way for a higher teacher than himself. Socrates certainly did not draw his inspiration from the festivals or ritual of the Greek religion. Neither the Greek nor Roman religion professed to teach any high spiritual or moral doctrines. The sculptors and the philosophers were the true religious teachers of both nations.

The best ethical teachers whom the Greeks and Romans possessed were to be found in the Stoical philosophers. We are made better to-day, and also wiser, by reading the works of Epictetus, Marcus Antoninus, and Seneca. They insist on all the manlier virtues, temperance, fortitude, truth, justice, purity. They make of life a discipline, a scene of moral gymnastics. You would not wish to live always in a gymnasium, only practicing athletic exercises, but as a strengthening process, to be used occasionally, there are few better helps than the writings of these great Stoics.

§ 8. *Ethics of Buddhism.*

Buddhism is a highly ethical religion. It is more a system of morality than a religion. Its moral impulse seems to have been derived from the life of its founder, and his character may be traced in all its history. A man of intense moral earnestness, profoundly sincere and truthful, he was still more profoundly humane. The woes of the world pressed heavily on his benignant heart. The whole system of Hindu caste, with its odious distinctions, was abhorrent to him. To his large mind all men were equal, and he sought to raise them to a peace of soul like his own, by showing them the laws of the universe and persuading them to accept these eternal laws as their rules of life. Obedience to the moral law, he believed, would remove at last all sin and all misery from the world. Consequently he went about, teaching this moral code, and his disciples have ever since done the same. Some of their ethical teachings are intended for the instruction of the Buddhist monks, and their minute analysis of right and wrong reminds us of the voluminous casuistry of the mediæval theology.

The Dhammapada is an ancient Buddhist work of the highest authority. The following extracts from the Dhammapada much resemble the tone of Jewish ethics as contained in the Book of Proverbs: —

"Earnestness is the path of immortality (Nirvâna), thoughtlessness the path of death. Those who are in earnest do not die; those who are thoughtless are as if dead already."

"By rousing himself, by earnestness, by restraint and control, the wise man may make for himself an island which no flood can overwhelm."

"Fools follow after vanity; men of sense, wisdom. The wise man keeps earnestness as his best jewel. Let the wise man guard his thoughts, for they are difficult to perceive, very artful, and they rush wherever they list: thoughts well guarded bring happiness. Long is the night to him who is awake; long is a mile to him who is tired; long is life to the foolish who do not know the true law."

"If a traveler does not meet with one who is his better, or his equal, let him firmly keep to his solitary journey; there is no companionship with a fool."

"The fool who knows his foolishness is wise at least so far. But a fool who thinks himself wise, he is called a fool indeed. He who drinks in the law lives happily with a serene mind; the sage rejoices always in the law, as preached by the elect (Aryas). The gods even envy him whose senses, like horses, well-broken in by the driver, have been subdued, who is free from pride, and free from appetites. . . . His thought is quiet, quiet are his word and deed, when he has obtained freedom by true knowledge, when he has thus become a quiet man. Though a man recite a hundred Gâthâs made up of senseless words, one word of the law is better, which, if a man hears, he becomes quiet."

"If one man conquer in battle a thousand times thousand men, and if another conquer himself he is the greatest of conquerors."

"He who always greets and constantly reveres the aged, four things will increase to him, viz: life, beauty, happiness, power."

"But he who lives a hundred years, vicious and unrestrained, a life of one day is better if a man is virtuous and reflecting."

"Let no man think lightly of evil, saying in his heart, 'It will not come nigh unto me.' Even by the falling of water-drops a water-pot is filled; the fool becomes full of evil, even if he gather it little by little."

"He who has no wound on his hand may touch poison with his hand; poison does not affect one who has no wound; nor is there evil for one who does not commit evil."

"If a man offend a harmless, pure, and innocent person, the evil falls back upon that fool like light dust thrown up against the wind."

"Self is the lord of self, who else could be the lord? With self well subdued, a man finds a lord such as few can find."

"Rouse thyself! do not be idle! follow the law of virtue! The virtuous rests in bliss in this world and in the next."

"Let us live happily then, not hating those who hate us! Among men who hate us let us dwell free from hatred! Health is the greatest of gifts, contentedness the best riches; trust is the best of relationships: Nirvâna the highest happiness. A man is not an elder because his head is gray; his age may be ripe, but he is called 'Old-in-vain.'"

"He in whom there is truth, virtue, love, restraint, moderation; he who is free from impurity, and is wise, he is called an elder."

§ 9. *Ethics in ancient Egypt. The oldest book of the world.*

The oldest texts of the Egyptian religion show the stress laid on morals in that ancient system of thought. I quote as follows, on this subject, from the Hibbert Lectures of Rhys Davids: —

"The triumph of right over wrong, of right in speech and action (for the same word signifies both truth and justice), is the burden of nine-tenths of the Egyptian texts which have come down to us. Right is represented as a goddess ruling as mistress over heaven and earth, and the world beyond the grave. The gods are said to live by it. Although funereal inscriptions are less to be depended upon when they describe the virtues of the deceased, than when they give the dates of his birth and death, they may at least be quoted in evidence of the rule of conduct by which actions were estimated. We are not obliged to believe that this or that man possessed all the virtues which are ascribed to him, but we cannot resist the conviction that the recognized Egyptian code of morality was a very noble and refined one. 'None of the Christian virtues,' M. Chabas says, 'is forgotten in it; piety, charity, gentleness, self-command in word and action, chastity, the protection of the weak, benevolence towards the humble, deference to superiors, respect for property in its minutest details, all is expressed there and in extremely good language."

The following are specimens of the praises which are put into the mouth of departed worthies: —

"Not a little child did I injure. Not a widow did I oppress. Not a herdsman did I ill-treat. There was no beggar in my days; no one starved in my time. And, when the years of famine came, I plowed all the lands of the province to its northern and southern boundaries, feeding its inhabitants, and providing their food. There was no starving person in it, and I made the widow to be as though she possessed a husband."

Of another great personage it is said that, in administering justice, "he made no distinction between a stranger and those known to him. He was the father of the weak, the support of him who had no mother. Feared by the ill-doer, he protected the poor; he was the avenger of those whom a more powerful one had deprived of property. He was the husband of the widow, the refuge of the orphan."

It is said of another that he was "the protector of the humble, a palm of abundance to the destitute, food to the hungry and the poor, largeness of hand to the weak;" and another passage implies that his wisdom was at the service of those who were ignorant.

The tablet of Beka, now at Turin, thus describes the deceased: —

"I was just and true without malice, placing God in my heart, and quick in discerning his will. I have come to the city of those who dwell in eternity. I have done good upon earth; I have done no wrong; I have done no crime; I have approved of nothing base or evil, but have taken pleasure in speaking the truth. There is no lowly person whom I have oppressed; I have done no injury to men who honored their gods. The sincerity and goodness which were in the heart of my father and my mother my love (paid back) to them. My mouth has always been opened to utter true things, not to foment quarrels. I have repeated what I have heard just as it was told to me."

Great stress is always laid in these inscriptions upon the strictest form of veracity, as, for instance, "I have not altered a story in the telling of it." The works of charity are commonly spoken of in terms which are principally derived from the Book of the Dead: —

"Doing that which is right and hating that which is wrong, I was bread to the hungry, water to the thirsty, clothes to the naked, a refuge to him that was in want; that which I did to him, the great God hath done to me."

"I was one that did that which was pleasing to his father and his mother; the joy of his brethren, the friend of his companions, noble-hearted to all those of his city. I gave bread to the hungry; I received (travelers?) on the road; my doors were open to those who came from without, and I gave them wherewith to refresh themselves. And God hath inclined his countenance to me for what I have done; he hath given me old age upon earth, in long and pleasant duration, with many children at my feet."

God's reward for well-doing is again mentioned in the inscription now at Miramar in honor of a lady who had been charitable to persons of her own sex, whether girls, wives, or widows: —

"My heart inclined me to the right when I was yet a child, not yet instructed as to the right and good. And what my heart dictated I failed not to perform. And God rewarded me for this, rejoicing me with the happiness which he has granted me for walking after his way."

We are acquainted with several collections of precepts and maxims on the conduct of life. The most venerable of them is the work of Ptahhotep, which dates from the age of the pyramids, and yet appeals to the authority of the ancients. It is undoubtedly, as M. Chabas called it, "The most ancient book of the world." The manuscript at Paris, which contains it, was written centuries before the Hebrew lawgiver was born. These books are very similar in character and tone to the Book of Proverbs in our Bible. They inculcate the study of wisdom, the duty to parents and superiors, respect for property, the advantages of charitableness, peaceableness, and content; of liberality, humility, chastity, and sobriety; of truthfulness and justice; and they show the wickedness and folly of disobedience, strife, arrogance, and pride; of slothfulness, intemperance, unchastity, and other vices.

The maxims of Ptahhotep speak of "God forbidding" and "God commanding": —

"If any one beareth himself proudly he will be humbled by God, who maketh his strength." "If thou art a wise man bring up thy son in the love of God." "Happy is the man who eateth his own bread. Possess what thou hast in the joy of thy heart. What thou hast not, obtain it by work. It is profitable for a man to eat his own bread; God grants this to whoever honors him." "Pray humbly with a loving heart, all the words of which are uttered in secret."

Another section is upon maternal affection. It describes the self-sacrifice of an affectionate mother from the earliest moments of the child's existence, and continues as follows: —

"Thou wast put to school, and whilst thou wast being taught letters she came punctually to thy master, bringing thee the bread and the drink of her house. Thou art now come to man's estate; thou art married and hast a house; but never do thou forget the painful labor which thy mother endured, nor all the salutary care which she has taken of thee. Take heed lest she have cause to complain of thee; for fear that she should raise her hands to God and he should listen to her prayer."

The religion of Zoroaster must be considered as highly moral in its influence, insisting on purity of thought, word, and action; on courage to oppose wrong and evil. It lays its chief stress on the truth-cycle of goodness, on the manly virtues. Herodotus said of the ancient Persians: "Lying is regarded as the most discreditable thing by them; next to that the incurring of debt, and chiefly for this reason, that the debtor must often tell lies."

§ 10. *Influence of Religion on Morality.*

We may now ask what is the influence exercised by the religions of mankind on the development of human morality.

Some attempt to produce good conduct, and to repress evil, by the hope of future reward, and the fear of future punishment. This was done very fully, as we have seen, in the Egyptian religion, which gave every Egyptian a full and detailed account of his resurrection, transmigrations, and future judgment before Osiris. Brahmanism and Buddhism are equally minute in their accounts of rewards and punishments hereafter, by the passage of the soul through innumerable heavens and hells, and transmigration through many bodies of animals, plants, and men.

How far such descriptions avail to prevent evil and encourage good is quite uncertain. A far-off and only half-believed retribution affects the imagination feebly. It is a curious and very noticeable fact that the religion of Moses teaches no such doctrine of future retribution. It appears nowhere in the Old Testament. A few texts may be strained to indicate something of the sort, but there is no plain, strong statement of a future judgment or moral retribution. Moses was acquainted with the whole Egyptian mythology on this subject, and must have deliberately refused to make use of this doctrine of future retribution as a sanction for his law. Reward and punishment in this world — not in the next — is the doctrine of the Old Testament. The moral influence of the teaching of Moses and the prophets is that they show the grandeur and nobleness of goodness; they rouse the higher nature in man; they purify and elevate all the moral sensibilities. Besides this, they show God, not far off, in another world, but close by in this present life. They give the sense of a watchful, ever-present Providence, Guardian, Judge. Such a sense of a Divine presence must always be the best defense and inspiration of the moral nature. For if the society and companionship of good or bad men exercises such an influence, how much more the society of a being who knows our inmost thoughts, and is the ideal of all moral purity.

There is still another influence exercised on morality by religion. This is the enthusiasm for goodness created by the sight of generous and noble lives. The ethical systems of books are dead and dry compared with this power which comes from a soul made alive by truth and love. Such souls are the great inspiration of the race, and virtue goes out of them, transmitted from age to age, to make the world better.

The great Brahmanical religion has its moral code in the Laws of Menu. They are very elaborate and go into many details. A large part of this book is devoted to ritual and priestly observances, to questions of rites and ceremonies, fasts and penances, and the details of the caste system. Here and there we find interesting passages; such, for instance, as these: —

> "The man who perceives in his own soul the supreme soul present in all creatures, acquires equanimity toward all, and will be resolved at last into the divine essence."
>
> "A Brahman should shun worldly honor as he shuns poison, and seek disrespect as he seeks nectar."
>
> "Let him say what is true, and also what is pleasing; let him speak no harsh truth, let him speak no pleasant falsehood."
>
> "The act of repeating the divine name is a hundred times better than sacrifice; if said alone, better still; if said in the depths of the soul, best of all."

Let us now return to our original definition of a moral act, which makes it consist in the three elements of sentiment, belief, and effort, or a feeling that we ought to do what is right, a belief that a certain act is right, and an effort to do what we believe is right. These constitute the spirit, the ethics, and the moral character of each race and each religion.

As we ascend from the lower races to the higher we find the moral sense to become more earnest, the ethical system more clear and elaborate, and the conduct more upright, truthful, benevolent, and pure. Morality is developed along this line of ascent through the races and religions of man. In some races there is more of one element; in others more of another element.

Finally, if we compare the morality of the New Testament with that of other sacred books and other religions, we see that its preëminence consists, not in giving any new ethical rules or methods, but in that it unites other moral teaching in a fullness of spiritual life. It gives to man the greatest work: to make God's kingdom come and cause his will to be done on earth as it is done in heaven. It furnishes the highest motive, — the love and grace of God dwelling in the heart. It sets before us the noblest ideal of goodness in the life and character of Jesus. It does not reveal maxims or laws of right never known before, but it turns duty into happiness, writes the law in the heart, helps us to walk in the spirit of love, and thus becomes a power to lift the world to the highest plane of peace and goodness.

CHAPTER XI.

IDEA OF A FUTURE STATE IN ALL RELIGIONS.

§ 1. Universal belief in a future state of existence. § 2. Notions concerning it among the Childlike Races. § 3. Belief of the ancient Etruscans. § 4. Of the Egyptians. § 5. Of Brahmanism. § 6. Of Buddhism. Meaning of Nirvâna. § 7. Of the Jews. The argument of Jesus with the Sadducees. § 8. How Religion produces faith in Immortality. § 9. The Poets and Philosophers. § 10. Two Sources of belief in a Future Existence. § 11. Modern scientific Unbelief. Spiritualism, and its evidences.

§ 1. *Universal belief in a future state of existence.*

PERHAPS the most remarkable fact in the comparative history of religions is the universal belief of mankind in a future state of existence after death.

"Placed on this isthmus of a middle state," with an unknown eternity behind him, and an unknown eternity before him, with a great gulf between this globe and the worlds which surround it, man has everywhere believed in a hereafter. No traveler returns from that bourne to tell us anything about it, at least, none return to throw light on the condition of departed souls. The wise, the good, the lovely no less than the ignorant, the vicious, the criminal, pass on in a long and never-ending procession into that darkness, and no one comes back to say to us where they have gone. But notwithstanding this, men have universally believed in another life. This is not because one race has received this faith as a tradition from another. It has sprung up, independently, in all parts of the world, and in all ages, among the ancient Egyptians and ancient Hindus, those who have lived in the frozen zone, and those who inhabit the burning regions of central Africa. The travelers who visited for the first time the Esquimaux of Greenland, or the negro tribes on the Niger, who first saw the natives of the islands of Oceanica, and the Papuans of the Eastern archipelago, found among them all a well-developed belief concerning a future life. This did not come by any process of reasoning, it came as the result of some instinctive operation of the mind itself.

The often-quoted saying of the intelligent missionary Charlevoix, that "the belief best established among the aboriginal Americans is that of the immortality of the soul," is confirmed by the careful researches of later writers. Brinton, in his "Myths of the New World," says that among all the Indians of North and South America there was only one clan found, and that a very small one, who seemed to have no notion of a future state.

This was the "Pend d' Oreilles," of Oregon, and even they believed in charms, omens, dreams, and guardian spirits. The Iroquois, Algonquins, Sioux, Dakotas, Navajos, Natchez, and the rest of the many varieties of North American Indians shared this common belief. The red men mostly believed in the sun as their future home, says Brinton. The Mexicans had a future paradise, and said to the dying: "Sir, or lady, awake, the dawn appears, the light is approaching, the birds begin their songs of welcome," for to them, when the man died, he awoke out of this dream of life into a future reality.

Brinton also mentions one curious analogy of belief in many nations. We learn that the Greeks supposed that every soul must cross the river Styx in Charon's boat; that the Persians thought the departed must cross above the abyss of woe on the arch of the rainbow; and that the Koran teaches that they must go over on the bridge el Sirat, whose blade is sharp as a scimitar; and even Christians speak of passing over a mythical Jordan. The early missionaries were told by the Hurons and Iroquois that the soul after death must cross a deep, rapid river on a bridge made of a slender and ill-poised tree; another tribe believed in crossing a river in a stone canoe, another in going over the stream on a bridge made of an enormous serpent. The Indians of Chili, the Aztecs, and the Esquimaux had similar legends. All these notions sprang up naturally. Among primitive people, before bridges were built, the chief difficulty a traveler encountered was in crossing a river, or a branch of the sea. They naturally thought that in the long journey from this world to the next, some similar difficulty would be found.

We saw in a previous chapter that a belief in ghosts is almost universal among primitive races. The negroes of Africa are tormented by the fear of ghosts, who are thought to return and haunt their homes.

The Nicaragua Indians, in 1528, gave their views concerning the departure of the soul, saying that, when one dies, the soul comes out of the mouth in a form like that of the living person. It is that which made them live, they said. A like phenomenon seems to have been accepted as a possibility by two of the most sharp-sighted observers, and ablest scientific men of our time. The late Dr. Edward Clarke told Dr. O. W. Holmes that once, as he sat by the side of a dying woman, he saw, at the moment of death, "a something rise from the body, which seemed like a departing presence." The conviction, he says, forced upon his mind, that something at that moment departed from the body, was stronger than words could express. Dr. Holmes adds that he heard the same experience told, almost in the same words, by a lady whose testimony was eminently to be relied on. While watching her parent, she felt aware, at the moment of death, of a "something" which arose as if the spirit was perceived in the act of leaving the body. Dr. Edward Clarke and Dr. Holmes seem both to have attached a certain weight to these phenomena.

§ 2. *Notions concerning it among the childlike races.*

It is curious to find among the childlike races a dread of the ghosts of ancestors, as of beings disposed to do harm even to their surviving friends, a dread which has now wholly disappeared. There are thousands to-day, perhaps millions, in our own country, who firmly believe that they receive communications from what they call "the spirit land," and no fear is excited by such intercourse. But among primitive people there is a great dread of the malignant disposition of the departed spirits. Precautions are taken against their return. The Hottentots and Siamese break an opening through the wall of the house to carry out the dead, rebuilding it again as soon as the body is removed. The notion seems to be that the dead man can only return by the passage through which he departed. What a dreadful idea is that of the vampire, described in one of the most striking passages of Byron.[1]

[1] See the passage in *The Giaour*.

The notion of the childlike races concerning the hereafter is usually that of a continuation of this life in another world on much the same plane. The North American Indians, being hunters, believe in happy hunting-grounds. The Esquimaux in a place where the sun never sets, the land of a midnight sun, where there are plenty of walrus and fishes. The people of Kamschatka in a subterranean city, like the world above, only far better. The New Zealanders, like the Romans, placed their heroes among the stars. They thought that the Pleiades were the eyes of seven heroes killed in battle. The Peruvians believed in the resurrection of the body, and in two future worlds: an abode of hard work below the earth for the wicked, and a pleasant heaven above for the good. The Mexicans believed in many future worlds like this, and they dressed the dead man in his best clothes, put his passports in his hand, and buried with him his valuables. The Druids believed in three worlds, and in transmigration from one to the other: in a world above this, in which happiness predominated; a world below, of misery; and this present state. This transmigration was to punish and reward, and also to purify the soul. In the present world, said they, good and evil are so exactly balanced that man has the utmost freedom, and is able to choose or reject either. The Welsh Triads tell us there are three objects of metempsychosis, to collect into the soul the properties of all being, to acquire a knowledge of all things, and to get power to conquer evil. There are, also, they say, three kinds of knowledge: knowledge of the nature of each thing, of its cause, and its influence. There are three things which continually grow less: darkness, falsehood, and death. There are three which constantly increase: light, life, and truth.

§ 3. *Belief of the ancient Etruscans.*

There was a wonderful nation, existing in a highly civilized condition in Italy before the rise of the Roman Republic. They excelled in arts and in arms, they had an artistic faculty like that of the Greeks, and an energy which long resisted and nearly crushed the growing power of the City of the Seven Hills. The safety of Rome was in the fact that the twelve cities of Etruria were only a confederacy and not a union. They carried on war independently of each other, and, therefore, might be defeated separately; whereas if they had been united, the Roman power could never have been developed. A half-Greek race, they were fond of decoration and drawing. Their faith in immortality shows itself in their tombs and inscriptions. Everything except the massive walls of some of their cities has disappeared. But the tombs of the Tarquins, of Lars Porsena, and other mighty Etruscan chiefs, still remain, vast monuments of the grandeur of the race. These graves are tumuli, in great numbers and of large proportions. They are still found in the extensive cemeteries of the Etruscans, in Tuscany, arranged in rows, like houses in streets. They can be counted, says Fergusson, by hundreds, and in some places by thousands. Though many of them have been opened and plundered of their precious contents, some have remained untouched until recently, and have yielded to their discoverers rich collections of the gold and bronze instruments buried with the dead, nearly three thousand years ago. The largest tomb yet opened is more than two hundred and forty feet in diameter and one hundred and fifteen feet high. The tomb of Lars Porsena, as described by Pliny, was a cluster of pyramids supporting other pyramids, which Mr. Fergusson thinks may have reached the height of four hundred feet, which is loftier than any spire or tower on this continent. These tombs were filled with golden ornaments worked with great taste and skill, elegant furniture, beautiful vases, mirrors, rings, engraved gems, bronze statues. The art of working in bronze was carried so far that in one Etruscan city there are said to have been two thousand bronze statues, and they understood engineering so well that the oldest monument in Rome, the Cloaca Maxima, still remains as a proof of their ability in sewerage.

The inscriptions in the Etruscan tombs indicate firm faith in immortality. One says, "While we depart to nought, our essence rises;" another, "We rise like a bird;" another, "We ascend to our ancestors;" another, "The soul rises like fire." They have pictures of the soul seated on a horse, and with a traveling-bag in its hand.

The opinions of the Etruscans may be said to have belonged to the ethnic class, but we know little more than that they had this intense belief in a future life. Like the Egyptians, they seemed to have thought more of dying than of living. The tomb was the permanent home of both people.

§ 4. *Of the Egyptians.*

In a previous chapter we have seen what precise views the Egyptians took of the hereafter; how fully and minutely they described the progress of the soul onward through its long cycle of change, till its final judgment before the tribunal of Osiris. Omitting what has been before described concerning the adventures of the soul after death until it reaches this day of judgment, I will add some further details of that transaction.

Conducted by Anubis, the soul traverses the labyrinth, and by the aid of a clew, guiding it through its windings, at last penetrates to the judgment hall, where Osiris awaits it seated on his throne, assisted by forty-two terrible assessors.

There the decisive sentence is to be pronounced, either admitting the deceased to happiness, or excluding him forever. Then commences a new interrogatory much more solemn than the former. The deceased is obliged to give proof of his knowledge: he must show that it is great enough to give him the right to be admitted to share the lot of glorified spirits. Each of the forty-two judges, bearing a mystical name, questions him in turn; he is obliged to tell each one his name, and what it means. Nor is this all: he is obliged to give an account of his whole life. This is certainly one of the most curious parts of the funereal ritual; Champollion called it the "Negative Confession;" it would perhaps be better described by the word "apology." The deceased addresses successively each of his judges, and declares for his justification that he has not committed such and such a crime. We have therefore here all the moral laws obligatory upon the Egyptian conscience: —

"I have not blasphemed," says the deceased; "I have not stolen; I have not smitten men privily; I have not treated any person with cruelty; I have not stirred up trouble; I have not been idle; I have not been intoxicated; I have not made unjust commandments; I have shown no improper curiosity; I have not allowed my mouth to tell secrets; I have not wounded any one; I have not put any one in fear; I have not slandered any one; I have not let envy gnaw my heart; I have spoken evil, neither of the king nor my father; I have not falsely accused any one; I have not withheld milk from the mouths of sucklings; I have not practiced any shameful crime; I have not calumniated a slave to his master."

The deceased does not confine himself to denying any ill conduct; he speaks of the good he has done in his life-time. "I have made to the gods the offerings that were their due. I have given food to the hungry, drink to the thirsty, and clothes to the naked." On reading these passages we may well be astonished at this high morality, superior to that of all other ancient people, which the Egyptians had been able to build up on the foundation of their religion. Without doubt it was this clear insight into truth, this tenderness of conscience, which obtained for the Egyptians the reputation for wisdom, echoed even by our own Scriptures.

Besides these general precepts, the apology acquaints us with some police regulations for public order raised by common interest in Egypt to the rank of conscientious duties. Thus the deceased denies ever having intercepted the irrigating canals, or having prevented the distribution of the waters of the river over the country; he declares that he has never damaged the stones for mooring vessels on the river. Crimes against religion are also mentioned; some seem very strange to us, especially when we find them classed with really moral faults. The deceased has never altered the prayers nor interpolated them. He has never touched any of the sacred property, such as flocks and herds, or fished for the sacred fish in the lakes of the temples, or stolen offerings from the altar.

The deceased, who now receives the name of the god Osiris, is fully justified; his heart has been weighed in the balance with "truth" and has not been found wanting; the forty-two assessors have stated that he possesses the necessary knowledge. The great Osiris pronounces his sentence, and Thoth, as recorder to the tribunal, having inscribed it in his book, he at last enters into bliss.

Here commences the third part of the ritual, more mystical and obscure than the others. We see the Osiris-soul, henceforth identified with the sun, traversing with him, and as him, the various houses of heaven and the lake of fire, the source of all light. Afterwards the ritual rises to a higher poetical flight, even contemplating the identification of the deceased with a symbolical figure comprising the attributes of all the deities of the Egyptian Pantheon.

Thus we see the faith of Egypt in a hereafter was not only full and entire, but that the Egyptians also had a distinct idea in their minds of the whole process of development in another world. No other theory, until we come to that of Swedenborg, professes to give such full details concerning the future life.

§ 5. *Of Brahmanism.*

The ancient Brahmanic religion made the gods Yama and Varuna the rulers of the world of spirits. Varuna judges the soul and thrusts the wicked down into an abyss of darkness. Yama, who was the Adam of this mythology — three letters out of the four being the same in each name — assembles around himself the good among his descendants. But before this ultimate result they are all obliged, as in Egypt, to pass through a long process of transmigration, the object of which is the punishment of past evil, discipline, and reform.

The last book of the Laws of Manu is on transmigration and final beatitude. The principle is here laid down that every human action, word, and thought bears its appropriate fruit hereafter, good or evil. Out of the heart proceed three sins of thought, four sins of the tongue, and three of the body, namely: covetous, disobedient, and atheistic thoughts; scurrilous, false, frivolous, and unkind words; and acts of theft, bodily injury, and licentiousness. He who controls his thoughts, words, and actions is called a triple commander. There are three qualities of the soul, giving it a tendency to goodness, to passion, and to darkness. The first leads to knowledge, the second to desire, the third to sensuality. To the first belong study of Scripture, devotion, purity, self-command, and obedience. From the second proceed hypocritical actions, anxiety, disobedience, and self-indulgence. The third produces avarice, atheism, indolence, and every act which a man is ashamed of doing. The object of the first quality is virtue; of the second, worldly success; of the third, pleasure. The souls in which the first quality is supreme rise after death to the condition of deities; those in whom the second rules pass into the bodies of other men; while those under the dominion of the third become beasts and vegetables. Manu proceeds to expound, in great detail, this law of transmigration. For great sins one is condemned to pass a great many times into the bodies of dogs, insects, spiders, snakes, or grasses. The change has relation to the crime; thus, he who steals grain shall be born a rat; he who steals meat, a vulture; those who indulge in forbidden pleasures of the senses shall have their senses made acute to endure intense pain.

On the other hand, every good action performed in this world leads to a higher birth hereafter; and it is even taught that a tree used for sacrifice in this world shall attain an exalted birth in the next; and he who lives a religious life with great devotion, will escape transmigration altogether, and after death ascend immediately to the highest heaven.

§ 6. *Of Buddhism. Meaning of Nirvâna.*

It has been repeatedly stated, on the authority of the most learned scholars, that the highest object of desire in Buddhism is to obtain Nirvâna or annihilation. I ventured to deny this as long ago as 1868, when I published an account of Buddhism in the "Atlantic Monthly," and chiefly on the ground that such a belief is not in accordance with human nature. I believe that Tennyson is perfectly right when he says: —

"Whatever crazy sorrow saith,
No life that breathes with human breath
Hath ever truly longed for death.

'Tis life of which our nerves are scant,
O life, not death, for which we pant,
More life, and fuller that we want."

I also opposed this opinion that a third of the human race longed to be annihilated, on the ground that the word Nirvâna means a peace and bliss which the Buddhists declare can be attained in this life, and that the Buddha himself entered Nirvâna long before his death. At present the best Buddhist scholars incline to the belief that Nirvâna does not mean annihilation but immovable rest. It probably means what Christianity means by the rest of the soul hereafter in God; what Jesus meant when he said: "Peace I leave with you, my peace give I unto you."

The Greeks and Romans firmly believed in the immortality of the soul, down to a late period, when their faith was shaken by the philosophy of Epicurus. Festivals of the dead were held by the Romans, and the dead father and mother accounted gods. Yet a certain terror of ancestral spectres was shown by the practice of driving them out of the house by lustrations.

Reviewing what we have thus seen, we notice that all nations and races have held to a future state of existence, that the primitive races believe that the dead are near by, and that their occupations are much the same as those of this life. Future existence is continued along the plane of the present life.

When we come among the ethnic races we find a difference. The dead are no longer close by, unless in exceptional cases. They have a world of their own, a heaven or a hell, or both in one. The world of the departed is an underworld, below this, where there is little light, or comfort of any kind. Such was the belief of the Greeks and Romans, and the Jews borrowed their conception of Hades from the same source. They also believed in a dark underworld, where both the good and bad went; the evil to be placed in Tartarus, and the good in the Elysian fields.

§ 7. *Of the Jews. The argument of Jesus with the Sadducees.*

We thus come to the religion of the Jews. The striking fact in this connection is that Moses taught nothing concerning a future life, and that there is no passage in the Old Testament which teaches this important doctrine. This has been fully shown by Mr. Alger, in his valuable monograph on the doctrine. The Jews, in the time of Jesus, generally believed in a resurrection and a hereafter. And, in the Old Testament, though the doctrine is not taught, there is a belief in a sheol, or underworld, dark and undesirable, to which souls go after death.

Jesus quotes one passage from the Old Testament in proof of immortality. It is the one where God is represented as speaking from the bush to Moses, and saying: "I am the God of Abraham, Isaac, and Jacob." Jesus infers from this passage the immortality of Abraham, and Isaac, and Jacob, though it is not taught there. He infers that those who belong to God must live — they cannot die. "God is not the God of the dead, but of the living."

And this is, in truth, the deepest source of faith in immortality. Faith in God himself as friend and father inevitably creates faith in immortal life.

"God is not the God of the dead but of the living." This is not an argument to convince a doubter. Jesus did not use it as a logical proof of a hereafter. It is not a syllogism to create a belief, but it produces faith. Whoever lives in the light of God's presence and love feels himself to be immortal. The sense of death passes away. It is the same announcement of immortality used by Christ afterward: "He who liveth and believeth in me shall never die." Create a sense of life in the soul and you overcome all fear of death, all thought of death.

§ 8. *How religion produces faith in immortality.*

Christianity, therefore, like Judaism, does not teach immortality as a doctrine or dogma; but creates faith in a hereafter by filling the soul now with spiritual life. It teaches a present resurrection or ascent of the soul to God. "I *am* the resurrection," says Jesus. He raises us up now, and that convinces us that he will raise us up at the last day.

The Jews, without any distinct doctrine of immortality, yet believed in it because they believed so firmly in the Providence of God. Trust in a divine presence and love here, creates faith in the future life. As to the form of that existence, they seem to have borrowed from the Greeks their idea of the under world as a dark region below. This appears in the famous passage in Isaiah, where Babylon, after its rod of cruel oppression was broken, is personified as going down into Hades, leaving the earth above at rest and in peace. The whole dark underworld is stirred at the coming of the imperial city. "Hell [or hades] from beneath is moved to meet thee at thy coming; the countless myriads of the dead rise up; the kings of nations stand up on their thrones and say: 'Art thou become like one of us?' How art thou fallen from heaven, O Lucifer, son of the morning!"

Not only all primitive religions, but all the great ethnic religions, have awakened in man's soul the same belief in a future life. It is the instinct of consciousness which creates this faith. Man, as a conscious personal being, a centre of life, feeling himself to be a thinking, feeling, and choosing person, sees no reason why he should cease to exist when his body is dissolved. He says: "Life does not die." Body dies off of it; the life continues elsewhere. And the more full of life he is, the less fear of death he has. This is the evidence of those who trust to their instincts. They have faith in immortality because it is natural to believe in it. They are made so.

§ 9. *The Poets and Philosophers.*

All sentiment, all affection, all imagination come to reënforce this feeling. The poetry of the world in its noblest aspiration has always expressed this faith. Even skeptical poets, like Byron and Shelley, find it hard to question a future existence. Byron says, in a well-known poem: —

"When coldness wraps this suffering clay
Ah! whither strays the Immortal mind?
It cannot die — it must not stay —
But leaves its darkened dust behind."

And Shelley says of Keats: —

"He hath outsoared the shadow of our night.
Envy, and jealousy, and rage, and pain,
And that unrest that men miscall delight,
Can touch him not, nor torture him again."

"Peace! peace! he is not dead, he doth not sleep;
He hath awakened from the dream of life."

"Thou canst not soar where he is sitting now,
Dust to the dust — but the pure spirit shall flow
Back to the burning fountain whence it came,
A portion of the Eternal, which must glow
Through time and change, unquenchably the same."

The philosophers, with few exceptions, have held this great faith in immortality: Pythagoras, Plato, Socrates, Cicero; and in modern times the best thinkers: Milton, Dante, Descartes, Leibnitz; and among ourselves, Channing, Emerson, and Theodore Parker.

Listen to what Goethe, certainly an unprejudiced thinker, said, in a private conversation: —

"I should be the very last man to be willing to dispense

with faith in a future life. Nay, I would say with Lorenzo di Medici, that all those are dead, even for the present life, who do not believe in another. I have a firm conviction that our soul is an existence of an indestructible nature, whose working is from eternity to eternity. It is like the sun, which seems indeed to set, but really never sets, shining on in unchangeable splendor."

The last great postulate of science, the persistence of force, is a new proof of immortality. For spiritual force is the only force we really know. We only know force at all by the consciousness of the efforts which we put forth from that mysterious centre of existence, the soul. And if this force is persistent, then the soul must continue. If any one asks me how I know that I have a soul, the reply is that I know it by a surer evidence than I know my body. I know of body by the sensations and thoughts which it awakens in my soul. We know the soul at first-hand; but matter we know only at second-hand.

If any one says, "There is no thought without molecular movements in the brain; no consciousness unless the body is in order; in short, that the soul depends for its activity here and now on the condition of the body," we readily admit it. But what then? The very point to be proved is: "Will the soul hereafter need this present body with which to act?" To say that it will is a pure assumption, an argument from ignorance to knowledge.

§ 10. *Two sources of belief in a future existence.*

In truth this is a case in which instinct is higher and surer than reasoning. Many philosophical and metaphysical arguments can be brought to prove immortality or the opposite. But neither does the one kind convince us that we are to live, nor does the other persuade us that when we die we die forever. Our conviction of a future life comes from two sources: a consciousness of the personality and activity of the soul, which is the instinct of immortality; and faith in God as a wise and loving father. If there be a God, all-wise and all-good, then he cannot have created mind, the highest thing we have in the universe, and educated it by all the experiences of life, all the long development of humanity, to let it come suddenly to an end at the very moment when it is in its fullest activity.

Nor, if there be a God, could he have put into the soul this longing for continued existence, and this faith in a hereafter, merely to deceive and delude us. What an inconsequence, to make men to live a few brief years, and then perish forever, and meantime to put into their minds the universal conviction that they are to live hereafter! Even we ourselves take a certain pride and pleasure in what we have made. We do not willingly destroy anything on which we have expended thought and love. Will God create souls with these noble powers, with minds capable of reading the laws of the universe, consciences able to cleave to the right in the midst of temptation, hearts made to love him, and then throw them carelessly away as of no value in his eyes? I could sooner believe that he does not let anything die. I would sooner believe that every animal down to the smallest insect has an immortal soul, fitted to ascend higher and higher, through innumerable bodies, than that God will destroy the human mind and human heart.

Everything here in our life is only just begun. We have just begun to understand a little of the mystery of creation; begun to adore the ineffable beauty and grandeur of the universe. Shall all this knowledge, aspiration, energy, be stopped at its very commencement?

We admire and reverence great souls. We learn to know and love the pure, the generous, the self-denying, the good. In the midst of their noblest work they are taken away. We say, Why is this? and the answer is, because there is another and higher world to which they have gone, other and higher duties, other and sweeter joys. This satisfies both our mind and heart. But if death ends all, then life becomes, not merely an inexplicable mystery, but an unmeaning tissue of contradictions.

Finally we are made to love, with undying and indestructible affections. Our beloved ones go, and as the years pass, we love them not less but more. They live in our hearts forever. Why did God make us thus, if we are never to see them again?

All then, finally, resolves itself into this: faith in immortality is inseparably connected with faith in God, and the higher we go up, the nobler our faith becomes, the more sure we are of immortal life. The highest being who ever lived on earth, was the surest of all. To him death was nothing, only a transient sleep.

§ 11. *Modern scientific unbelief. Spiritualism, and its evidences.*

It is a somewhat striking fact, however, that at the present time we see two movements of thought, two great currents of opinion, in exactly opposite directions. One is the English and German unbelief in a future life, based on certain scientific facts or theories. The other is the new faith in a hereafter, founded on a supposed intercourse with the world of spirits.

A large number of serious scientific thinkers have come to question immortality, and even to declare it an impossibility, because they think it contrary to the facts of physical science. A recent English work tells us that "our positive scientific thinkers, reasoning independently from the verified conclusions of science, have come to the conclusion that the belief in a future life must be finally given up. A cunning arrangement of material atoms is the essence of all the phenomena of life, and their disarrangement must be the end of it all." These thinkers deny that there is any real self, or ego in man, independent of the body. Thought, emotion, volition, are inseparably bound up with the brain and nervous system, whose functions they are, just as it is the function of the heart to pump up the blood, and of the lungs to oxygenate it. Thought cannot go on without the brain, which is the thinking organ. It is incredible and impossible that man should live again.

Meantime, as if by a natural reaction against this doctrine of despair, or as if sent by Providence to save mankind from such dreary unbelief, there has grown up in all parts of the civilized world a vast faith in an actual present intercourse with the souls of the departed. There are probably many millions who are convinced that they talk with disembodied spirits just as certainly as they talk with those in the body. Nor is this altogether a new faith, though it has increased very rapidly within a few years. There are on record, in all times, numerous instances of similar intercourse. To those who believe, as I do, in the continued existence of souls after death, and also that they may be still near to us, there is no antecedent impossibility or even improbability in such intercourse. All we want is to have sufficient evidence of it.

The difficulty in obtaining such evidence arises from the fact that most people are so credulous, so easy to be deluded, so ready to deceive themselves, and are such inaccurate observers. I am not implying anything disrespectful to mankind in saying this. I include myself in the same category. It requires trained habits of observation to verify such facts. I have been present on many occasions at spiritual *séances*, and have seen many inexplicable phenomena. But I have also witnessed a great deal of delusion and some positive deception, so that I do not feel qualified to decide how much or how little of truth there may be in such supposed intercourse. I should be glad to believe in it, especially for the benefit of those who are deficient in the instinct of immortality, or who have not much faith in the divine presence and love. But I confess that what I have seen in this movement has not been very edifying.

That which commonly comes from what is called Spiritualism has a negative value; it produces a conviction that death is *not* the end of our being. It has not, as yet, revealed much concerning the nature of the hereafter. Perhaps it is not meant that we should think about it, while immersed in the pursuits and duties of the present life. It might take our minds too far away from what we ought to be doing now. It seems evident, from man's experience, that he was made to believe in a future life, but was not made to know much about it. We know enough when we know this: that since God sends death to all his creatures, as he sends life to all, it must be just as great a blessing to die as it is to live, perhaps greater. And we also know that the same Being who has made this world, — with all its variety and beauty, all its opportunities for knowledge, work, growth, love, — has made all other worlds. We shall not go away from his presence, or his care, no matter where we go.

In all times, then, and in all lands, men have believed and continue to believe in a future life. The only exceptions are in the case of those too much immersed in sense, or too stupefied by ignorance to rise to the conception; and in those who, following some narrow path of reasoning, suppose themselves logically obliged to disbelieve. Meantime the race looks across the boundary, and reaches out its longings and hopes into the great beyond.

I will close this chapter with Blanco White's lines on this great theme. Coleridge and Leigh Hunt both have called it the finest sonnet in the English language. Without going so far as this, we must at least admit that it is one of the best, and it is truly wonderful that a native of Spain, brought up to manhood only speaking the Spanish language, should have written *one* of the best sonnets in another tongue: —

"Mysterious night! When our first parent knew
Thee from report divine, and heard thy name,
Did he not tremble for this lovely frame,
This glorious canopy of light and blue?
Yet, 'neath the curtain of translucent dew,
Bathed in the rays of the great setting flame,
Hesperus with the host of heaven came,
And lo! creation widened in man's view.
Who could have thought such darkness lay concealed
Within thy beams, O Sun! or who could find,
While fly, and leaf, and insect lay revealed,
That to such countless orbs thou mad'st us blind!
Why do we, then, shun death with anxious strife?
If Light can thus deceive, wherefore not Life?"

CHAPTER XII.

THE FUTURE RELIGION OF MANKIND.

§ 1. Man a religious being. His continued interest in religious questions. § 2. Religious faith necessary to progress in Science, Literature, and Art. Individualism insufficient. § 3. The essence of Christianity. § 4. Christianity the religion of Civilized Man. § 5. Progress and power of Christian Nations. § 6. Chief of the three Catholic Religions. § 7. Its fullness of life. § 8. Its corruptions. Their origin in its power of assimilation. Persecution. Monasticism. § 9. Will the basis of the church of humanity be a Ritual, a Creed, or a Person? § 10. The personality of Jesus. Examples of the influence of Prophets on national life. § 11. Will the world outgrow the teaching of Jesus? Future prospects.

§ 1. *Man a religious being. His continued interest in religious questions.*

IN this work we have examined several of the chief religions of the world. We have seen pass before us, in majestic march, the grand faiths of mankind, Brahmanism and Buddhism, the systems of Zoroaster, Moses, and Mohammed, the religions of Egypt, Greece, and Scandinavia; and now we have to institute a brief comparison between Christianity and those other forms of human faith, to see what right, if any, Christianity has to claim superiority over the others.

But before proceeding to give an opinion on this subject, I wish to make one or two preliminary remarks.

First, our studies must have impressed us with the conviction that man is a religious being, and that he cannot do without religion. Long before he can secure the comforts and luxuries, or even what we consider the necessaries of life, he begins to adore the invisible, to pray to some unseen power. He finds that he cannot live by bread alone, but also needs some word which proceeds out of the mouth of God. Half-starved savages worship; all the races of men worship; the most civilized portions of the earth worship; worship reaches back to the beginning of history. Thousands of years before Christ, our Aryan ancestors worshipped on the plateau of Central Asia; the Chinese worshipped on the Hoang-Ho and Yang-tze-Kiang, the Hindus on the Ganges, the Hebrews, Assyrians, and Babylonians on the Euphrates and Tigris, the Egyptians on the Nile,— and there are no symptoms that this religious need is less at the present time.

Looking at the history of the world from the beginning, we may say that religion has been and is the chief concern of mankind.

And it is not only of great interest to those who

need its comfort, guidance, and strength. It is not simply that it feeds the soul with bread from heaven, gives increased peace and joy to those on whom society lays hard burdens, brings consolation to the wounded heart, but it also continues to be the most interesting subject of intellectual investigation. After all the speculations of thousands of years in regard to creation and providence, God and immortality, there are still no more interesting questions than these. The Positivists have told us that man goes through three stages of thought: (1) Theological, (2) Metaphysical, and (3) Scientific; and that we have now passed out of the two first into the last, in which only scientific questions are interesting. But the curious fact is, that science itself has gone largely into religious and metaphysical investigations. Tyndall publishes a volume which he calls "Fragments of Science" in which one essay is on "Prayer," another on "Miracles and Special Providence," and another on the appearance of Spirits. Darwin gives us a new cosmogony or origin of things, and sets all the world to discuss again old questions concerning creation. Professor Clifford, an eminent scientist, writes about the ethics of religion, and the influence on morality of a decline in religious belief. Huxley publishes almost as many papers on religious as on scientific questions. If any popular lecturer is anxious to secure an overflowing audience he has only to take for his subject the mistakes of Moses, or to deny some fundamental points of religious belief. It does not then appear that human interest has passed from religious questions to those of science. One writer lately gave it as his opinion that the world had lost its interest in religion, on the ground that the churches in Boston and Chicago were never well filled. If he had consulted the United States census he would have seen that the basis of his induction was too narrow; and that, taking the whole United States during a decade of years, there has been a constant and large increase in the amount of church property, church accommodation, and church attendance.

Some people think that science, art, literature, and philanthropy may take the place of religion. But each of these occupies its own department, each meets a separate need of the human soul. Science can no more take the place of religion than religion can take the place of science. Knowledge belongs to one region of the soul, faith, hope, and love to another. Physical science teaches us the facts and laws of the outward visible universe. Religion teaches us the facts and laws of the unseen and eternal world.

§ 3. *Religious faith necessary to progress in science, literature, and art. Individualism insufficient.*

More than this. It is highly probable that man, if deprived of religious faith, would after a while cease to have any science, art, literature, or philanthropy. For, as we have seen in the course of this work, the deep power which moves this world is faith in another world. Thus far history has shown us religion as the root of civilization. And it is so still, whether men are conscious of it or not. Take away religious hope from man; confine him to the present world and the present life; and deprive him of his faith in a Divine Providence, a guardian care, a progress upward of all being, a heavenly world beyond of purer joys and nobler love, and he would probably lose his interest even in this life. There is profound significance in the text which speaks of certain persons as being "without God and without hope in the world." Man is so great that unless he can lay hold of the infinite he soon tires of the finite. In a universe of dead laws and iron fate, of matter and force, a world without meaning, purpose, or love, men would not care enough for *anything* to pursue science, art, literature, or philanthropy. For a time, indeed, from force of habit and from the acquired faith of the past, from habits of hope stored up in the soul, an atheistic community might continue to think and work as before. But they would be like people living on their capital, instead of on their income. The old stock of beliefs, inherited from the past, would soon be used up, and then the legitimate fruits of the death of faith in anything divine would appear in a steadily increasing weariness and indifference to life. A train will run some time after the engine is taken off, from acquired momentum, but it gradually moves more and more slowly, and at last stops.

Nor will the needs of the religious nature be met by any voluntary association assembled for free inquiry in religious matters. Freedom alone tends to pure atomism; it will turn an association into a heap of sand; it cannot organize life. And without life no growth, progress, or development. Religion must be free; but then it must be religion first, in order to be free at last. And religion is faith in something divine. Men united in some common faith may freely develop that faith. The religious nature, for its growth and satisfaction, needs union, coöperation, and sympathy. Human beings can no more develop the religious life alone than they can develop civilization, art, science, and literature. Robinson Crusoe on his desert island might reproduce some of the arts of life which he had learned before in the society of man. The anchorites in the desert might reproduce there some of the religious emotions which they took with them from their former Christian education. But neither did the anchorite nor Robinson Crusoe make much progress, and both were glad to get back to some human companionship. Individualism in religion, as in the desolate island, may cry —

> "I am monarch of all I survey,
> My right there is none to dispute" —

But it pays the penalty of that autocratic supremacy when forced to add, —

> "I am out of humanity's reach,
> I must finish my journey alone."

Pure individualism will never be the religion of the future. To freedom there must be added union, coöperation, some kind of church relation, and brotherhood.

Man will always have a religion and religious faith. The question is, "What faith will it be?" We have examined the other religions with some minuteness, but have not thus far inquired into the nature or future of our own religion. What is the relation of Christianity, then, to other religions, and what reason is there to think that Christianity, in some form, will become the faith of mankind?

§ 3. *The essence of Christianity.*

But first we must endeavor to define Christianity, and say what it is and what it is not. The essence of Christianity cannot, perhaps, be better stated than in the famous words of a high Roman Catholic authority. Essential Christianity is that which has been received by all Christians, always and in all places: "*Quod ubique, quod semper, quod ab omnibus.*"

It follows that no one church is the exclusive and only church, for no one church has ever included all Christians. No one creed is the exclusive and only creed, for there have always been those who rejected it. Christianity is rather a spirit of life, which has come to us from the first century, a method of feeling, thinking, and acting. It has always held to Jesus as its founder, teacher, and leader. It has always worshipped one God, the Father. It has clung to the law of love, as the rule of duty. It has had faith in an immortal life beyond and above this. These sentiments and convictions have been held by all Christians, everywhere, and always; and will therefore, probably, last as long as Christianity lasts. Taking Christianity in this large way, and including in its sphere all professed believers in Christianity, and also the Christendom which holds by Christ's name, we shall see that Christianity differs from other religions in some very important particulars.

§ 4. *Christianity the religion of civilized man.*

Christianity is the religion of the most civilized and the only progressive nations of the world.

Other forms of civilization have been arrested or have come to an end. The wonderful development of knowledge, art, power, industrial progress in ancient Egypt, gradually faded away. So it was with the national life of Greece and of Rome, of Babylonia, Assyria, Phœnicia, and Persia. That of China has been long arrested, and has remained motionless. That of India, after a long period of intellectual growth, entered upon a season of dilapidation and decay. Mohammedanism no longer makes much progress. Its early life has died out of it. Buddhism has also long since ceased from further advances, and remains in a condition of apathy. But Christian civilization is still progressive. Whether there is anything in it to prevent its sharing the fate of the others, remains to be seen. But at present, we may certainly say that the Christian religion, and Christian civilization, are the only ones which are in a condition of constant progress.

§ 5. *Progress and power of Christian nations.*

Among the religions and civilizations of earth, one, and only one, continues to make progress outwardly and inwardly; by new developments within and new accessions of power without. The evident fact in the history of mankind is, that Christianity and Christendom alone are in a state of steady development and progress. Every country which professes the Christian faith is advancing, all others are relatively stagnant. In Christian states, the vast increase of wealth has not brought enervating luxury or weakness. The inhabitants of the little island of England, possessing incredible wealth, are able to conquer and keep possession of vast continents, and to master populations ten times more numerous than their own. The islands of Great Britain and Ireland contain one hundred and twenty-one thousand square miles, and they govern countries which contain eight million square miles. The inhabitants of the United Kingdom are thirty-one millions; they rule in Asia, Africa, Australia, Oceanica, and America, two hundred millions of people. And yet Great Britain is not at the head of the Christian powers of Europe to-day. The power of Christendom is vastly greater than that of all the rest of the world combined. This power is accompanied with wealth, with means of enjoyment, comfort, luxury; in comparison with which the heaped-up treasures of oriental despots are pauperism. The experience of all nations outside of Christendom has been that power brought wealth, wealth brought luxury, luxury brought weakness and ruin. Thus far there are no symptons of such results in European civilization. The young aristocracy of England are, on the whole, as full of energy as though they were young savages. They spend their superfluous strength not only in athletic exercises at home, boating, hunting, etc., but they climb mountains in Himalaya and Colorado, shoot tigers in India, and rhinoceroses in Africa, throw themselves on grim death in Balaklava charges, and lead the forlorn hope in Abyssinia or Affghanistan.

Christendom is a confederation of mighty nations, armed with power which defies the danger of any future overflow of barbaric conquerors. Were it possible for new hordes, like the Goths, Huns, or Saracens, to renew the assaults on Christendom which threatened its life in the fifth and eighth centuries, such attacks would now be ridiculous. Either one of five or six nations in Christendom could now defeat Alaric, Attala, or Saladin. But besides this vast force organized in national life, and besides the great wealth of these nations, the only progress now seen in science, art, and literature belongs to the same Christian groups of nations. What discoveries are made to-day in Arabian observatories? Who goes to the universities of China to learn science? Where were invented the electric telegraph, the steam-engine, the locomotive and railroad, the daguerreotype, the photograph, the spectroscope? In Christendom only. Who have deciphered the hieroglyphics of Egyptian monuments, the cuneiform inscriptions on the rocks of Behistan? Who have rediscovered Nineveh and the site of Troy; the temple of Ephesus and the treasury of the Atrides at Argos? The scholars of Christendom. Where are the chief manufactures and commerce of the world? In Christendom.

Again, we ask, where are we to go for good governments, for well-organized nationalities, for governments of laws not men, for political institutions which unite order and freedom, liberty and law? Still, we may say, these are found among Christian nations, not outside of them; strictly co-extensive with the faith of Christ and the knowledge of the Christian Scriptures.

And finally, I ask, where are the only persistent, systematic, and scientific attempts made to relieve the human race from the great miseries and wrongs under which it has groaned from the beginning: from war, from slavery, pauperism, crime, disease? War has not ceased, but it has been restrained and regulated. The great nations of Europe have what they call the "balance of power," which means that no one or two of them shall unite to oppress the rest. The idea of peace, the desire for peace, the general conviction of the importance of peace, is the prevailing sentiment in all Christian countries. Just as slavery has been overthrown by these sentiments and convictions, so will war be overthrown. Ideas make and unmake institutions. Fill the world with an idea, and the appropriate outward result must follow.

The ideas of universal peace, of social progress, of philanthropy, of reform schools, of universal education; these, to-day, fill the minds not only of advanced thinkers, but make the warp and woof of public opinion.

Thus while all other forms of human civilization are arrested and stationary, or else have come to an end, Christendom is advancing, in wealth, power, science, art, social improvements, development of industry and new inventions and discoveries. In the nations which profess Christianity there is a motive power at work not to be found outside of them. Exactly those nations which profess the Christian religion are actuated by this spirit of progress, and those outside of Christianity are mostly in a condition of relative stagnation. Is this, then, merely an accidental coincidence, or is there anything in their faith which is the spring of this progress?

Without assuming now that Christianity, as a faith, is the cause of Christian civilization, we must agree at least that the two are associated together and in sympathy. Christianity goes with the most advanced civilization of the world. The two seem certainly to belong together. Every Christian country, England, France, Germany, Italy, Spain, Norway, Denmark, Russia, Austria, Greece, and the States of North and South America, have some common features which difference them from the nations outside of their community. Christian nations are governed by law; even despotisms like Russia and Austria are despotisms tempered by law. In Christian nations law stands above kings and rulers, in other parts of the world the will of the ruler stands above law. Every one of the twenty or more states which profess Christianity is making progress in government, law, popular education, art, literature, and efforts to humanize, reform, and elevate man. None of the nations outside are thus progressive. This association of Christianity and progress can hardly be an accident.

§ 6. *Chief of the three Catholic Religions.*

The second peculiarity of Christianity is that it is the chief among the catholic religions; that is, of those which overleap the boundaries of race and nation, and aim at converting all races. Most of the religions are ethnic, or confined to a single race or nation. Thus Brahmanism never went out of India; the religion of Zoroaster was confined to the Persians, that of Egypt to the Egyptians, that of Greece to the Hellenic races, that of Rome to the Latin races, that of the Eddas to the Teutonic nationalities, that of the Druids to the Keltic tribes. Each of these was limited by the boundaries of a race or nation, and never sought to go beyond them. Even Buddhism, which has many of the traits of a catholic religion and which has converted many nationalities, has never succeeded in making converts outside of the great Mongol race. We may say that only Judaism, Christianity, and Mohammedanism are truly and absolutely catholic religions.

These three have attempted to convert different races, and have succeeded in doing so. The Jews compassed sea and land to make proselytes; that which marred the catholicity of their work was that they insisted on making proselytes to their outward visible church, instead of making converts to God. The Mohammedans afterwards fell into the same error. They wished to make, not converts, but subjects. They were satisfied with outward conformity, and so neglected inward conversion. They did not ask for faith, but submission. This is always the fault of sectarianism, that it wishes to make proselytes to its sect, rather than converts to truth. Christians have fallen into the same condemnation. But the spirit of their religion is much broader. This was seen at first in Christ's treatment of Samaritans, Romans, and Phœnicians. It has since appeared in all noble missionary work, where the simple gospel of love has been carried, without regard to making proselytes. These three missionary religions are all Monotheisms, for only belief in one God can prompt the faith that all mankind are his children, and sustain the effort to bring them all to him.

§ 7. *Its fullness of Life.*

A third peculiarity of Christianity, which makes it capable of becoming the religion of mankind, is its fullness of religious and moral life. By comparing it with other religions we see that it is a pleroma, possessing the truths and supplying the deficiencies in the other systems.

Thus Brahmanism is an eminently spiritual religion. Passages may be quoted from its sacred books which fill the soul with a sense of a divine presence. But it is deficient on the human side. Its system of castes is a denial of human brotherhood, and the source of countless forms of inhumanity and oppression.

Buddhism was a revolt from Brahmanism because of this inhumanity. It took the opposite direction, and has everywhere taught the brotherhood of man. It has made the whole East of Asia more tender and less cruel; it has softened the hard hearts of the Mongols, and so has done vast good. But it has lost the idea of the Infinite and Eternal. It loves man, but omits the love of an infinite God. Reverent, humane, and moral, it is weak on the side of faith in the Unseen and Eternal.

The Egyptian religion saw the divine element in nature, perceived its plastic life, felt a sacred mystery in all animal and vegetable organization, but it missed unity in the contemplation of variety, and became at last a broken and divided Polytheism.

The Greek religion beheld God revealed in man, and made every human form divine. The Greeks deified courage as Mars, wisdom as Pallas, beauty as Aphrodite, glory and art as Apollo. But they also lost unity, and pushed separate qualities to extremes. This led at last to the dilapidation and decay of their religion and national life.

Mohammedanism taught the sovereignty of God, and represented him as Infinite Will. Hence came its merits and its defects; its power at first, and its weakness afterward. Absolute submission to the divine decree gave valor to the followers of Omar, as it afterward inspired with like courage the troops of Cromwell. Looking at God as Will, develops the will of man, until it passes into despotic hardness and isolation, and so tends to dissolve society into mere lonely particles.

When we compare Christianity with these systems we see how it possesses a fullness of life which includes and completes them all. It has developed a spiritual life in its saints like that of Brahmanism; a humanity in its philanthropists which allies it with Buddhism; a sense of the divine presence in nature and life, like that of Egypt; it has, like Greece, seen in the One Supreme Being the human qualities of power, knowledge, justice, love, which the Greeks distributed among their Pantheon. It has, with Islam, taught divine decrees, and a divine predestination, but always has modified the doctrine by leaving room for human freedom. Thus Christianity has shown itself as a fullness, a pleroma, or, to use the modern phrase, an all-sidedness, which marks it for a still larger catholicity hereafter.

§ 8. *Its corruptions. Their origin in its power of assimilation. Persecution. Monasticism.*

When we speak of Christianity as all-sided, and hospitable to all truth, we shall immediately be told that it has been most exclusive, and that it has denounced, persecuted, and attempted to destroy all outside of its own pale. It has had its crusades against Mohammedans and Albigenses, its *auto-da-fés* of Jews, Moors, and heretics. It has burned witches and hung Quakers. And when I say that it is a system which teaches a kingdom of heaven here, I shall be told that salvation from a future hell into a future heaven has been the main motive of its efforts. Instead of making religion a part of human life to redeem and educate it, it has taken it from life into monasteries and nunneries, and made it consist not in practical goodness, but ritual, ceremony, and sacraments. There is, no doubt, truth in all this.

But I cling to my definition of the type of each religion, and I assert that these tendencies and habits were no part of original Christianity, and have not been permanent in it, but local and temporary. They are, therefore, corruptions and accretions, and not normal developments coming properly from its germ.

That so many of these corruptions are found in Christianity results, in fact, from its very catholicity. Its receptive power is so great that it easily assimilates from other systems many kinds of belief and practice, and only afterward throws off what it finds out of harmony with its own type. Christianity has had its Papal inquisitions and its Protestant persecutions, certainly. But is it not evident that neither of these were present in its original form? And is it not also evident that persecution has been almost wholly eliminated from it at the present time, by its self-reforming and self-purifying quality?

All religions, as we have seen, divide themselves into popular and personal; that is, those which originate in a popular tendency, and those which originate in a single prophet. To the first class belong five great systems, namely, those of India, Egypt, Greece, Rome, Scandinavia. In the other class, each founded by a prophet, are the six systems, of Confucius, Buddha, Moses, Zoroaster, Mohammed, and Christ.

Christianity belongs to the last class, each of which has its origin in a prophet, and we are able to study in the life of Jesus the marks which belong to its earliest type. That persecution was alien to his idea, appears from such instances as that in which he rebukes the disciples for wishing to call down fire on those who refused to admit them, saying that "the Son of Man has not come to destroy men's lives but to save them;" from his commands to "bless them that curse you, and do good to them that despitefully use you and persecute you;" from his parable of the Good Samaritan, his treatment of the Samaritan woman, his teaching that those who had helped their suffering brethren had really helped him; his announcing that those should be forgiven who spoke against him, but not those who denied the spirit of truth in their own souls; his declaration that "not every one who saith unto me, Lord, Lord, shall enter into the kingdom of heaven, but they who do the will of my Heavenly Father."

Take another instance, Monasticism. At one period this system almost took possession of the Christian church, and it still continues as an important element in the Roman Catholic and Greek communions. But it is apparent that its period of supreme importance has passed by, and that its influence has long been declining. So little power has it over the convictions of the people, that the governments of the most Catholic countries in Europe have not hesitated to abolish the monasteries, and to secularize their property; and in countries like England and America people no longer enter these institutions to save their souls by ascetic practices, but rather to make themselves useful as teachers or as nurses. That Jesus never countenanced the idea which is the root of monasticism, namely, that the best way of saving the soul is to retire from the world and live a separate life in the practice of self-denial, is very plain. He points out the distinction between his own spirit and that of John the Baptist (who was an anchorite) by saying: "John the Baptist came neither eating nor drinking; the Son of Man has come eating and drinking." His first miracle, of making wine at Cana (whether you call it a fact or a myth) shows that it was a principle with him not to go out of the world, or to renounce innocent pleasures for religious purposes. Unless he had considered that a principle was at stake, he would not have needlessly exposed himself to such calumnies, for, as appears in the incident of his paying taxes, he did not unnecessarily offend the prejudices of others merely to claim his own rights.

§ 9. *Will the basis of the church of humanity be a Ritual, a Creed, or a Person?*

If man then is not only to be always a religious being, but also needs religious institutions, a church, what church shall he have? The basis of a church union must be one of three things: (1) a ritual, or priesthood and form of worship; (2) a creed, or system of belief; (3) a personal prophet. Many religions have had one of these, or a combination of them, for their bond of union.

Some of those we have been examining were united by a hierarchy and a ritual. Such were those of Egypt and India, Greece and Rome. These had neither creed nor prophet for their foundation; they rested on priesthood and worship. A certain belief concerning the gods and the future life was taught by the priests to the people, both in India and Egypt; but the real union was the power of the hierarchy. All these systems based on ritual and priesthood came to an end. The same was the case in Peru and Mexico on this continent. A hierarchy seems to sap the life of a nation, and at last the nation and the priestly religion go down together in a common fall.

A creed, by itself, is quite inadequate to maintain long the life of a religion. A creed means belief, belief implies thought. As soon as men begin to think, they differ. All creeds tend toward a multiplication of sects; which in itself is not an evil, provided there is still some common bond of union among them. But a creed *alone* will not give this union.

The strongest basis of union is faith in a prophet or inspired teacher. The great prophetic religions have shown themselves lasting. The systems of Buddha and Confucius, founded five centuries before Christ, are still active, though not progressive. That of Moses, which began a thousand years earlier than either, holds together the six or seven millions of Jews, in their dispersion over the world, and continues to maintain their national existence. Mohammed is a centre of unity to a hundred million of disciples in Europe, Asia, and Africa. Even Zoroaster, whose epoch goes far back into times before the days of Moses, is still able to unite a few small bodies of Parsee disciples who read his books and maintain his teachings to-day.

The religion of the future is likely, therefore, to be a prophetic religion. And if so, what inspiration ever rose so high as that of Jesus. Among all prophets, he by common consent stands supreme. This is no place to examine his claims to preëminence, nor is it necessary. Even those students of history who do not claim to be his disciples readily admit it.

§ 10. *The personality of Jesus. Examples of the influence of prophets on national life.*

But this we may say, that from the fullness of life in the soul of Jesus has proceeded the fullness of life in his religion. If Christianity does justice to the different sides of human nature, and meets the various needs of the soul, it is because the same all-sided development was in the life of Jesus himself. When he said: "I am not come to destroy, but to fulfill," he indicated the large character of his influence and work. He was able to sympathize with all forms of goodness, to accept truth from all quarters. His work was not to destroy anything, but to fulfill everything by supplying its deficiencies.

In the records of the life and teachings of Jesus, we see a union of those elements usually separated in men. He united love to God with love to man; courage and caution; perfect freedom from forms, and reverence for the substance in all forms; hatred for sin, and love for the sinner.

It really seems as if the soul of a prophet (as that of Zoroaster, Buddha, Mohammed, Luther, Wesley, Swedenborg, Fox, Channing) is like a seed, which brings forth plants and fruit after its kind. It has, wrapped in it, involved and latent, a whole system of belief and conduct, which is gradually evolved in the history of the religion. All that is essential in Mohammedanism was in the soul of Mohammed; all that is essential in Buddhism was in Sakya-Muni; all that is essential to Judaism was in Moses; all that is essential in Christianity was in Jesus.

Christianity is as spiritual as Brahmanism, as humanė as Buddhism, developing as much of the self-denying and ascetic virtues as any religion, yet also feeding the springs of thought, invention, discovery, of poetry and art, of science, of earthly improvement and progress in comfort, luxury, and taste. Yet it does not sink, enervated and corrupted by luxury, as other civilizations have done.

Christianity teaches the love of God and love of man, divine providence and human freedom, piety and morality, self-denial and development, a kingdom of God here and a kingdom of God hereafter, a divine life now and an immortality to come.

There is a memorable example of the influence of religion on national life, in the sudden awakening of the Arabs to a vast energy of will, by the teaching and life of Mohammed. Here the cause and effect are seen in immediate relation one to the other. The Bedouin tribes, children of Esau and Ishmael, had been roving their deserts during twenty or thirty centuries, with no influence on mankind, until the doctrines of Mohammed united them in one compact organization, inspired them with a fiery enthusiasm, and sent them forth to conquer half the world, and to produce a sudden outburst of intellectual activity in science, art, and literature. This shows the power of religion to create civilization.

Another illustration of this power of religious ideas to produce and maintain a special form of social order is to be found in the Jews. They have existed now for perhaps three thousand years, as a distinct nationality, formed into a nation by the institutions of Moses, and held together by those same institutions.

Another illustration is to be seen in the influence of Luther in originating that form of civilization which exists in Northern Europe and in Protestant nations. When Luther came, the southern countries of Europe, Italy, Spain, Austria, Portugal, France, were superior in wealth and power to the northern nations. The scale has turned the other way, and the invention, the arts, the commerce, the literature of Europe preponderate in Germany and England, Norway, and Sweden. Only France, a semi-Catholic country, stands in these respects among the leading powers. Spain, which, in the sixteenth century, monopolized the largest part of the force and wealth of Europe; Italy, which, in that same period, was supreme in art and literature, have both sunk to a second-rate position in the scale of European civilization.

I am well aware that the tendency of the present time is to disparage and discredit prophets and men of genius, and to substitute for them a worship for humanity in general. These great souls are not considered providential men, sent to create a new epoch, but as themselves the result of their time. This sort of explanation may be carried too far. Concerning this let us listen to Carlyle, who thus speaks: —

"This is an age which, as it were, denies the existence of great men; denies the desirableness of great men. Show our critics a great man, a Luther for example, they begin to, what they call, 'account for him'; not to worship him, but take the dimensions of him and bring him out to be a very little kind of man. He was 'the creature of the time' they say; the time called him forth; the time did everything, he nothing but what we, the little critic, could have done too! This seems to me but melancholy work. The time call forth? Alas! we have known times call loudly enough for their great man, but not find him when they called! He was not there. Providence had not sent him. The time, calling its loudest, had to go down to confusion and wreck because he would not come when called."

"I liken common, languid times, with their unbelief, distress, perplexity; their languid doubting character, impotently crumbling down through ever worse distress into final ruin, — all this I liken to dry, dead fuel, waiting for the lightning out of heaven which shall quicken it. The great man, with his free force direct out of God's own hand, is the lightning. All blazes now around him. The critic thinks the dry mouldering sticks have called him forth. They wanted him greatly, no doubt; but as to calling him forth! They are critics of small vision, who think that the dead sticks have created the fire."

"To lose faith in God's divine lightning, and to retain faith only in dead sticks, this seems to me the last consummation of unbelief."

So far Carlyle.

My opinion is this, and this is what I have tried to show in this and the previous chapters: —

1. That Christianity alone now keeps alive a steadily advancing civilization.

2. It does this because of the breadth and universality of the convictions which inspire it.

3. It derived these from the faith and inspiration of its founder.

4. Christianity does not differ from other religions in being alone true while they are false, but in possessing the whole of which they possess parts.

§ 11. *Will the world outgrow the teaching of Jesus. Future prospects.*

There remains then to be considered only the possibility that the world will outgrow the teaching and example of Jesus, and leave him behind. But in what respect will the world outgrow him? Not in his teaching concerning God, of whom he declares that he is a Spirit, and that those who worship him must worship him in spirit and in truth. Higher than this, worship cannot go. With this Jesus connected the doctrine of the unity and supreme goodness of God. "Hear, O Israel! the Lord our God is one Lord." "There is none good but one, that is God." When you have reached the unity of all things in one supreme being of perfect goodness, it would seem impossible to go higher. In the same way Jesus has posited the highest possible law of ethics when he teaches us to love God and love man. These ideas may be infinitely developed and unfolded, as Christ himself foresaw and foretold. He avoided limiting truth by the letter of his own statements, but declared that the Spirit of Truth would lead his followers into all truth.

He himself thus opened the way for indefinite progress; but these foundation-truths, when once seen, must remain as foundations always. A truth once recognized continues always true. These are, —

"Truths which wake
To perish never."

We may build a multitude of additions on such a basis, but "other foundation can no man lay than that is laid." The foundation of faith once laid, *that* work is done.

Christianity in the past has gone through a long cycle of change; it has altered its type from age to age; taken up and dropped again many beliefs and many practices. It will probably continue to do so, developing more and more into the character of which the life of Jesus is the type. As it does this, it will become better able to convert the world to him. It will not offer to mankind a creed and a ritual, but the life of the Master himself, —

"Most human and yet most divine,
The flower of man and God."

Christianity was never so vigorous as to-day. It differs from other religions in obeying this law of development. It is moving onward. Catholicism itself develops new doctrines. Even that cannot stand still. Protestantism is fermenting with the new wine of a growing faith. Germany goes ever deeper into the study of religious philosophy. In England, such leaders as Gladstone, Dean Stanley, Jowett, and others have carried aloft the banner of advancing thought. Christianity is alive in every part of the world.

The bitter sectarian animosities which have disgraced the past will disappear. All churches and confessions will hear each other speaking in their own tongue wherein they were born. They will no more undertake to teach every man his neighbor, and every man his brother, saying: "Know the Lord in my way, for I am right, I have the truth, mine is the only safe creed, the only church which can teach with authority;" for it will be seen that the Spirit of God has not left itself without a witness in the humblest sect, the most despised and heretical party, and that all know him, from the least of them to the greatest of them.

This is the way by which Christ will put all enemies under his feet; this is the way in which every knee shall at last bow to him, and every tongue confess that he is Lord, to the glory of God the Father.

The doubter and infidel will not have to renounce any of their freedom of mind. No one will be obliged to submit his reason to unintelligible mysteries, or to accept blindly what contradicts his common sense. Science shall not give up any part of its domain to faith, nor the reign of natural law be violated by a single rent in the vast web of universal order. No innocent pleasure, no natural joy of life, nothing beautiful in art, literature, society, home, will be sacrificed to Christian faith. But all men will come to Jesus, because they find in him the mightiest influence to lift up their aspirations to his Father and their own; the fullest revelation of pardon, peace, hope, immortal life, needed by us all for the perfect development of our being; and through him they will catch glimpses in their most barren lives of "that immortal sea which brought us hither," "and hear its mighty waters rolling evermore."

APPENDIX.

NOTE I. *The Nirvâna.*

[From Oldenberg, "Buddha, his Life," etc.]

"IT is not an anticipation in parlance, but it is the absolutely exact expression of the dogmatic thought, when not merely the hereafter, which awaits the emancipated saint, but the perfection which he already attains in this life, is called the Nirvâna. What is to be extinguished has been extinguished, the fire of lust, hatred, bewilderment. In unsubstantial distance lie hope and fear; the will, the hugging of the hallucination of egoity, is subdued, as a man throws aside the foolish wishes of childhood. What matters it whether the transitory state of being, the root of which is nipped, lay aside its indifferent phenomenal life instantaneously or in after ages?

"Max Müller's researches, which could under the then circumstances of the case be based on only a portion of the authentic texts bearing on this branch of the subject, did not fail to attract the attention of native literati in Ceylon, the country which has preserved to the present day Buddhist temperament and knowledge in its purest form. And by the joint labors of eminent Singhalese students of Buddhist literature, such as the late James d'Alwis, and European inquirers, among whom we may mention especially Childers, Rhys Davids, and Trenckner, literary materials for the elucidation of the dogma of Nirvâna have been amply unearthed and ably treated. I have endeavored to complete the collections, for which we have to thank these learned scholars, in that I have submitted all the testimony of the sacred Pali canon, that contained in the discourses of Buddha as well as that in the writings upon the rights of the Order, to a detailed examination, so that I believe I am in a position to hope that no essential expression of the ancient dogmatics and doctrinal poets has been omitted. Before I undertook this task, it was my conviction that there is in the ancient Buddhist literature no passage which directly decides the alternative whether the Nirvâna is eternal felicity or annihilation. So much the greater, therefore, was my surprise, when in the course of these researches I lit not upon one passage, but upon very numerous passages, which speak as expressly as possible upon the point regarding which the controversy is waged, and determine it with a clearness which leaves nothing to be desired. And it was no less a cause of astonishment to me when I found that in that alternative, which appeared to have been laid down with all possible cogency, namely, that the Nirvâna must have been understood in the ancient Order to be either the Nothing or a supreme felicity, there was finally, neither on the one side nor on the other, perfect accuracy.

"King Pasenadi of Kosala, we are told, on one occasion, on a journey between his two chief towns, Sâketa and Sâvatthi, fell in with the nun Khemâ, a female disciple of Buddha, renowned for her wisdom. The king paid his respects to her, and inquired of her concerning the sacred doctrine.

"'Venerable lady,' asked the king, 'does the Perfect One (Tathâgata) exist after death?'

"'The Exalted One, O great king, has not declared: the Perfect One exists after death.'

"'Then does the Perfect One not exist after death, venerable lady?'

"'This also, O great king, the Exalted One has not declared: the Perfect One does not exist after death.'

"'Thus, venerable lady, the Perfect One does exist after death, and at the same time does not exist after death? thus, venerable lady, the Perfect One neither exists after death, nor does he not exist?'

"The king is astonished. 'What is the reason, venerable lady, what is the ground, on which the Exalted One has not revealed this?'

"'O great king, if the existence of the Perfect One be measured by the predicates of corporeal form, these predicates of the corporeal form are abolished in the Perfect One, their root is severed, they are hewn away like a palm tree, and laid aside, so that they cannot germinate again in the future. Released, O great king, is the Perfect One from this, that his being should be gauged by the measure of the corporeal world; he is deep, immeasurable, unfathomable as the great ocean. "The Perfect One exists after death," this is not apposite; "the Perfect One does not exist after death," this is not apposite; "the Perfect One at once exists and does not exist after death," this also is not apposite; "the Perfect One neither does nor does not exist after death," this also is not apposite.'

"When such a reason is assigned for the waiving of the question as to whether the Perfect One lives forever, is not this very giving of a reason itself an answer? And is not this answer a Yes? No being in the ordinary sense, but still assuredly not a non-being; a sublime positive, of which thought has no idea, for which language has no expression, which beams out to meet the cravings of the thirsty for immortality in that same splendor of which the apostle says: 'Eye has not seen, nor ear heard, neither have entered into the heart of man, the things which God hath prepared for them that love him.'"

Note 2. *Mohammedanism.*

[From "Islam under the Arabs," by R. D. Osborn, 1876. See also "Islam under the Khalifs of Baghdaad," by the same author.]

"Muhammad was neither philosopher nor metaphysician. No speculative difficulties troubled him as to the sources of creative power, or the relations between man and God. An omnipotent, self-conscious Being was the first cause. He had said, 'Be!' and the universe had started into existence. That was the whole account of the matter. Muhammad deemed it a monstrous absurdity to suppose that the attributes of man gave him any peculiar claims on the consideration of God. But it was worse than an absurdity; it was blasphemy to suppose that man could claim any spiritual kinship with his Creator, that any particle of the Divine essence had been breathed into him. 'Almost,' he cries in horror, 'might the very heavens be rent thereat, and the earth cleave asunder and the mountains fall down in fragments. Verily, there is none in the heavens and the earth but shall approach the God of Mercy *as a slave.*' God sits in awful and unapproachable majesty. He has fashioned man as an artificer fashions an image out of clay. There is no living bond between them. God is called the Merciful and Compassionate, not because love is of the essence of His nature, but because, though all powerful, He forbears to use His might for man's destruction. He might smite man with plagues; He might cause him to perish of famine or the lingering agonies of thirst; He might envelop the earth in perpetual darkness; but out of His mercy and compassion He does none of these things; He gives men rain and fruitful seasons, and genial sunshine. But He is not less the inscrutable despot, acting upon no principle but the caprices of His will. He creates the soul, and 'breathes into it its wickedness and piety.' He 'misleadeth whom He will, and guideth whom He will.' 'Whomsoever God shall please to direct, He will open his breast to receive the faith of Islam; but whomsoever He shall please to lead into error, He will render his breast straight and narrow as though he were climbing up into Heaven. Thus doth God inflict a terrible punishment on those who believe not.'

"Hope perishes under the weight of this iron bondage. There are in the Koran no forward glances to a coming golden age when the earth shall be filled with the knowledge of the

Lord as the waters cover the sea, such as irradiate the hymns and prophecies of the Old Testament. There is no communion of man's spirit with the Spirit of God, none of that loving trust which casteth out fear. There are not even any aspirations after spiritual perfection as bringing a man nearer to God.

"Fatalism is thus the central tenet of Islam. It suffices to explain the degraded condition of Muhammadan countries. So long as Muhammad lived and God did stoop to hold communication with men, the effects flowing from it were in a measure obscured. But when he died, the Deity seemed to withdraw altogether from the world He had created. The sufferings, sorrows, crimes, hopes, and struggles of men became a wild and ghastly orgy without meaning or ulterior purpose. The one rational object which a sober-minded, practical man could set before him was, in this life, to keep aloof from all this senseless turmoil, and, by a diligent performance of the proper rites and ceremonies, to cheat the Devil in the next. And so it has been always. History repeats itself in Muhammadan countries with a truly doleful exactness. The great bulk of the people are passive; wars and revolutions rage around them; they accept them as the decrees of a fate it is useless to strive against. All power passes accordingly into the hands of a few ambitious and turbulent spirits, unencumbered with scruples of any kind, animated by no desires except those of being rich and strong. There is never a sufficient space of rest to allow institutions to grow up.

"The Koran pulverizes humanity into an infinite number of separate atoms. The one common duty laid upon the Faithful is to be the agents of God's vengeance on those who believe not. These are to be slaughtered until they pay tribute, when they are to be allowed to go to Hell in their own way without further molestation.

"The mind of Muhammad was one but lightly burdened with the sense of mystery. It was thoroughly materialistic in all its conceptions. The first crude conception of an explanation seemed to him always a perfectly satisfactory one. He saw no difficulties. The earth was flat and kept steady by the mountains: that appeared to him a cosmogony as satisfactory as it was simple. There were seven heavens, — good, solid, substantial firmaments, — and the lowest, a magazine of fiery darts for hurling at the djinns: that seemed to him a sound and reasonable explanation of the blue sky and the stars."

Note 3. *Chaldean Account of the Creation.*

[From "Records of the Past," vol. ix.]

"The discovery of these tablets has greatly raised the reputation of the ancient author Damascius, for it is now seen that his account of the Creation was derived from genuine Babylonian sources. He says (see Cory's 'Ancient Fragments,' page 318, compared with the original), 'The Babylonians speak not of *One* origin of all things, for they make two original beings, Tauthe and Apason, making Apason the husband of Tauthe, whom they call the mother of the gods. Their only son (eldest son?) was Moymis. And another race proceeded from them, namely, Dakhė and Dakhos. And again a third race proceeded from the same (parents), namely, Kissaré and Assoros.'"

The First Tablet.

1. When the upper region was not yet called heaven,
2. and the lower region was not yet called earth,
3. and the abyss of Hades had not yet opened its arms,
4. then the chaos of waters gave birth to all of them
5. and the waters were gathered into one place.
6. No men yet dwelt together: no animals yet wandered about:
7. none of the gods had yet been born.
8. Their names were not spoken: their attributes were not known.
9. Then the eldest of the gods
10. Lakhmu and Lakhamu were born
11. and grew up

12. Assur and Kissur were born next
13. and lived through long periods.
14. Anu

[The rest of this tablet is lost.]

The Fifth Tablet.

[This fifth tablet is very important, because it affirms clearly, in my opinion, that the origin of the Sabbath was coeval with Creation.]

1. He constructed dwellings for the great gods.
2. He fixed up constellations, whose figures were like animals.
3. He made the year. Into four quarters he divided it.
4. Twelve months he established, with their constellations three by three.
5. And for the days of the year he appointed festivals.
6. He made dwellings for the planets: for their rising and setting.
7. And that nothing should go amiss, and that the course of none should be retarded,
8. he placed with them the dwellings of Bel and Hea.
9. He opened great gates, on every side :
10. he made strong the portals, on the left hand and on the right.
11. In the centre he placed luminaries.
12. The moon he appointed to rule the night
13. and to wander through the night, until the dawn of day.
14. Every month without fail he made holy assembly days.
15. In the beginning of the month, at the rising of the night,
16. it shot forth its horns to illuminate the heavens.
17. On the seventh day he appointed a holy day,
18. and to cease from all business he commanded.
19. Then arose the sun in the horizon of heaven in (glory).

[It has been known for some time that the Babylonians observed the Sabbath with considerable strictness. On that day the king was not allowed to take a drive in his chariot; various meats were forbidden to be eaten, and there were a number of minute restrictions.

But it was not known that they believed the Sabbath to have been ordained at the Creation. I have found, however, since this translation of the fifth tablet was completed, that Mr. Sayce has recently published a similar opinion. See the Academy, of November 27, 1875, p. 554.

This account falls short of the majesty of the Hebrew Genesis, especially where the writer implies that the heavenly movements might possibly go wrong, and it was therefore necessary that the gods Bel and Hea should watch over them and guard against misfortune.]

NOTE 4. *Buddhism in Siam.*

[From "The Wheel of the Law. Buddhism, illustrated from Siamese Sources." By Henry Alabaster. London. 1871.]

"Of the three hundred and sixty-five millions of men, the third of the human race who, according to a common estimate, profess in some form the religion of Buddha, the four million inhabitants of Siam are excelled by none in the sincerity of their belief and the liberality with which they support their religion. No other Buddhist country, of similar extent, can show so many splendid temples and monasteries. In Bangkok alone there are more than a hundred monasteries, and, it is said, ten thousand monks and novices. More than this, every male Siamese, some time during his life, and generally in the prime of it, takes orders as a monk, and retires for some months or years to practice abstinence and meditation in a monastery.

"All Buddhists, throughout the wide range of countries where the doctrines of Buddha prevail, call their religion the doctrine of 'The Wheel of the Law.' I have adopted the name for this book, because it is peculiarly appropriate to a theory of Buddhism, which the book in some degree illustrates. I refer to the theory that all existence of which we have any conception is but a part of an endless chain or circle of causes and effects; that so long as we remain in that wheel there is no rest and no peace; and that rest can only be obtained by escaping from that wheel into the incomprehensible Nirwana. Buddha taught a religion of which the wheel was the only proper symbol; for his theory, professing to be complete, dealt with but a limited round of knowledge; ignored the beginning, and was equally vague as to the end. He neither taught of a God, the Creator of existence, nor of a heaven, the absorber of existence, but restrained his teaching within what he believed to be the limits of reason.

"I will now give a sketch of the chief points of Buddhist belief and practice mentioned in the 'Life.'

"The first essential idea is that of transmigration, — transmigration not only into other human states, but into all forms, active and passive.

"Gods and animals, men and brutes, have no intrinsic difference between them. They all change places according to their merits and demerits. They exist because of the disturbance caused by their demerits. How they began to exist is not even asked; it is a question pertaining to the Infinite, of which no explanation is attempted. Even in dealing with the illustrious being who afterwards became Buddha, no attempt is made to picture a beginning of his existence, and we are only told of the beginning of his aspiration to become a Buddha, and the countless existences he subsequently passed through ere he achieved his object.

"Having thus declared the fact of transmigration, and the principle which causes its various states, Buddhism teaches that there is no real or permanent satisfaction in any state of transmigration; that neither the painless luxuries of the lower heavens nor the tranquillity of the highest angels can be considered as happiness, for they will have an end, followed by a recurrence of varied and frequently sorrowful existences. Here is one of the great distinctions, the irreconcilable differences, between Buddhism and Christianity.

"Take this one point alone: Christians profess that their existence is the effect of the benign providence of God, and that they have something to thank God for.

"But Buddhists, rich or poor, acknowledge no providence, and see more reason to lament existence than to be grateful for it.

"Nirwana, the extinction of all this kind of existence, must therefore be the object of the truly wise man. What this extinction is may, perhaps, have never been defined. Certainly it has been the subject of endless contention by those who think themselves capable of dealing with the infinite, and analyzing the beginning and the end. All I can see of it in this 'Life' is that it is now considered to be peace, rest, and eternal happiness. The choicest and most glorious epithets are lavished on it by the Siamese, but we are left as ignorant of it as we are of the heaven of Christians. We may call heaven an existence, but we are even less capable of realizing that existence than we are of realizing what Barthélemy St. Hiliare calls, with professed horror, the annihilation or non-existence of Nirwana.

"I believe that most men recognize sleep as a real pleasure. Certain it is that after a hard day's toil, bodily or mental, man longs for sleep; and if his overtasked body or too excited brain deprives him of it, he feels that the deprivation is pain. Yet, what is sleep? It is, to all intents and purposes, temporary non-existence, and during its existence we do not appreciate its temporariness. The existence during sleep, when sleep is perfect, appreciates no connection with the waking existence. When it is imperfect, it is vexed by dreams connected with waking existence, but that is not the sleep which men long for.

"The ordinary Siamese never troubles himself about Nirwana, he does not even mention it. He believes virtue will be rewarded by going to heaven (Sawan), and he talks of heaven, and not of Nirwana. Buddha, he will tell you, has entered Nirwana, but, for his part, he does not look beyond Sawan.

"The Buddhist who differs from us in recognizing a law of nature, without seeking for a Maker of that law, also differs from us in assuming a continuation of existence, without defining a soul as that which is continued. For all practical purposes we may speak of a soul as that which passes from one state of existence to another, but such is not the Buddhist idea, at least, not the idea of Buddhist metaphysicians.

"In my explanation of Buddhist ideas, I at times use the word soul, because it facilitates the comprehension of the idea I want to convey, and because I have not been able to find any other way of conveying it. The Buddhist tells me there is no soul, but that there is continuation of individual existence without it. I cannot explain his statement, for I fail thoroughly to understand it, or to appreciate the subtlety of his theory.

"The main rules of a virtuous life, that is, the five principal commandments, are:—

1. Not to destroy life.
2. Not to obtain another's property by unjust means.
3. Not to indulge the passions, so as to invade the legal or natural rights of other men.
4. Not to tell lies.
5. Not to partake of anything intoxicating.

"Of the practice of charity, it is not requisite to say much here. The whole character of Buddha is full of charity, insomuch that, although his perfection was such that at almost an infinite period before he became Buddha, he might, during the teaching of an earlier Buddha, have escaped from the current of existence, which he regarded as misery, he remained in that current, and passed through countless painful transmigrations, in order that he might ultimately benefit, not himself, but all other beings, by becoming a Buddha, and helping all those whose ripe merits could only be perfected by the teaching of a Buddha.

"I have lived long among Buddhists, and have experienced much kindness among them. Above all things I have found them exceedingly tolerant."

Note 5. *Buddhism and Christianity.*

[From the "Hibbert Lectures," pp. 233, 234, 236, by A. Kuenen, 1882.]

"What is the nature of the proofs alleged by those who maintain that Buddhistic influences were at work in the production of Christianity? Positive evidence that Buddhistic ideas had penetrated to Western Asia is not forthcoming till a far later time. The Indian Gymnosophists whom Philo mentions once or twice are not Buddhists at all, and, moreover, he only knows them by vague report. Clement of Alexandria is the first who mentions the Buddha, and he speaks of him as the human founder of a religion, whom his followers, 'because he was so surpassingly venerable,' reverenced as a god. What he has to tell us leaves the impression that even in those days, about the beginning of the third century of our era, Buddhism was still a remote phenomenon." "But the total absence of historical witnesses should make us very cautious in assuming such an 'actio in distans,' and renders it at least our imperative duty to submit the quality of the proofs which are usually urged in support of the theory of Buddhistic influences to a very close examination. The well-known volume on 'The Angel Messiah of the Buddhists, Essenes, and Christians' no doubt teems with parallels of every description; but alas! it is one unbroken commentary on Scaliger's thesis that errors in theology — or, as he really puts it, 'disputes in religion' — all rise from neglect of philology. A writer who can allow himself to bring the name of 'Pharisee' into connection with Persia has once for all forfeited his right to a voice in the matter. But the very title of the book ought really to have preserved us from any illusion as to its contents. 'The Angel-Messiah' of the Buddhists, who know nothing either of angels or a Messiah, and of the Essenes, who were certainly much occupied with the angels and their names, but of whose Messianic expectations we know nothing, absolutely nothing! By such comparisons between unknown or imaginary quantities, instituted without any kind of accuracy, we could prove literally anything. Unquestionably there are points of agreement between the Gospel narratives, especially in Luke and John, and the legend of the Buddha, and also between the preaching of Jesus and that of his great predecessor. To make a complete collection of these parallels, and to illustrate both them and the no less noteworthy points of difference, I hold to be far from a superfluous task; and it is satisfactory to know that it has actually been undertaken by a competent hand, with results that have quite recently been given to the world. [1] It would be premature as yet to pronounce a final judgment on the outcome of the running comparison thus instituted; but meanwhile I think I may safely affirm that we must abstain from assigning to Buddhism the smallest direct influence on the origin of Christianity. The utmost that can be maintained is, that a few features in the evangelical tradition may have been borrowed from it; and even this must remain very doubtful, inasmuch as the resemblances upon which the hypothesis is built present themselves, remarkably enough, in some of the stories which are dependent on the Old Testament, and in which, of course, the coincidence with certain traits in the life of Câkya-Muni *cannot* by any possibility be more than accidental. In a word, however attractive the hypothesis that brings Jesus into connection with the Buddhists may possibly appear, and however readily it may lend itself to romantic treatment, yet sober and strict historical research gives it no support, and indeed condemns it."

[1] Professor Seydel.

NOTE 6. *On the Connection between the Buddhist Books and the New Testament.*

[By T. W. Rhys Davids, "Sacred Books of the East," vol. ii., 1881.]

"Very little reliance can be placed, without careful investigation, on a resemblance, however close at first sight, between a passage in the Pali Pitakas and a passage in the New Testament.

"It is true that many passages in these two literatures can be easily shown to have a similar tendency. But when some writers on the basis of such similarities proceed to argue that there must have been some historical connection between the two, and that the New Testament, as the later, must be the borrower, I venture to think they are wrong. There does not seem to me to be the slightest evidence of any historical connection between them; and whenever the resemblance is a real one — and it often turns out to be really least when it first seems to be greatest, and really greatest when it first seems least — it is due, not to any borrowing on the one side or on the other, but solely to the similarity of the conditions under which the two movements grew.

"This does not of course apply to the later literature of the two religions, and it ought not to detract from the very great value and interest of the parallels which may be adduced from the earlier books. If we wish to understand what it was that gave such life and force to the stupendous movement which is called Buddhism, we cannot refrain from comparing it, not only in the points in which it agrees with it, but also in the points in which it differs from it, with our own faith. I trust I have not been wrong in making use occasionally of this method, though the absence of any historical connection between the New Testament and the Pali Pitakas has always seemed to me so clear that it would be unnecessary to mention it. But when a reviewer who has been kind enough to appreciate, I am afraid too highly, what he calls my 'service in giving, for the first time, a thoroughly human, acceptable, and coherent' account of the 'life of Buddha' and of the 'simple groundwork of his religion' has gone on to conclude that the parallels I had thus adduced are 'an unanswerable indication of the obligations of the New Testament to Buddhism,' I must ask to be allowed to enter a protest against an inference which seems to me to be against the rules of sound historical criticism."

NOTE 7. *The Lamentations of Isis and Nephthys.*

[From "Records of the Past," vol. ii., p. 117.]

[This papyrus was found by the late Mr. Passalaqua in the ruins of Thebes, in the interior of a statue representing Osiris. It is divided into two parts, very distinct. The first contains chapters of the funeral ritual in the hieroglyphic writing; the second, of which a translation here follows, consists of five pages of a fine hieratic writing of the lower epoch, probably about the time of the Ptolemies.]

TRANSLATION.

Recital of the beneficial formulæ made by the two divine sisters in the house of Osiris, who resides in the West, Great God, Lord of Abydos, in the month of Choiak, the twenty-fifth day. They are made the same in all the abodes of Osiris, and in all his festivals; and they are beneficial to his soul, giving firmness to his body, diffusing joy through his being, giving breath to the nostrils, to the dryness of the throat; they satisfy the heart of Isis as well as [that] of Nephthys; they place Horus on the throne of his father, [and] give life, stability, tranquility to Osiris-Tentrut born of Takha-aa, who is surnamed Persais, the justified. It is profitable to recite them, in conformity with the divine words.

EVOCATION BY ISIS.

She says: —

Come to thine abode, come to thine abode!
God An, come to thine abode!
Thine enemies [exist] no more.
O excellent Sovereign, come to thine abode!
Look at me; I am thy sister who loveth thee.
Do not stay far from me, O beautiful youth.
Come to thine abode with haste, with haste.
I call thee in [my] lamentations
[even] to the heights of Heaven,
and thou hearest not my voice.
I am thy sister who loveth thee on earth;
no one else hath loved thee more than I,
[thy] sister, [thy] sister.

EVOCATION BY NEPHTHYS.

She says: —

O excellent Sovereign, come to thine abode!
Rejoice, all thine enemies are annihilated!
Thy two sisters are near to thee,
protecting thy funeral bed;
calling thee in weeping,
thou who art prostrate on thy funeral bed.
Thou seest [our] tender solicitude.
Speak to us, Supreme Ruler, our Lord.
Chase all the anguish which is in our hearts.
Thy companions, who are gods and men,
when they see thee [exclaim]:
Ours by thy visage, supreme Ruler, our Lord;
life for us is to behold thy countenance;
let not thy face be turned from us;
the joy of our hearts is to contemplate thee;
[O] Sovereign, our hearts are happy in seeing thee.
I am Nephthys, thy sister who loveth thee.
Thine enemy is vanquished,
he no longer existeth!
I am with thee,
protecting thy members forever and eternally.

INVOCATION BY ISIS.

She says : —

Hail [O] God An!
Thou, in the firmament, shinest upon us each day.
We no longer cease to behold thy rays.
Thoth is a protection for thee.
He placeth thy soul in the barque Ma-at,
in that name which is thine, of God Moon.
I have come to contemplate thee.
Thy beauties are in the midst of the Sacred Eye,
in that name which is thine, of Lord of the sixth day's festival.
Thy companions are near to thee;
they separate themselves no more from thee.
Thou hast taken possession of the Heavens,
by the grandeur of the terrors which thou inspirest,
in that name which is thine, of Lord of the fifteenth day's festival.
Thou dost illuminate us like Ra each day.
Thou shinest upon us like Atum.
Gods and men live because they behold thee.
Thou sheddest thy rays upon us.
Thou givest light to the Two Worlds.
The horizon is filled by thy passage.
Gods and men [turn] their faces towards thee;
nothing is injurious to them when thou shinest.
Thou dost navigate in the heights [of Heaven]
and thine enemy no longer exists!
I am thy protection each day.
Thou who comest to us as a child each month,
we do not cease to contemplate thee.
Thine emanation heightens the brilliancy
of the stars of Orion in the firmament,
by rising and setting each day.
I am the divine Sothis behind him.
I do not separate myself from him.
The glorious emanation which proceedeth from thee giveth
life to gods and men.
Hail to the divine Lord!
There is no god like unto thee!

Heaven hath thy soul;
earth hath thy remains;
the lower heaven is in possession of thy mysteries.
Thy spouse is a protection for thee.
Thy son Horus is the king of the worlds.

INVOCATION BY ISIS.

She says: —

Come to thine abode, come to thine abode!
Excellent Sovereign, come to thine abode!
Come [and] behold thy son Horus
as supreme Ruler of gods and men.
He hath taken possession of the cities and the districts,
by the grandeur of the respect he inspires.
Heaven and earth are in awe of him,
the barbarians are in fear of him.

When this is recited,
the place [where one is]
is holy in the extreme.
Let it be seen or heard by no one,
excepting by the principal Kher-heb and the Sam.
Two women beautiful in their members,
having been introduced,
are made to sit down on the ground
at the principal door of the Great Hall.
[Then] the names of Isis and Nephthys
are inscribed on their shoulders.
Crystal vases [full] of water
are placed in their right hands;
loaves of bread made in Memphis
in their left hands.
Let them pay attention to the things done
at the third hour of the day,
and also at the eighth hour of the day.
Cease not to recite this book
at the hour of the ceremony!

It is finished.

NOTE 8. *Religion of Zoroaster.*

[From the "Vendidad, Fargard III."]

1. Creator of the corporeal world, Pure One!
2. What is in the first place most acceptable to this earth?
3. Then answered Ahura-Mazda: Where a holy man walks about, O holy Zarathustra,
4. Offering-wood in the hand, Bĕrĕçma in the hand, the cup in the hand, the mortar in the hand,
5. In accordance with the law speaking these words: Mithra with his broad territories will I invoke, and Râma-saçtra.
6. Creator of the corporeal world, Pure One!
7. What is in the second place most acceptable to this earth?
8. Then answered Ahura-Mazda: That a holy man should build himself there a habitation,
9. Provided with fire, provided with cattle, provided with a wife, children, and good flocks.
10. Then is there in this habitation abundance of cattle, abundance of righteousness, abundance of provender, of dogs, of women, of youths, of fire, of all that is requisite for a good life.
11. Creator of the corporeal world, Pure One!
12. What is in the third place most acceptable to this earth?
13. Then answered Ahura-Mazda: Where by cultivation there is produced, O holy Zarathustra, most corn, provender, and fruit-bearing trees.
14. Where dry land is watered, or the water is drained from the too moist land.
15. Creator of the corporeal world, Pure One!
16. What is in the fourth place most acceptable to this earth?
17. Then answered Ahura-Mazda: Where most cattle and beasts of burden are born.

26. What is in the second place most displeasing to this earth?
27. Then answered Ahura-Mazda: Where most dead dogs and dead men are buried in it.

38. Creator of the corporeal world, Pure One!
39. Who first rejoices this earth with the greatest joy?

40. Then answered Ahura-Mazda : He who especially digs up where dead men and dogs are buried.
75. Creator of the corporeal world, Pure One!
76. Who rejoices this earth with the greatest joy?
77. Then answered Ahura-Mazda : He who most cultivates the fruits of the field, grass, and trees which yield food, O holy Zarathustra.
78. Or, he who provides waterless land with water, or gives water to the waterless land.
79. For the earth is not glad which lies long uncultivated.
91. He who does not cultivate this earth, O holy Zarathustra, with the left arm and the right, with the right arm and left,
92. Then this earth speaks to him : Man! thou who dost not cultivate me with the left arm and right, with the right arm and left,
93. Always thou standest there, going to the doors of others to beg for food.
94. Always they bring food to you, thou who beggest lazily out of doors.

Note 9. *Transmigration and Final Beatitude.*

[From the "Laws of Manu," chapter xii.]

1. O Thou, who art free from sin, (said the devout sages,) thou hast declared the whole system of duties ordained for the four classes of men : explain to us now, from the first principles, the ultimate retribution for their deeds.
2. Bhrigu, whose heart was the pure essence of virtue, who proceeded from Manu himself, thus addressed the great sages : Hear the infallible rules for the fruit of deeds in this universe.
3. Action, either mental, verbal, or corporeal, bears good or evil fruit, as itself is good or evil ; and from the actions of men proceed their various transmigrations in the highest, the mean, and the lowest degree :
4. Of that three-fold action, connected with bodily functions, disposed in three classes, and consisting of ten orders, be it known in this world, that the heart is the instigator.

5. Devising means to appropriate the wealth of other men, resolving on any forbidden deed, and conceiving notions of atheism or materialism, are the three bad acts of the mind :
6. Scurrilous language, falsehood, indiscriminate backbiting, and useless tattle are the four bad acts of the tongue :
8. A rational creature has a reward or a punishment for mental acts, in his mind; for verbal acts, in his organs of speech; for corporeal acts, in his bodily frame.
9. For sinful acts mostly corporeal, a man shall assume after death a vegetable or mineral form ; for such acts mostly verbal, the form of a bird or a beast; for acts mostly mental, the lowest of human conditions:
10. He, whose firm understanding obtains a command over his words, a command over his thoughts, and a command over his whole body, may justly be called a tridandi, or triple commander ; not a mere anchoret, who bears three visible staves.
11. The man who exerts this triple self-command with respect to all animated creatures, wholly subduing both lust and wrath, shall by those means attain beatitude.
24. Be it known, that the three qualities of the rational soul are a tendency to goodness, to passion, and to darkness ; and endued with one or more of them, it remains incessantly attached to all these created substances :
26. Goodness is declared to be true knowledge ; darkness, gross ignorance ; passion, an emotion of desire or aversion : such is the compendious description of those qualities which attend all souls.
27. When a man perceives, in the reasonable soul, a disposition tending to virtuous love, unclouded with any malignant passion, clear as the purest light, let him recognize it as the quality of goodness.
30. Now will I declare at large the various acts, in the highest, middle, and lowest degrees, which proceed from those three dispositions of mind.
31. Study of scripture, austere devotion, sacred knowledge, corporeal purity, command over the organs, performance of duties, and meditation on the divine spirit, accompany the good quality of the soul :

32. Interested motives for acts of religion or morality, perturbation of mind on slight occasions, commission of acts forbidden by law, and habitual indulgence in selfish gratifications, are attendant on the quality of passion.

NOTE 10. *Japan and the Japanese.*

[From Baron Hübner's "Ramble Round the World in 1871," page 420.]

"Before the arrival of the Europeans the people were happy and contented. . . . Public order was rarely troubled in Japan. Life and property were better protected than in any other pagan nation. The cultivation of the soil, the development of certain branches of industry, the taste for a practice of the fine arts, bespoke a long-established civilization. Doubtless this civilization is imperfect, for Christianity has never shed its light freely over the land. Certain barbarous customs tarnish the spirit of chivalry and the feeling of honor which distinguish this people. Gross superstitions darken and hinder the aspirations of their souls, which are dissatisfied with the Buddhist doctrines. Although Buddhism is the religion of the majority, the spirit of scepticism has invaded and enervated the whole of the upper classes. The family forms the basis of the political institutions of the state; but woman, though more free and respected than in any other pagan society, still waits her enfranchisement. Hence arises a deplorable laxity of morals. Respect for parental authority, fidelity to the head of the clan, bravery, and voluntary death, when exacted by honor, were and are the chief virtues of this gay, polite, careless, chivalrous, and amiable people.

Every one in these days knows that the Japanese people are gentle, amiable, civil, gay, good-natured, and childish; that the men of the lower classes have skins bronzed by the sun, and often tattooed red and blue like the designs on the lacquer-work of their country; that men of all classes have their heads shaved, saving a little tail which is agreeably balanced above the occiput; that in summer they leave off their narrow trousers, and content themselves with a simple tunic of silk or cotton, according to the rank of the individual, and when they are at home, with the fundashi. From the Mikado down to the lowest coolie, this waistband or sash forms the principal part of the toilet of every respectable Japanese. Every one except the merchants, who are the lowest in the social scale, belongs to some one, not as a serf or slave, but as a member of a clan, which, divided into a great many different castes, forms only one great family, of which the prince or daimio is the chief. He has his counsellors, his vassals, his samurais, or knights with two swords (the others having only one), his men of war, and servants of all grades. Each one wears on his back, and on the sleeves of his tunic, the coat of arms of the prince or the corporation whom he serves, a flower or certain letters inscribed in a circle. The sabres of the gentlemen, their inkstands, their pipes, their purses fastened to their waistbands, — all this is well known. As to the women, all authors speak of them with delight. They are not exactly beautiful, for they are wanting in regularity of feature. Their cheek-bones are too prominent. Their beautiful, large, brown eyes are too decidedly of an almond shape, and their thick lips are wanting in delicacy; but that does not spoil them. But what no pen or pencil can ever truly render is the sight of the streets, with their busy, picturesque crowd of men and women, smiling courteously at one another and bowing profoundly to each other; or, if it be a question of some great personage, prostrating themselves on the ground; but with an agility and a dignity which takes off what might appear humiliating in the action, and only gives it the appearance of an excess of politeness and deference. The Japanese people are happy and contented with the conditions in which they are placed, or rather, in which they have been placed until now. Misery is unknown amongst them, but so, also, is luxury. The simplicity of their habits, an extreme frugality, and the absence of those wants which Europe could and would satisfy, are, it appears to me, so many obstacles to a vast exchange of European products with those of Japan. "The Japanese have adopted the civilization, religion, and even the handwriting of the Chinese;" this was told me by a man who has long been resident here. Now they are trying to imitate Europeans. They cannot help copying others; it is their nature. Only compare a Japanese and Chinese servant. The former will watch the minutest habit of his master, and conform himself to it with the most wonderful facility; only he must not act by his own inspiration, for he has no head. The Chinese remain always Chinese. They observe and copy less, but they do better when they are left to follow their own imaginations.

The Japanese, provided you keep them in their place and make them observe the etiquette of their own country, are gentle, merry, and very affectionate towards their master. If he beats them, they are not the less attached; besides the bamboo brings with it no dishonor. They are only children whom a father has chastised. But if you treat them as you would a European servant, they become familiar, rude, and positively insupportable. The Chinaman, on the other hand, can never be made to love the master he serves. He is proud, vindictive, and very susceptible, but always of an exquisite politeness. At the slightest observation you make to him, he leaves your service, either under the pretext of the illness of his mother, or telling you, very respectfully, and with the peculiar smile of his race when announcing disagreeable intelligence, that there is between you and him an incompatibility of character. Having said this, nothing stops him, and he leaves you. The Japanese are wonderful lovers of nature. In Europe a feeling for beauty has to be developed by education. Our peasants will talk to you of the fertility of the soil, of the abundance of water, so useful for their mills, of the value of their woods, but not of the picturesque charms of the country. They are not perhaps entirely insensible to them; but if they do feel them, it is in a vague, undefined sort of way, for which they would be puzzled to account. It is not so with the Japanese laborer. With him the sense of beauty is innate. This extraordinary love and feeling for nature is reflected in all Japanese productions. A taste for the fine arts is common among the very lowest classes, and to a degree which is not found in any country in Europe. In the humblest cottage, you will find traces of this — an artificial flower, an ingenious child's toy, an incense-burner, an idol, heaps of little ornamental things, the only use of which is to give pleasure to the eye. With us, except in the service of religion, this kind of art is the privilege of the rich and of people in easy circumstances.

NOTE 11. *The Ethics of Buddhism.*

[From "A Manual of Buddhism." By Spence Hardy.]

There are three sins of the body: 1. The taking of life, Murder. 2. The taking of that which is not given, Theft. 3. Impurity.

There are four sins of the speech: 1. Lying. 2. Slander. 3. Abuse. 4. Unprofitable Conversation.

There are three sins of the mind: 1. Covetousness. 2. Malice. 3. Scepticism.

There are also five other evils that are to be avoided: 1. The Drinking of Intoxicating Liquors. 2. Gambling. 3. Idleness. 4. Improper Associations. 5. The Frequenting of Places of Amusement.

There are five things necessary to constitute the crime of taking life: 1. There must be the knowledge that there is life. 2. There must be the assurance that a living being is present. 3. There must be the intention to take life. 4. With this intention there must be something done, as the placing of a bow or spear, or the setting of a snare; and there must be some movement towards it, as walking, running, or jumping. 5. The life must be actually taken.

There are eight causes of the destruction of life: 1. Evil Desire. 2. Anger. 3. Ignorance. 4. Pride. 5. Covetousness. 6. Poverty. 7. Wantonness, as in the sport of children. 8. Law, as by the decree of the ruler.

This crime is committed, not only when life is actually taken, but also when there is the indulgence of hatred or anger; hence also lying, stealing, and slander may be regarded in some sense as including this sin.

Under certain circumstances one's own life may be given up, but the life of another is never to be taken.

The crime is not great when an ant is killed; its magnitude increases in this progression: a lizard, a guana, a hare, a deer, a bull, a horse, and an elephant. The life of each of these animals is the same, but the skill or effort required to destroy them is widely different. Again, when we come to men, the two extremes are the sceptic and the rakat (as no one can take the life of a supreme Buddha).

In a village near Danta, there was a husbandmàn. One of his oxen having strayed, he ascended a rock that he might look for it; but while there he was seized by a serpent. He had a goad in his hand, and his first impulse was to kill the snake; but he reflected that if he did so he should break the precept that forbids the taking of life. He therefore resigned himself to death, and threw the goad away; no sooner had he done this, than the snake released him from its grasp, and he escaped. Thus, by observing the precept, his life was preserved from the most imminent danger.

A certain king commanded an upásaka to procure him a fowl and kill it. As he refused, the king issued a decree that he should be taken to the place of execution, where a fowl was to be put into his hand, and if he still refused to kill it, he was to be slain. The upásaka, however, said that he had never broken the precept that forbids the taking of life, and that he was willing to give his own life for the life of the fowl. With this intention he threw the fowl away unhurt. After this he was brought back to the king, and released, as he had been put to this test merely to try the sincerity of his faith.

In the city of Wisála there was a priest, who one day, on going with the alms-bowl, sat down upon a chair that was covered with a cloth, by which he killed a child that was underneath. About the same time there was a priest who received food mixed with poison into his alms-bowl, which he gave to another priest, not knowing that it was poisoned, and the priest died. Both of these priests went to Buddha, and in much sorrow informed him of what had taken place. The sage declared, after hearing their story, that the priest who gave the poisoned food, though it caused the death of another priest, was innocent, because he had done it unwittingly; but that the priest who sat upon the chair, though it only caused the death of a child, was guilty, as he had not taken the proper precaution to look under the cloth, and had sat down without being invited by the householder.

THEFT.

When anything is taken that is not given by the owner, whether it be gold, silver, or any similar article, and it be hidden by the person who takes it, in the house, or in the forest, or in the rock, the precept is broken that forbids the taking of that which is not given; it is theft.

There are five things necessary to constitute the crime of theft: 1. The article that is taken must belong to another. 2. There must be some token that it belongs to another. 3. There must be the intention to steal. 4. There must be some act done, or effort exerted, to obtain possession. 5. There must be actual acquirement.

LYING.

To deny the possession of any article in order to retain it is a lie, but not of a heinous description; to bear false witness in order that the proper owner may be deprived of that which he possesses, is a lie to which a greater degree of culpability is attached. When any one declares that he has not what he has, or that he has what he has not, whether it be by the lips, or by signs, or in writing, it is a lie.

Four things are necessary to constitute a lie: 1. There must be the utterance of the thing that is not. 2. There must be the knowledge that it is not. 3. There must be some endeavor to prevent the person addressed from learning the truth. 4. There must be the discovery by the person deceived that what has been told him is not true.

It is said by the Brahmans that it is not a crime to tell a lie on behalf of the guru, or on account of cattle, or to save the person's own life, or to gain the victory in any contest: but this is contrary to the precept.

On one occasion Buddha said that when a lie is uttered knowingly it is pàràjikà, or excludes from the priesthood; yet on another occasion he said that it is a venial or minor offence. It was in this manner that it occurred. A number of priests kept near a river; but as the people were remiss in providing them with food and other requisites, they falsely gave out that they had entered the first path and had become rakats, by which means they obtained abundance of all that they wanted. At the conclusion of the ceremony they went to Buddha, who, after inquiring about their welfare, began to reprove them and said, "Foolish men, for the sake of the belly you have assumed to yourselves the glory of the Dharmma, as if you yourselves had promulgated it. Better would it have been for you, than to have practiced this deception for the sake of a little food, to have had your intestines torn out, or to have swallowed molten metal."

Note 12. *Buddhist Ascetics before Christ.*

Extracts from "The Toy Cart," a Sanskrit Drama. Translated into English in Wilson's "Hindu Drama."

[These extracts show: —

1. That Buddhism existed in India together with Brahmanism, and tolerated by it, at least one hundred years before Christ.

2. That Buddhism in those days as now (1) set aside caste, (2) laid stress on moral conduct, (3) made its priests take the vows of poverty, celibacy, and monastic life; that they were mendicants; must not touch women.

3. That the King or Rajah of the Province appointed the heads of the Buddhist monasteries, so that Buddhism was a part of the established religion of India.]

ACT VIII.

Enter the SRAMANKA, *or* BAUDDHA *mendicant, with a wet garment in his hand.*

SRAMANKA (*sings*).

Be virtue, friends, your only store,
And restless appetite restrain,
Beat meditation's drum, and sore
Your watch against each sense maintain;
The thief that still in ambush lies,
To make devotion's wealth his prize.

Cast the five senses all away
That triumph o'er the virtuous will,
The pride of self-importance slay,
And ignorance remorseless kill;
So shall you safe the body guard,
And Heaven shall be your last reward.

Why shave the head and mow the chin
Whilst bristling follies choke the breast?
Apply the knife to parts within
And heed not how deformed the rest.
The heart of pride and passion weed,
And then the man is pure indeed.

My cloth is heavy with the yet moist dye. I will enter this garden belonging to the Rájá's brother-in-law, and wash it in the pool, and then I shall proceed more lightly. (*Does so.*)

(*Behind.*) What ho! you rascally Sramanka, what are you doing there?

Sram. Alas, alas! here he is, Samsthánaka himself. He has been affronted by one mendicant, and whenever he meets another he sends him off with his nose slit like an ox. Where shall I fly to? The lord Buddha be my refuge!

Vit. In that case I suspect he will not have long followed the profession.

Sams. How so?

Vit. Observe: his head shines as if it had only been lately shaven; and his garment has been so little worn that there are no scars on his shoulder. The ochry dye has not yet fully stained the cloth, and the open web yet fresh and flaccid hangs loosely over his arms.

Sram. I do not deny it, worthy sir; it is true I have but lately adopted the profession of a beggar.

Sams. And why so; why did you not become a beggar as soon as you were born, you scoundrel? (*Beats him.*)

Sram. Glory to Buddha!

Sams. He shall neither go, nor stay, nor move, nor breathe. Let him fall down and be put to death.

Sram. Glory to Buddha! Mercy, mercy!

Enter the SRAMANKA *as mendicant, as before.*

I have washed my mantle, and will hang it on these boughs to dry. No, here are a number of monkeys. I'll spread it on the ground. No, there is too much dust. Ha! yonder the wind has blown together a pile of dry leaves, that will answer exactly; I'll spread it upon them. (*Spreads his wrapper over Vasantasénâ and sits down.*) Glory to Buddha! (*Repeats the moral stanzas as above.*) But enough of this. I covet not the other world until in this I may make some return for the lady Vasantasénâ's charity. On the day that she liberated me from the gamester's clutches she made me her slave forever. Holloa! something sighed amidst yon leaves! or perhaps it was only their crackling, scorched by the sun, and moistened by my damp garment. Bless me, they spread out like the wings of a bird. (*One of Vasantasénâ's hands appears.*) A woman's hand, as I live, with rich ornaments, — and another; surely I have seen that hand before. It is, it is — it is the hand that once was stretched forth to save me. What should this mean! (*Throws off the wrapper and leaves, and sees Vasantaséná.*) It is the lady Vasantaséná, the devoted worshiper of Buddha. (*Vasantaséná expresses by signs the want of water.*) She wants water: the pool is far away, what's to be done? Ha! my wet garment. (*Applies it to her face and mouth and fans her.*)

Vas. (*reviving.*) Thanks, thanks, my friend. Who art thou?

Sram. Do you not recollect me, lady? You once redeemed me with ten suvernas.

Vas. I remember *you;* aught else I have forgotten. I have suffered since.

Sram. How, lady?

Vas. As my fate deserved.

Sram. Rise, lady, rise; drag yourself to this tree: here, hold by this creeper. (*Bends it down to her, she lays hold of it and rises.*) In a neighboring convent dwells a holy sister; rest awhile with her, lady, and recover your spirits. Gently, lady, gently. (*They proceed.*) Stand aside, good friends, stand aside, make way for a young female and a poor beggar! It is my duty to restrain the hands and mouth, and keep the passions in subjection. What should such a man care for kingdoms? His is the world to come.

Enter the Sramanka *and* Vasantaséna.

Sram. Bless me, what shall I do? Thus leading Vasantaséná, am I acting conformably to the laws of my order? Lady, whither shall I conduct you?

Vas. To the house of Chárudatta, my good friend.

Sram. Quick, lady! Worthy servant of Buddha, hasten to save Chárudatta! Room, good friends, make way!

Chár. And who is this?

Vas. To him I owe my life;
His seasonable aid preserved me.

Chár. Who art thou, friend?

Sram. Your Honor does not recollect me. I was employed as your personal servant. Afterwards becoming connected with gamblers, and unfortunate, I should have been reduced to slavery, had not this lady redeemed me. I have since then adopted the life of a mendicant; and coming in my wanderings to the Rájá's garden, was fortunately enabled to assist my former benefactress.

Ser. Lady Vasantaséná, with your worth
The King is well acquainted, and requests
To hold you as his kinswoman.

Vas. Sir, I am grateful. (*Servillaka throws a veil over her.*)

Ser. What shall we do for this good mendicant?

Chár. Speak, Sramaṇaka, your wishes.

Sram. To follow still the path I have selected,
For all I see is full of care and change.

Chár. Since such is his resolve, let him be made
Chief of the monasteries of the Buddhas.

Ser. It shall be so.

INDEX

OF SUBJECTS TREATED IN THIS WORK.

Important Religious Books

Published by

HOUGHTON, MIFFLIN & COMPANY

BOSTON

The Riverside Press, Cambridge

A. Barth.

THE RELIGIONS OF INDIA. Translated from the French by REV. J. WOOD. 8vo, gilt top, $5.00.

A masterly treatise on the religious thought, worship, and history of one of the most interesting people on the face of the earth. — *Advertiser* (Boston).

E. E. Beardsley, D.D.

THE HISTORY OF THE EPISCOPAL CHURCH IN CONNECTICUT, from the Settlement of the Colony to the Present Time. 2 vols. 8vo, $6.00.

Buddhist Birth Stories.

BUDDHIST BIRTH STORIES; or, Jataka Tales. Translated by T. W. RHYS DAVIDS. 8vo, gilt top, $5.00.

Many a wonder-story with which the little inmates of American nurseries are charmed to sleep was told, long centuries ago, under the shadows of the Himalayas. They present a nearly complete picture, quiet, unaffected by European intercourse, of the social life and customs and popular beliefs of the common people of Aryan tribes closely related to ourselves, just as they were passing through the first stages of civilization, a priceless record of the childhood of our race. — *Tribune* (New York).

John Bunyan.

THE PILGRIM'S PROGRESS. 16 full-page illustrations. 16mo, 75 cents.

THE SAME. New *Popular Edition*, from new plates. With Archdeacon Allen's Life of Bunyan (illustrated), and Macaulay's Essay on Bunyan. 62 wood-cuts. 12mo, $1.00.

THE SAME. *Holiday Edition*, comprising, in addition to the Popular Edition, a Steel Portrait of Bunyan, and Eight Colored Plates. 8vo, full gilt, $2.50.

James Freeman Clarke, D. D.

TEN GREAT RELIGIONS. An Essay in Comparative Theology. With an Index. 8vo, $3.00; half calf, $5.50.

CONTENTS: Ethnic and Catholic Religions; Confucius and the Chinese; Brahmanism; Buddhism, or the Protestantism of the East; Zoroaster and the Zend Avesta; The Gods of Egypt; The Gods of Greece; The Religion of Rome; The Teutonic and Scandinavian Religion; The Jewish Religion; Mohammed and Islam; The Ten Religions and Christianity.

He treats the ten condemned faiths in a spirit of the fullest reverence, anxious to bring to light whatever of good is contained in them, regarding each as in reality a religion, an essay toward the truth, even if only a partially successful one. . . . A great body of valuable and not generally or easily accessible information. — *The Nation* (New York).

Nothing has come to our knowledge which furnishes evidence of such voluminous reading, such thorough study and research, and such masterly grasp of the real elements of these religions, as does the volume before us. James Freeman Clarke has accomplished a work here of solid worth. — *Missionary Review* (Princeton).

TEN GREAT RELIGIONS. Part II. A Comparison of all Religions. 8vo, $3.00; half calf, $5.50.

CONTENTS: Description and Classification; Special Types, Law of Development; Origin and Development of all Religions; The Idea of God in all Religions: Animism, Polytheism, Pantheism, Ditheism, Tritheism, and Monotheism; The Soul and its Transmigrations in all Religions; The Origin of the World in all Religions; Evolution, Emanation, and Creation; Prayer and Worship in all Religions; Inspiration and Art in all Religions; Ethics in all Religions; Idea of a Future State in all Religions; The Future Religion of Mankind.

COMMON-SENSE IN RELIGION. A Series of Essays. 12mo, $2.00.

CONTENTS: Common Sense and Mystery; Common-Sense View of Human Nature; On the Doctrine Concerning God; The Bible and Inspiration; The True Meaning of Evangelical Christianity; The Truth about Sin; Common-Sense and Scripture Views of Heaven and Hell; Satan, according to Common-Sense and the Bible; Concerning the Future Life; The Nature of Our Condition Hereafter; Common-Sense View of the Christian Church; Five Kinds of Piety; Jesus a Mediator; The Expectations and Disappointments of Jesus; Common-Sense View of Salvation by Faith; On not being Afraid; Hope; The Patience of Hope; Love; The Brotherhood of Men.

As the common-sense of religion is the most certain reality of all life, the title of these essays is admirably chosen. It must arrest attention in face of the conservative determination to relegate religion to the domain of darkness, dreams, disease, myths, and other uncertainties. — *Advertiser* (Boston).

He writes, not for the learned, but for the simple; and there is hardly a child but might follow his course of thought, and take delight in his fresh and striking illustrations. — *Atlantic Monthly.*

Joseph Cook.

BOSTON MONDAY LECTURES.

These wonderful lectures stand forth alone amidst the contemporary literature of the class to which they belong.—London Quarterly Review.

BIOLOGY. With Preludes on Current Events. Seventeenth edition. 3 colored illustrations. 12mo, $1.50.

TRANSCENDENTALISM. With Preludes on Current Events. 12mo, $1.50.

ORTHODOXY. With Preludes on Current Events. 12mo, $1.50.

CONSCIENCE. With Preludes on Current Events. 12mo, $1.50.

HEREDITY. With Preludes on Current Events. 12mo, $1.50.

MARRIAGE. With Preludes on Current Events. 12mo, $1.50.

Mr. Cook did not take up the work he has accomplished as a trade, or by accident, or from impulse; but for years he had been preparing for it, and prepared for it by an overruling guidance. . . . He lightens and thunders, throwing a vivid light on a topic by an expression or comparison, or striking a presumptuous error as by a bolt from heaven. — JAMES McCOSH, D. D.

Professor J. L. Diman.

THE THEISTIC ARGUMENT AS AFFECTED BY RECENT THEORIES. Edited by Professor GEORGE P. FISHER. 8vo, $2.00.

The author has succeeded in making it clear that recent science impels us to a point where the necessity of admitting the existence of God is irresistible; that its most elevated conceptions and widest generalizations render it necessary to accept the presence and constant efficient energy of God as realities, and that the modes of operation which science discloses are in harmony with the fundamental principles and postulates of Christianity. — *British Quarterly Review.*

Dr. Diman concedes to his opponents every advantage of debate, adopts their phraseology, follows their methods of reasoning, grants to them every principle that they have established wholly or approximately, and, indeed, a great deal that is scarcely more than conjecture; and yet he is able to present a defense of theistic doctrine that will seem most admirable and most consolatory to its adherents and most embarrassing to some of its enemies. He has conducted the whole discussion with rare ability, and has furnished sound reasoning at every successive step. — *Times* (New York).

Orations and Essays, with selected Parish Sermons. A Memorial Volume, with a Portrait. 8vo, gilt top, $2.50.

Contents: A Commemorative Discourse. J. Lewis Diman. By the Rev. James O. Murray. — *Literary and Historical Addresses:* The Alienation of the Educated Class from Politics; The Method of Academic Culture; Address at the Unveiling of the Monument to Roger Williams in Providence; The Settlement of Mount Hope; Sir Henry Vane. — *Reviews:* Religion in America, 1776–1876; University Corporations. — *Sermons:* The Son of Man; Christ, the Way, the Truth, and the Life; Christ, the Bread of Life; Christ in the Power of His Resurrection; The Holy Spirit, the Guide to Truth; The Baptism of the Holy Ghost; The Kingdom of Heaven and the Kingdom of Nature.

I think it is not the partiality of personal friendship which leads me to regard these productions of Professor Diman as not surpassed by any other writings of the same class in our literature. — Professor George P. Fisher.

One cannot read these pages without becoming conscious of contact with the workings of a strong and an earnest mind. The words betoken culture, scholarship, and, what is more important, they show that he who wrote them lived near to God. — *The Churchman* (New York).

The rich contents of this volume assure his place among our noblest teachers and scholars. — *Christian Register* (Boston).

The Dhammapada.

Texts from the Buddhist Canon, commonly known as Dhammapada, with accompanying Narratives. Translated from the Chinese, by Samuel Beal, Professor of Chinese, University College, London. 8vo, gilt top, $2.50.

This is a most important addition to our knowledge, as the Pali texts of this work, hitherto available to scholars, and translated by Professor Max Müller and others, contain only two thirds of the matter which has survived in the Chinese version. — *The Athenæum* (London).

Joseph Edkins, D. D.

Religion in China. Containing a brief account of the Three Religions of the Chinese, with Observations on the Prospects of Christian Conversion among that People. 8vo, gilt top, $2.50.

Dr. Edkins writes with the firmness and clearness of a mind that has mastered its subject; and few scholars will require a completer statement of the principles of the Chinese theologies, their development, present phase, and contrasted character, than he furnishes. — *Tribune* (New York).

Chinese Buddhism. A volume of Sketches, Historical, Descriptive, and Critical. 8vo, gilt top, $4.50.

With the purpose constantly in mind to speak for the advancement, the civilization, and the Christianization of the Chinese, Dr.

Edkins has here written a work fit to serve, for ordinary readers at least, the double purpose of a history of Buddhism and a critical examination of its effects upon the intellect and life of China. It is a work of great interest and of permanent value. — *Evening Post* (New York).

Ludwig Feuerbach.

THE ESSENCE OF CHRISTIANITY. Translated from the Second German Edition by MARIAN EVANS (George Eliot). 8vo, gilt top, $3.00.

I confess that to Feuerbach I owe a debt of inestimable gratitude. Feeling about in uncertainty for the ground, and finding everywhere shifting sands, Feuerbach cast a sudden blaze into the darkness, and disclosed to me the way. — S. BARING-GOULD, in *The Origin and Development of Religious Belief.*

Washington Gladden.

THE LORD'S PRAYER. Seven Essays on the Meaning and Spirit of this universal Prayer. 16mo, gilt top, $1.00.

Often as we offer this prayer, and much as we have studied over it to give proper expositions of it from the pulpit and in the catechism, we shall henceforth pray it more intelligently than we ever have before; nay, we have learned, we think, to pray better in all our supplications, and to comprehend more in them than has been our wont. — *Lutheran Quarterly* (Philadelphia).

W. R. Greg.

THE CREED OF CHRISTENDOM. Its Foundations contrasted with the Superstructure. 2 vols. 8vo, gilt top, $5.00.

A model of honest investigation and clear exposition, conceived in the true spirit of serious and faithful research. — *Westminster Review* (London).

Dr. Martin Haug.

ESSAYS ON THE SACRED LANGUAGE, WRITINGS, AND RELIGION OF THE PARSIS. Second Revised Edition, by Dr. E. W. WEST. 8vo, gilt top, $4.50.

It supplies the most accurate knowledge now accessible of one of the noblest forms of historic religion, and is the product of genuine and thorough scholarship. — *Christian Register* (Boston).

Hindu Pantheism (A Manual of).

THE VEDANTASARA. Translated, with Annotations, by Major G. A. JACOB, Bombay Staff Corps. With Preface by E. B. COWELL, M. A., Professor of Sanskrit in the University of Cambridge. 8vo, gilt top, $2.50.

The Vedântasâra, acknowledged to be the best presentation of the modern phase of these tenets, is in this little book translated, and its fourteen sections are explained, one by one, with large critical annotation. The notes show wide research in the realm of curious speculation, while the translation may be accepted as accurate and faithful. — *Christian Union* (New York.)

Hymns of the Ages.

HYMNS OF THE AGES. First, Second, and Third Series. Each in one volume, illustrated with steel vignettes, after TURNER. 12mo, $1.50 each; half calf, $9.00 a set; morocco, $12.00.

They date all the way from the sixth century to to-day. But, oldest and newest, they deal with that which is older than the ancientest, and newer than the latest of them. And this is the ground of their excellence, and of the esteem in which they are held, — that worthily and sincerely they deal with that truth in souls whose infinite variety age cannot wither and custom cannot stale, and with which every heart, as it is pure, finds itself at home in a dear and sacred kinship. — *Christian Examiner.*

Henry James.

THE SECRET OF SWEDENBORG. Being an Elucidation of his Doctrine of the Divine Natural Humanity. 8vo, tinted paper, $2.50.

We admire the metaphysical acuteness, the logical power, and the singular literary force of the book, which is also remarkable as carrying into theological writing something besides the hard words of secular dispute, and as presenting to the world the great questions of theology in something beside a Sabbath-day dress. — *Atlantic Monthly.*

SOCIETY THE REDEEMED FORM OF MAN, AND THE EARNEST OF GOD'S OMNIPOTENCE IN HUMAN NATURE. Affirmed in Letters to a Friend. Crown 8vo, $2.00.

Samuel Johnson.

ORIENTAL RELIGIONS, AND THEIR RELATION TO UNIVERSAL RELIGION. By SAMUEL JOHNSON.

INDIA. 8vo, 802 pages, $5.00; half calf, $8.00.

Samuel Johnson's remarkable work is devoted wholly to the religions and civilization of India; is the result of twenty years' study and reflection by one of the soundest scholars and most acute thinkers of New England, and must be treated with all respect, whether we consider its thoroughness, its logical reasoning, or the conclusion, unacceptable to the majority, no doubt, at which it arrives. — *Republican* (Springfield).

CHINA. 8vo, 1,000 pages, $5.00; half calf, $8.00.

Altogether the work of Mr. Johnson is an extraordinarily rich mine of reliable and far-reaching information on all literary subjects connected with China. . . . He decidedly impresses us as an authority on Chinese subjects. — E. J. EITEL, Ph. D., Editor of *The China Review* (Hong Kong).

Thomas Starr King.

CHRISTIANITY AND HUMANITY. Sermons. Edited, with a Memoir, by EDWIN P. WHIPPLE. Fine steel portrait, 12mo, $2.00; half calf, $4.00.

CONTENTS: The Experimental Evidence of Christianity; Cries from the Depth; The Supremacy of Jesus; Christian Thought of the Future Life; True Spiritual Communications; Life more Abundantly; Lessons of the Drought; The Christian and the Heathen Dollar; The Divine Estimate of Death; Distribution of Sorrows; Deliverance from the Fear of Death; The Two Harvests; The Organ and its Symbolism; The Supreme Court Decision and our Duties; Living for Ideas and Principles; The Heart and the Issues of Life; Salt that has lost its Savor, or Religion Corrupted; Lessons from the Sierra Nevada; Living Waters from Lake Tahoe; The Comet of July, 1861; Religious Lessons from Metallurgy; Christian Worship.

The Koran.

SELECTIONS FROM THE KORAN. By EDWARD WILLIAM LANE. A new edition, revised and enlarged, with an introduction by STANLEY LANE POOLE. 8vo, gilt top, $3.50.

Alvan Lamson, D. D.

THE CHURCH OF THE FIRST THREE CENTURIES; or, Notices of the Lives and Opinions of the Early Fathers, with special reference to the Doctrine of the Trinity; illustrating its late origin and gradual formation. Revised and enlarged edition. 8vo, $2.50.

Dr. Lamson was a Unitarian in opinion, but in this book he does not advocate his views except by showing how they are supported by history.

Rev. J. Long.

EASTERN PROVERBS AND EMBLEMS ILLUSTRATING OLD TRUTHS. 8vo, $3.50.

This curious collection of proverbs, gleaned principally from among the Eastern peoples, illustrates the analogy of the old truths of Scripture with the common sayings in every-day use in the East.

Samuel Longfellow and Samuel Johnson.

HYMNS OF THE SPIRIT. 16mo, $1.25.

A collection of remarkable excellence.

W. A. McVickar, D. D.

LIFE OF THE REV. JOHN MCVICKAR, S. T. D. With portrait, crown 8vo, $2.00.

Hundreds of scholars in all professions and vocations, now living, will be delighted with this admirable biography of their revered master, who for fifty years stood foremost among the eminent men who filled the professors' chairs in Columbia College. — *Journal* (Albany).

William Mountford.

EUTHANASY; or, Happy Talk towards the End of Life. New edition, 12mo, $2.00.

It is the product of a mind cultivated, gentle, and reverent, appealing to the subtle intuitions of the spirit, and aiming to persuade the soul to rest in the peace of confidence in the goodness of God. — *Advertiser* (Boston).

Elisha Mulford, D. D.

The Republic of God. 8vo, $2.00.

It is the mirror of the age, the gospel of the age, the embodiment of the thought of the age, and yet, for the most part, it is the statement of the truth of all ages as it concerns the spiritual life of man. The prime thought of the book can no more be shaken than the eternal hills, and whether men accept or dispute different points in its development, it is one of the few books that sooner or later create a new world for men to live in. — *Times* (New York).

No book on the statement of the great truths of Christianity at once so fresh, so clear, so fundamental, and so fully grasping and solving the religious problems of our time, has yet been written by any American. — *Advertiser* (Boston).

It is the most important contribution to theological literature thus far made by any American writer. — *The Churchman* (New York).

A book which will not be mastered by hasty reading, nor by a cool, scientific dissection. We do not remember that this country has lately produced a speculative work of more originality and force. . . . The book is a noble one — broad-minded, deep, breathing forth an ever-present consciousness of things unseen. It is a mental and moral tonic which might do us all good. — *The Critic* (New York).

Rev. T. T. Munger.

On the Threshold. Familiar Lectures to Young People on Purpose, Friends and Companions, Manners, Thrift, Self-Reliance and Courage, Health, Reading and Intellectual Life, Amusements, and Faith. 16mo, gilt top, $1.00.

This book touches acts, habits, character, destiny; it deals with the present and vital thought in literature, society, life; it is the hand-book to possible careers; it stimulates one with the idea that life is worth living; there are no dead words in it. The production of a book of this sort is not an every-day occurrence: it is an event; it will work a revolution among young men who read it; it has the manly ring from cover to cover. — *Times* (New York).

The Freedom of Faith. Sermons. 16mo, $1.50.

Contents: Prefatory Essay: The New Theology; On Reception of New Truth; God our Shield; God our Reward; Love to the Christ as a Person; The Christ's Pity; The Christ as a Preacher; Land-Tenure; Moral Environment; Immortality and Science; Immortality and Nature; Immortality as Taught by the Christ; The Christ's Treatment of Death; The Resurrection from the Dead; The Method of Penalty; Judgment; Life a Gain; Things to be Awaited.

J. A. W. Neander.

General History of the Christian Religion and Church. Translated from the German by Rev. Joseph Torrey, Professor in the University of Vermont. With an Index volume. The set, with Index, 6 vols., $20.00. Index volume, separate, $3.00.

"Neander's Church History" is one of the most profound, carefully considered, deeply philosophized, candid, truly liberal, and independent historical works that have ever been written. In all these respects it stands head and shoulders above almost any other church history in existence. . . . Professor Torrey has executed admirably his part of the task; and I can say of his translation (what I can say about no other that I have ever seen), I now use the translation constantly in preference to the original. — Professor CALVIN E. STOWE, Andover, Mass.

Peep of Day Series.

PEEP OF DAY SERIES. Comprising "The Peep of Day," "Precept upon Precept," and "Line upon Line." 3 vols. 16mo, each 50 cents; the set, $1.50.

Elizabeth Stuart Phelps.

THE GATES AJAR. 16mo, $1.50.

Of all the books which we ever read, calculated to shed light upon the utter darkness of sudden sorrow, and to bring peace to the bereaved and solitary, we give, in many important respects, the preference to "The Gates Ajar." — *The Congregationalist* (Boston).

Physicus.

A CANDID EXAMINATION OF THEISM. By PHYSICUS. 8vo, gilt top, $2.50.

Prayers of the Ages.

PRAYERS OF THE AGES. Compiled by CAROLINE S. WHITMARSH, one of the editors of "Hymns of the Ages." $1.50.

I have long wished for something of the kind, a broad, liberal, catholic presentation of what must be regarded as the flower of the world's piety and devotion. The "Hymns of the Ages" are favorite volumes with me, and I have comforted the sick and sorrowing with them. But this last volume, it seems to me, I shall value highest. — JOHN G. WHITTIER.

George Putnam, D. D.

SERMONS BY GEORGE PUTNAM, D. D., late Pastor of the First Religious Society in Roxbury, Massachusetts. With fine steel portrait. 16mo, gilt top, $1.75.

CONTENTS: If Thou hadst been here; I have Trodden the Wine-Press alone; Life a Voyage; Jesus and Solomon; Almost and Altogether; Tekel; Christian Manliness — Doing and Standing; Go Quickly; True Religion; Unitarianism; Infidelity; One Faith; The Windows towards Jerusalem; Oh, that I knew! The One Foundation; The Offense of the Cross; Science and Theology; Hath God said it? Righteousness First; Hindrances; Anthropomorphism; Thou shalt say, No; The Miracle of Cana; Introductory I. and II.; Ordaining Address.

Rev. James Reed.

SWEDENBORG AND THE NEW CHURCH. 16mo, $1.25.

While the work is definite and positive in its affirmations, it is written in an admirable spirit, and is quite free from every taint of that narrow sectarianism or supercilious dogmatism which too often disfigures professedly religious works, and may be cordially recommended to any one who desires to acquaint himself with the principles of Biblical interpretation and the theological views of the Swedenborgians or New Church. — *Christian Union* (New York).

Edward Robinson, D. D., LL. D.

HARMONY OF THE FOUR GOSPELS, in Greek. 8vo, $1.50.

THE SAME, in English, 12mo, 75 cents.

BIBLICAL RESEARCHES IN PALESTINE. 3 vols. 8vo, with maps, $10.00. Price of the maps alone, $1.00.

Dean Stanley said of these volumes: "They are amongst the very few books of modern literature of which I can truly say that I have read every word. I have read them under circumstances which riveted my attention upon them while riding on the back of a camel; while traveling on horseback through the hills of Palestine; under the shadow of my tent, when I came in weary from the day's journey. These were the scenes in which I first became acquainted with the work of Dr. Robinson. But to that work I have felt that I and all students of Biblical literature owe a debt that can never be effaced."

It lays open, unquestionably, one of the richest discoveries, one of the most important scientific conquests, which has been made for a long time in the field of geography and Biblical archæology. — CARL RITTER.

PHYSICAL GEOGRAPHY OF THE HOLY LAND. A Supplement to "Biblical Researches in Palestine." 8vo, $3.50.

A capital summary of our present knowledge.—*London Athenæum.*

HEBREW AND ENGLISH LEXICON OF THE OLD TESTAMENT, including the Biblical Chaldee. From the Latin of WILLIAM GESENIUS, by EDWARD ROBINSON. *Twenty-second Edition.* 8vo, half russia, $6.00.

Gesenius is indispensable. No one has yet arisen who, with the same comprehensive mastery of the lexical material, can lay claim to the uniform sobriety of philological judgment and the all but absolute freedom from bondage to the trammels of theory which characterize Gesenius. He is still the "prince of Hebrew lexicographers." — Professor P. H. STEENSTRA, *Cambridge Episcopal Theological School.*

ENGLISH-HEBREW LEXICON: Being a complete Verbal Index to Gesenius' Hebrew Lexicon. By JOSEPH LEWIS POTTER, A. M. 8vo, $2.00.

Rev. Thomas Scott.

THE BIBLE, WITH EXPLANATORY NOTES, PRACTICAL OBSERVATIONS, AND COPIOUS MARGINAL REFERENCES. By Rev. THOMAS SCOTT. 6 vols. royal 8vo, sheep, $15.00.

I believe it exhibits more of the mind of the Spirit in the Scriptures than any other work of the kind extant. — Rev. ANDREW FULLER.

William Smith.

DICTIONARY OF THE BIBLE, comprising its Antiquities, Biography, Geography, and Natural History. By WILLIAM SMITH. Edited by Professor HORATIO BALCH HACKETT and EZRA ABBOT, LL. D. In four volumes, 8vo, 3,667 pages, with 596 illustrations. Cloth, beveled edges, strongly bound, $20.00; full sheep, $25.00; half morocco, $30.00; half calf, extra, $30.00; half russia, $35.00; full calf, or full morocco, gilt, $40.00; russia, or levant, $45.00.

There are several American editions of Smith's Dictionary of the Bible, but this edition comprises not only the contents of the original English edition, unabridged, but very considerable and important additions by the editors, Professors Hackett and Abbot, and twenty-six other eminent American scholars.

This edition has 500 more pages than the English, and 100 more illustrations; more than a thousand errors of reference in the English edition are corrected in this; and an Index of Scripture Illustrated is added. In view of the improvements made in this edition, Professor ROSWELL D. HITCHCOCK, of New York, said: "There cannot well be two opinions about the merits of Smith's Bible Dictionary. What was, to begin with, the best book of its kind in our language, is now still better." The *London Bookseller* remarked: "It seems that we have to thank America for the most complete work of the kind in the English, or, indeed, in any other language."

No similar work in our own or in any other language is for a moment to be compared with it. — *Quarterly Review* (London).

Robert South, D. D.

SERMONS PREACHED UPON SEVERAL OCCASIONS. With a Memoir of the author. 5 vols. 8vo, $15.00; sheep, $20.00; half calf, $25.00.

We doubt if, in the single quality of freshness and force of expression, of rapid and rushing life, any writer of English prose, from Milton to Burke, equaled South. — E. P. WHIPPLE, in *North American Review.*

South's sermons are adapted to all readers and all days. — *Retrospective Review* (London).

Harriet Beecher Stowe.

RELIGIOUS POEMS. Illustrated. 16mo, gilt, $1.50.

The poems are all characterized by the genius of Mrs. Stowe. . . . There is a profound appreciation of the *inner life* of religion, — a wrestling for nearness to God. — *American Christian Review.*

A Talmudic Miscellany.

A TALMUDIC MISCELLANY; or, A Thousand and One Extracts from the Talmud, the Midrashim, and the Kabbalah. Compiled and translated by P. I. HERSHON. With Introductory Preface by Rev. F. W. FARRAR. 8vo, gilt top, $4.50.

A scholarly and painstaking book — the volume has a solid value. — *Tribune* (New York).

It will interest theologians, historians, and thinkers. — *Advertiser* (Boston).

Henry Thornton.

FAMILY PRAYERS, AND PRAYERS ON THE TEN COMMANDMENTS, with a Commentary on the Sermon on the Mount, etc. By HENRY THORNTON. Edited by the late Bishop EASTBURN, of Massachusetts. 12mo, $1.50.

Probably no published volume of family prayers has ever been the vehicle of so much heart-felt devotion as these. They are what prayers should be — fervent, and yet perfectly simple. — *Christian Witness.*

Professor C. P. Tiele.

OUTLINES OF THE HISTORY OF RELIGION TO THE SPREAD OF THE UNIVERSAL RELIGIONS. 8vo, gilt top, $2.50.

His main object is to show how that one great psychological phenomenon which we call religion has developed and manifested itself in such various shapes among the different races and peoples of the world. By this outline sketch of the author we see how all religions, even those of highly civilized nations, have grown up from the same simple germs, and we also learn the causes why these germs have in some cases attained such a rich and admirable development, and in others have scarcely grown at all. — *Transcript* (Boston).

The book is one of uncommon and curious interest. — *Courant* (Hartford).

James M. Whiton.

THE GOSPEL OF THE RESURRECTION. 16mo, gilt top, $1.25.

A thoughtful and reverent study of one of the fundamental doctrines of Christianity. To those who are capable of rightly apprehending the spiritual conceptions which Dr. Whiton embodies in this volume, they will serve to clear away many mistaken and material ideas, and will help to make the sublime and inspiring truth of a life beyond the grave more intensely and vitally real. — *Journal* (Boston).

John Woolman.

THE JOURNAL OF JOHN WOOLMAN. With an Introduction by JOHN G. WHITTIER. 16mo, $1.50.

Get the writings of John Woolman by heart. — CHARLES LAMB.

A perfect gem. His is a beautiful soul. An illiterate tailor, he writes in a style of the most exquisite purity and grace. His moral qualities are transferred to his writings. His religion is love. His Christianity is most inviting: it is fascinating. — H. CRABB ROBINSON, in his *Diary.*

www.ingramcontent.com/pod-product-compliance
Lightning Source LLC
LaVergne TN
LVHW021129110826
845150LV00005B/974

9781425550745